ENDLESS PRESENT

ENDLESS PRESENT

Selected Articles, Reviews and Dispatches, 2010–23

RORY WATERMAN

All rights reserved. No part of this work covered by the
copyright herein may be reproduced or used in any means –
graphic, electronic, or mechanical, including copying, recording,
taping, or information storage and retrieval systems – without
written permission of the publisher.

Printed by imprintdigital
Upton Pyne, Exeter
imprintdigital.com

Typesetting and cover design by The Book Typesetters
hello@thebooktypesetters.com
07422 598 168
thebooktypesetters.com

Published by Shoestring Press
19 Devonshire Avenue, Beeston, Nottingham, NG9 1BS
(0115) 925 1827
shoestringpress.co.uk

First published 2024
© Copyright: Rory Waterman

The moral right of the author has been asserted.

ISBN 978-1-915553-44-7

ABOUT THE AUTHOR

Rory Waterman was born in Belfast in 1981, grew up mainly in Lincolnshire, and lives in Nottingham. He is Associate Professor of Modern and Contemporary Literature at Nottingham Trent University, where he has worked since completing a PhD in twentieth-century poetry at the University of Leicester in 2012. His most recent poetry collection is *Come Here to This Gate* (Carcanet, 2024), and his others, all published by Carcanet, are: *Tonight the Summer's Over* (2013), which was a Poetry Book Society Recommendation and was shortlisted for a Seamus Heaney Award; *Sarajevo Roses* (2017), which was shortlisted for the Ledbury Forte Prize for second collections, and *Sweet Nothings* (2020). His critical books include *Belonging and Estrangement in the Poetry of Philip Larkin, R. S. Thomas and Charles Causley* (Routledge, 2014), *Poets of the Second World War* (Liverpool University Press, 2016), and *Wendy Cope* (Liverpool University Press, 2021). He is also the editor of W. H. Davies, *The True Traveller: A Reader* (Fyfield, 2016) and *W. H. Davies: Essays on the Super-tramp Poet* (Anthem, 2021), and co-editor, with Anthony Caleshu, of *Poetry and Covid-19* (Shearsman, 2021). He co-edits the poetry pamphlet publisher New Walk Editions, and previously founded and co-edited *New Walk* magazine. He has been writing reviews, mainly of poetry books, since 2008.

CONTENTS

Introduction	1
Raising and Electrifying the Bar	5
A Monumental Task	17
Self's the Man	25
'I would sooner marry you than anyone else I know': Philip Larkin, Monica Jones and Marriage	35
Such Absences	45
R. S. Thomas, *The Stones of the Field* (Carmarthen: The Druid Press, 1946)	49
A Multiplicity of Belonging	56
To Me it Was Dilution	60
Almost-Instincts Almost True: Philip Larkin's 'Statement' of 1955	64
John Agard, *Travel Light, Travel Dark* (Bloodaxe, 2013)	68
Thoughts Trained to One Furrow	70
Battered, but Not at El Alamein	75
Reflections on the Underside	82
Kevin Powers, *Letter Composed During a Lull in the Fighting* (Sceptre, 2014)	85
Patience Agbabi, *Telling Tales* (Canongate, 2014)	87
This Last Gasp of Inspiration	89
The Art of Non-criticism, or The Sword is Mightier than the Pen	97
come come come and cull me	102
Line for Line	109
Togara Muzanenhamo, *Gumiguru* (Carcanet, 2014)	112
James Sutherland-Smith, *Mouth* (Shearsman, 2014)	114
I Didn't Qualify: Ian Parks, Mexborough, and the Quest for Identity	116
Just Like That	127
In Passing	133

All of Us Here	136
Moody Excavations	139
Songs We Still Sing	142
Romantic, Not Quixotic	147
Voice of Sense on Earth	149
A Series of Fits	152
Of Death and Consolation	163
Tippoo Charging Tennyson	166
Cans and Desert Thistles	169
Full of Soul	175
Hoping for Poetry	180
Jacks of All Trades	184
Inward, is Absorbed	187
Wendy Cope, *Anecdotal Evidence* (Faber and Faber, 2018)	190
Anne Haverty, *A Break in the Journey* (New Island, 2018)	192
Back into Slaughter	194
Pamphleting	197
Truth and Lies	203
Sick of Sadness	208
No Time for Innocence	211
Winners, All	213
Silent Strengthenings	218
Dr Bob Pintle, Senior Lecturer in Professional Creativity	220
The Sonnet	225
A Past Too Close	229
Candid Pain	234
Makeshift Flags	236
A Lifelong Fan	238
We Only Know	240
Blessed Breach	242
On 'Like Father'	245
(Good) Person Poems	249
I Was Nothing but a Heretic Cormorant	254
Endless Present	258
Andrew Waterman, 1940–2022	263

I Say Heart	270
Eye of the Storm	274
Let the Morbid Fancy Roam	277
Love and Shadow	286
First as Tragedy, then as Farce	288
To hear their voice bounce off the shape of things	292
Mature Methods	299
Saint Robert of Waco	301
Index	307

INTRODUCTION

In the fourteen years covered by this book, which ends with the last piece I published before my forty-second birthday, I've somehow written well over half a million words of commissioned literary criticism, in addition to those that have appeared in books. Choosing what to include here was therefore quite difficult – as was resisting the temptation to stick mainly to the newer pieces, all of which reflect what I think now and the way I choose to write now, as a man in his early forties. The initial challenge, then, was to decide upon grounds for elimination. This book does not include any of the essays I have published in academic journals, nor (of course) any excerpts from my critical books. In an attempt to ensure thematic unity, I have also omitted articles that do not focus directly on literary matters. Most of the reviews and other articles I have written during this period have also been left out, either because their time had clearly passed, because they were too terse to matter now, or because what I wrote displeases me too much. I have been particularly selective with the shorter pieces; very few of the reviews I have written for the *TLS* during this period are here, for example – with regret, in some instances. The same is true for most of the pamphlet round-ups I have published in *PN Review*, and some of my less substantial pieces in *Poetry Review*, *Poetry London* and elsewhere. On the whole, I think concentrating on the meatier reviews and articles makes for a stronger book, though I have left some of those out too, if I felt their moment had gone.

A lot can happen between the ages of twenty-seven and forty-one. In my case, that has included, to some extent, going from being an outsider looking in at what seemed a closed-off poetry world full of people I didn't know personally and was sure I never would, to something approaching its obverse, at least up to a point. I am confident this hasn't altered my critical responses: as a reviewer I have an obligation to what I think is true, and I take that obligation as seriously as ever. It has helped me to understand the efforts some people make, though – and the lack of effort (and manifest lack of talent) others get away with. I hope I retain plenty of my earlier fire in my more recent criticism, that I have grown up without growing old. In any case, this book includes some judgements I no longer agree with and in places adheres to positions that are no longer mine; but I have resisted the temptation to edit myself, other than to correct typos, or to restore phrases, sentences, etc that had not made it past the cutting floor of an editor, but which I though worth keeping. (For that reason, some of these reviews are not quite in the same form in which they first appeared in print, though overwhelmingly the changes are superficial.) I have left out all pieces I wrote before 2010, the year I began reviewing very regularly, and have opted to present the pieces in chronological order of publication, for no reason other than that I had to choose *some* way of doing it. This seems logical if you want to chart the development of this critic's work, though it is unlikely you do. However, it is also helpful, I think, if you wish to see how the last decade and a bit of British poetry is reflected in what I have written, and what I have been commissioned to write about.

A few further caveats. Philip Larkin dominates the early part of this book. For several years, I was repeatedly asked to write about him, partly because he was one of the three poets I concentrated on for my PhD (which I completed in 2012), and partly because several books about, or compiling, Larkin were published in the years 2010–15. I was happy to take these commissions, and happy to let him go. Secondly, I have also been very interested in multiple poetr*ies*, but again that is not necessarily reflected thoroughly in what I have been commissioned to write. Thirdly, the gender imbalance in the commissioned pieces is stark – with the exception of the pamphlet round-ups I've frequently written in recent years for *PN Review* (a few of which are included here) and once for the *TLS*, the year I judged the Michael Marks Awards. Historically, male poets are of course likely to have received more than their share of attention. In an era in which such things rightly come under greater scrutiny. I am, however, yet to see any statistics regarding the proportions of reviews of books by men written by men, and reviews of books by women written by women. I suspect this has become increasingly compartmentalised over time, as poets and critics have increasingly been slotted into demographic siloes. Finally, I haven't been asked to write about many poets who aren't white, either.

An intriguing addition to recent statistical endeavours regarding the demographics of reviewers would be to determine what proportion of British poets and reviewers in the more prestigious corners of the literary press did not attend a fee-paying school and/or did not proceed to Oxbridge (or perhaps 'Doxbridge', as a friend's self-aware son, a Durham graduate, once jokingly termed it). Moreover, what proportion grew up in rented accommodation, with a single parent? What proportion did not grow up in, or in their twenties move to, London? I suspect it would be hard to acquire funding for such a project, and that many requests for information would go unanswered, but anyone who gives it a moment's thought knows roughly what the results would be. I fit all of those categories, as does a huge proportion of the population, but it makes me a little unusual for a literary critic in England. I did, however, go on to become an academic, in which sense I am perhaps not unusual enough, and I had a father who was a poet. We did not live together (or even in the same country) after I was a toddler, but I did at least know a future as a writer need not be a wholly unrealisable ambition, even when I was getting expelled from school or finding out I had achieved four C grades at GCSE. There will be many potential poets and critics of acclaim out there who will never get the opportunity, nor realise they could have it. In the third decade of the twenty-first century, we have a literary and critical culture that still has little to no interest in finding them, and is in some cases actively, self-interestedly opposed to doing so.

I have always held to Wendy Cope's dictum that you shouldn't agree to review a book if you aren't prepared to be rude about it if you don't like it. She hasn't published any reviews, to my knowledge, so presumably she isn't prepared to be rude (in prose, anyway), which is understandable. I remember the poet and critic William Wootten once saying to me that essentially a reviewer of poetry books is answering one central question: is this book worth about £10 of your money? He is right, but of course there is no wholly objective way to tackle that question, and no 'general reader' to receive the verdict. I see no reason to write an excoriating review of a book hardly anyone is going to read, and little point in reviewing some of the books that are currently receiving orgasmic acclaim but which read as though they are the product of ChatGPT being asked to write like a poseur on acid. Nonetheless, writers with serious acclaim should be less precious about probing, challenging or critical reviews than some of them are, and critics should be more unafraid, and less keen to write to make influential friends, than many of them so very evidently are. I know I have been blackballed as a result of some of my critical pieces, and I have received some angry emails too. This always feels horrible: I like to be a nice person, and like to make friends. But no: you shouldn't agree to review a book if you aren't prepared to be rude about it if you don't like it. The flipside is that I must avoid hypocrisy, and must accept the judgements of other critics about my own poetry. They obviously have precisely the same right.

I am very grateful to John Lucas for wanting to publish this book, and to the past and present editors of the publications represented here. You have helped to keep my life intellectually stimulating, and your faith in me has always meant a lot. I owe special thanks to Michael Schmidt and Alan Jenkins, but also owe sincere thanks to the other editors who wanted these articles: Emily Berry, Gerry Cambridge, Michael Caines, Hilary Menos, Catharine Morris, André Naffis-Sahely, Dawn Potter, Camille Ralphs, and Christopher Ricks. I hope I haven't left anyone out. And last but never least, I owe many debts of gratitude to Francesca Hardy, who has read drafts of almost everything I've written since 2017.

RAISING AND ELECTRIFYING THE BAR

William Logan, *Our Savage Art: Poetry and the Civil Tongue* (Columbia University Press, 2009)

> The more criticism I write, the more I'm asked to write about criticism; and, the more I'm asked to write about criticism, the less I want to write about anything at all.

Thus begins *Our Savage Art: Poetry and the Civil Tongue*, William Logan's fifth tome of critical prose in twelve years. He goes on: 'then something gets under my skin', and this, for the fifth time, is a book about literature getting under the skin of one of the most tempestuous and exacting poet-critics of our – or any – generation. Before the opening paragraph has drawn to a close Logan is firing off a warning salvo, lambasting an individual editor for writing 'rubbish' and directing readers to the book's interior to find out exactly what the critic thinks of him and his opinions about contemporary poetry being 'too obscure, when it isn't half obscure enough'.

This willingness to fashion the critic's quill into a poisoned dart delights and confounds readers, of course. The book's title is a funny one because Logan spends so much of his time not being civil at all; his uncivil tongue must be firmly in his cheek. Moreover, he is also not afraid to take down big victims, from Billy Collins to Seamus Heaney. In fact, he seems positively to *enjoy* doing so. The book's blurb suggests that Logan 'might be considered a cobra with manners', but (to hold on to the metaphor and go for a long run with it) perhaps he can more accurately be described as an anaconda, constricting large prey (of his contemporaries Logan doesn't bother much with less famous names), swallowing it whole, and basking in any heat given off by the ensuing friction and furore.

Logan does not court ambivalence, and many people involved in modern poetry have fairly strong views about him:

I've been threatened by a few poets and told by two newspapers never to darken their doorways again. Years ago the editor of *Poetry*, rejecting a review he had commissioned, warned me never to publish it, because it would harm my reputation. I published it elsewhere, of course; but during his tenure the magazine never asked for another review.

The critic is showing his reader the battle scars that legitimise him as a representative of this 'minor art'. An editor or reader might disagree with his opinions to the point of despair, but that editor or reader can be sure Logan means what he says. No faint praise here. Permit me to recount a personal grievance: an American editor recently spiked one of my own reviews because 'it does not make a reader want to buy the book'. But why on earth should it? This editor did not want honest criticism, but free advertising, any praise as good as worthless. Logan's praise must be earned, earning it is astronomically difficult, and most of the books he receives are not deemed worth reviewing at all:

> When poetry books arrive at my door […] I look at them as I can, somewhat lazily and haphazardly, and sometimes after ten or twenty pages I put one down with a sigh and turn to another – there are so many waiting and so few I can review. In truth, if a poet doesn't catch your eye in twenty pages, he probably never will. Life is too short, and poetry books, however short, are too many.

So, what of the chosen few? Included in this book are ten of Logan's infamous 'Verse Chronicles': sequences of reviews of contemporary poetry books published biannually in *The New Criterion*. They are overwhelmingly negative, and it is not surprising that some of his terse witticisms and outright condemnations stick in the craw of respective poets and editors. After a while, one reads each review waiting for the *coup de grâce* – normally witty and always, well, *savage*: Rosanna Warren's 'well-meaning poems' (ouch) are mostly as 'conventional as cottage cheese' (as is that put-down, of course). Howard Nemerov 'could cram so many [abstractions] into a poem, they looked like frat boys stuffed into a phone booth'. Sherod Santos revels in moments which 'hover between sentiment and sententiousness. After a dozen of them you want to put your hand into a lawnmower blade'. A long poem by Carolyn Forché 'is the graveyard where unused lines go to die'. James Fenton is 'the best poet of his generation in Britain' but reading most of *The Love Bomb* is like 'chewing shoe leather'. The 'most accomplished poem' in Franz Wright's *Walking to Martha's Vineyard* 'collapses into the same kitschy sanctimoniousness that puts nodding Jesus dolls on car dashboards', and his poems are 'the Hallmark cards of the damned'. And all of this in the first twenty pages after the introduction. Logan's reviews are not formulaic, exactly, but so many of them begin in such a way that the reader cannot immediately tell what the reviewer thinks of a book, before he drops one of these little stinkbombs. Quite often he then drops another, and another, and another. But it is not the reviewer's job to sell books or ingratiate himself, and while we might be tempted to run from the room, or bring the critic down (or fetch a gas mask and join in), it is inescapable that Logan acts as he sees fit without letting any inimical politeness spoil the party, and can be guaranteed to get to the point (and sometimes stay there for a while).

So far, so amusing. Nonetheless, it is hard not to wish that more of this book was given over to poets and collections Logan *would* recommend. Very rarely, it must be said, he disarms the reader by actually praising something, though hardly in the sort of language that might grace the dust-jacket of a second edition. For example, the U.S. Poet Laureate Kay Ryan is 'a minor poet of a rare and agreeable sort'. One of the most alluring pieces in this book is an essay on 'The Forgotten Masterpiece of John Townsend Trowbridge', a poet from upstate New York whose life straddled the nineteenth and twentieth centuries – and about whom I must confess my complete prior ignorance. Never blithe in his flattery (ha!), one senses a genuine affection for Trowbridge's minor Byronic masterpiece *Guy Vernon*. Endeavouring to rescue what one believes to be a lost masterpiece is, on the face of it, a noble task – though most critics' 'discoveries' amount to no more than ego-pumping or – worse – belie a desire to bolster a political or ideological agenda under false pretences, before the 'rediscovered' old texts topple backwards into near-oblivion once more. However, Logan really sells Trowbridge's 'brilliance' to the reader, warts and all. But, alas, it is rare for this critic to make his reader want to pick up a book he discusses. In *New Criterion*, or *Poetry*, or any of the other forums in which his critical prose tends to appear, we can admire his standards, his eagle eye for detail, his individuality as a critic; but *in extenso* one first starts to wonder where the good bits have all gone, then grows incredulous. Considered in bulk, his short reviews read almost like one long, vitriolic and two-dimensional attack on contemporary literature and contemporary taste, and it is hard not to tire of so many utterly negative pieces as they hurtle past one after another. At the beginning of the book Logan writes that: 'A critic who does his job must be a good hater if he's to be a good lover, because if he likes everything he reads he likes nothing well enough'. Sure. But it too often seems as though even when he does find something to love he picks at the cracks, opens them up, then plugs them with dynamite and stands back, smirking. I have not counted the occurrences, but Logan is keen on writing 'a little of this goes a long way' and words to that effect; after reading the nth wittily condescending review one feels the same might be said about his criticism.

Which isn't to say he doesn't often have a point. Short shrift is given to what Logan considers the plague of dumbing-down that has overwhelmed modern poetry. Among the poets to receive the Logan haymaker on this account is, unsurprisingly, Billy Collins, who 'has been called a philistine'. 'He's something much worse, a poet who doesn't respect his art enough to take it seriously'. But Logan doesn't stop there, of course. Indeed, he gets more and more savage, funnier and funnier, angrier and angrier for a thousand words or so, broadening into an impassioned attack on so much dross that is, apparently, *like* Collins:

> Yet readers adore Billy Collins, and it feels almost un-American not to like him. Try to explain to his readers what "The Steeple-Jack" or "The River Merchant's Wife" or "The Snow Man" is up to, and they'll look at you as if you'd asked them to hand-pump a ship through the locks of the Panama Canal. Most contemporary poetry isn't any more difficult to understand than Collins – it's written in prose, good oaken American prose, and then chopped into lines.

Logan reserves a special, sad frustration for the established, esteemed poet worth admiration who has let readers down by becoming 'so secure in his tendencies he can't remember when he didn't have tendencies at all'. Moreover, he sees that many of our more established living poets have become weak parodies of their former selves, and his disappointment is almost palpable. Most of the poets that come onto the radar screen for this particular line of attack are certainly writers whom the critic obviously admires, some a great deal. Discussing Seamus Heaney's *District and Circle*, Logan writes: 'The things he does well he can still do brilliantly', before warning that 'If he's not careful, he'll become the equivalent of a faux Irish pub, plastic shamrocks on the bar, Styrofoam shillelaghs on the wall, and green ale on tap'. Heaney's compatriot Paul Muldoon 'never runs out of things to say, only things worth saying'. Moreover, 'There's nothing natural about Muldoon's poems now – they're full of artificial sweeteners, artificial colors, and probably regulated by the FDA'. Logan has great admiration for Richard Wilbur, but in a review of the 2004 *Collected Poems* he concentrates foursquarely on the generally 'muddled and listless' new poems, in which 'Wilbur sounds like an old fussbudget sorry he threw out his last pair of spats'. (What a shame Logan does not spare more room for the reasons why Wilbur's *Collected* 'deserves to be on the bookshelf of any serious reader' instead of indulging in this virtually meaningless comic assault.) Geoffrey Hill's four recent books, from the *Triumph of Love* (1998) to *Scenes from Comus* (2005), each have 'peculiar gifts' but have nevertheless 'diluted a career of painstakingly crafted, close-managed poems'. For half a century John Ashbery 'has pressed the limits of the expected and at last become an expectation itself', while Les Murray has been 'acting like a cartoon Aussie, the Crocodile Dundee of the poetry circuit'. (By the same token, Logan's criticism is often as American as a drive-by shooting.) At the heart of this is – must be – a love of putting the knife in wherever there is an exposed weak spot. But Logan is also driven by an honourable and unflagging thirst, in this age of critics and editors settling for and even lauding mediocrity, for literary greatness. And where he finds that such greatness has come and gone, he mourns its loss.

Most of the above quotations are from the short reviews in the aforementioned 'Verse Chronicles' that make up about half of the book. When Logan retracts his claws and stretches out a while – in, for example, the piece on Trowbridge or the review-essay 'Elizabeth Bishop Unfinished' – he can be fascinating and, by God, congenial. Logan reserves a special fondness for Bishop:

> The poems in her first book, stuffed with allegories and fables, betray too close a reading of George Herbert – sometimes she seems a Metaphysical, Third Class. […] Yet a poem like "Sestina," with its mournful old woman and trusting granddaughter, today appears painfully autobiographical; we know so much more about Bishop's life, it's easier to see, as in Eliot, where the personal wormed into the poetic. Even in Worcester, the child found small, obscure delights – the pansies on the back porch every spring; the two canaries, Sister and Dickie; even the quarreling neighbors (you can tell she was deprived because the pleasures were so small). She turned the ordinary into an Aladdin's cave of wonders because she had to.

It is as though one is suddenly reading a different critic altogether. When fascinated by his subject, rather than repulsed, disappointed or but mildly entertained, Logan warms up without losing any of his customary vigour and rigour. And his fascination can be infectious in these roomier pieces, not least because they are always extremely well written and informed – and normally entertaining, too: you're still never *quite* sure what he is going to say next. Logan cares about 'good poetry' – is a 'good lover' in his own terminology – and he wants you to care about it too. At times like this it almost seems a shame he has earned a reputation as the pantomime villain of American literary critics because he has talents beyond hacking his contemporaries in the shins.

A lively, lengthy review of Robert Lowell's *Letters* also sparkles with insight and humanity, for the most part. Logan saves the full force of his critical chastisement (which, when not at the fore, lurks in the background like an over-keen doorman) for Saskia Hamilton, the editor: 'Her attempt to gauge the precise stage of mania in which Lowell wrote certain letters is comically obtuse'. Typically, his word choice smacks of academic thuggery, though anyone who consults the *Letters* will be hard-pressed not to see his point. But is there any point in using an entire page to list mainly minor typing errors, or uncharitably suggesting that Hamilton's spelling is at fault for her writing 'British Navel Reserve', which is more likely to be another typo? (Elsewhere in this book Logan suggests that criticism is 'often wishful thinking', which is true, but his own is normally the opposite, not the absence of either.) He ends this section by declaring 'Enough cavils'. Quite.

But Logan's willingness to take on an exacting task can reap rewards – for the reader and also for broader literary standards. The fastidiousness that lies behind the emphasis on minor 'cavils' in the Lowell book results in the editor of *The Notebooks of Robert Frost*, Robert Faggen, being roundly found out. The first half of Logan's 25-page review of this book is essentially a critical perspective, typically intriguing and learned as is Logan's wont in such pieces. The second half (half!) comprises a thorough and ruthless deconstruction of the editorial practices of Faggen: 'in just about every way possible the edition goes wrong'; 'the index is helpful as far as it goes, and it goes only as far as being unhelpful'; 'after a while I wondered if he possessed the basic cultural knowledge necessary to interpret Frost'. And on each of these points the author is happy to give details. Too many of them, in fact: some passages here could be prescribed as sleep aids. But Logan vindicates himself utterly in his analysis of the transcriptions of Frost's notebooks, about which he has drawn some thunderously negative conclusions: 'the transcription is a scandal', he storms, before proving with several sizeable quotations that he isn't exaggerating:

> I would not normally stake my eyes against those of an editor who had spent years in company with these notebooks; yet, having requested a dozen or two photocopies from the Dartmouth library, where most of the books are housed, I shook my head in wonder at the editor's wild suppositions, casual sloppiness and simple inability to set down what was on the page before him. (I ordered another dozen, and another dozen, and kept going.) Words are added or subtracted, punctuation missing where it is present and present where it is missing, canceled words unrecorded, and sense rendered nonsensical.

This is not the place to quote quotations, but Logan makes the case very convincingly. (What Logan's book does not provide, unfortunately, are photofacsimiles: he notes in the book's 'Acknowledgments' that the Frost estate 'refused permission'.) It takes an astute critic of the highest rank to go to these scrupulous lengths and conclude, with several tons of evidence behind him, that 'Harvard University Press, if it has any regard for its reputation, should withdraw this edition and subject the transcripts to microscopic examination – and the final text to the hawkeyed copyediting and proofreading it somehow failed to enjoy'. And this is why we need critics like William Logan (and

James Sitar, who made similar points in a review in *Essays in Criticism*): no future edition of Frost's notebooks can refuse to take the serious misgivings of his review into account. This demolition probably haunts Faggen in his sleep. And it probably should.

On the subject of literary theory and academic criticism, Logan wins my sympathies without reservation. The essay 'Forward Into the Past: Reading the New Critics' should be compulsory reading on every undergraduate literary theory course in Britain and North America, not least among the conveners and tutors of such courses:

> In a literature class, the poem will be analysed, often as not, as a "text" that mirrors the world of its making, as if it had been written not by a poet but by Sir History or Dame Sociology. The professor will employ the cryptic jargon of methods that to their promoters reveal hidden tensions in language but to their detractors tar and feather poems for the sins of another day and force very different poets to sing the same tune.

Informing Logan's showering criticism of so many species of academic scavenger is a love – in theory at least (and if you'll excuse me) – of the art from which they feed:

> It's disheartening to see a poem raided for evidence of sins long defunct or treated with a forensics kit, as if it were a crime scene. I therefore find it hard to work up enthusiasm for the latest announcement of racism in *Oliver Twist* [...] or elitism in Shakespeare, or sexism in, well, in just about everything. There have been sophisticated and revealing studies on these subjects, but in the classroom what you tend to get is a professor who counts penis symbols – this reduces criticism to something like trainspotting.

I have sat through a conference paper on 'Queer *Oliver Twist*', and a public lecture in which tall buildings were described as phallic symbols of male oppression (and never mind those vaginal rooms, doorways, windows). The latter seemed to have a point, at least, but not one based on the evidence it provided. Aristotle apparently said that it is the mark of a great mind to be able to entertain a thought without accepting it. Perhaps I lack a great mind, but one of the principal values of Logan in these longer pieces is that he so often says, while lightly wearing an impressive cloak of erudition, what I hope I already thought and would like to have said myself. In the same essay he opines that 'contemporary theory remains largely inoculated against the way poems work. In the end, it is a very dull way to look at poetry' – which is all very well unless one has a professional reason for disagreeing, of course. It won't only be certain poets and editors who have found Logan contemptible, but myriad academics also (and often they are the same people, of course). Again, I am enthusiastic to add, this makes him all the more important. He dares to say what too many others do not, with a readability and acumen the vast majority of his detractors could never emulate.

Logan has a refreshing gift for peering over a miasma of opinions. Here he is on Philip Larkin, whose reputation (as a man, not as a poet) has come under severe scrutiny for racism in the past two decades, when that of others has not:

> If we're going to call [...] Larkin a racist, we ought to start drawing up an indictment of Sylvia Plath, who noted in her journals a girl's "long Jewy nose"; or Wallace Stevens, who wrote, "I went up to a nigger policeman", or Marianne Moore, who mentioned in a letter that a "coon took me up in the elevator"; or William Carlos Williams, whose letters are peppered with references to wops, niggers and Jews. Until very recently such remarks were so prevalent in Britain and America, we do ourselves no credit by turning into scapegoats the writers who merely succumbed to the bigotry of the age.
>
> We are no better if we condemn such opinions without seeing where Larkin rose above them, sometimes merely by exposing the

> insecurity and self-loathing at their heart. His poems may be the
> record of how a man converts his basest feelings to something more
> humane [...].

This risks being offensively forgiving, but nonetheless there is a perspicacity to it that is lacking in Andrew Motion's generally dependable biography of Larkin, which sparked much of the furore about Larkin's personality, or the far-fetched, knee-jerk criticism of Tom Paulin, Lisa Jardine, and many other commentators. Logan's is a point that might be made by Larkin's friends and those with a closer interest in the self-designated 'Hermit of Hull', but this critic is altogether more detached and this makes his comments all the more necessary. (They should be emailed to the author of the 'phallic buildings' lecture I mentioned earlier.)

It is perhaps strange to see two reasonably long pieces on Thomas Pynchon in a book subtitled *Poetry and the Civil Tongue*, but both strive to earn their places: the first because it deals (in somewhat longwinded fashion) on the 'poetic' qualities (whatever that means) of Pynchon's novel *Mason & Dixon*, and the second because it can be bloody entertaining:

> Pynchon's attorneys might mutter that [his] jokes are never "bad"
> in an absolute or moral sense but merely the projection in our
> "time-stream" of a humor (call it a "variant stimulus to laughter") in
> common use in the future but not yet available to us. They are
> therefore not prochronistic, rotting away any slim foundation of
> realism that remains, but always already anticlimactic.

Of course, when Logan takes on a novelist he gets out the same familiar weapons:

> *Against the Day* [...] starts in the air, high-minded as a kite, and
> gradually flutters groundward, dragged down by subplots galore
> and characters thrown in willy-nilly, as if a novel's only virtue were
> how many characters it could stuff into a phone booth.

Another phone booth full of flesh aching to be pipe-bombed, and I'm not convinced the essay that makes this point need run to a full twenty-three pages.

And this sums up the book: it is a work of devilish wit, necessary arrogance, insight and intellect; but too often he roots out the bad whilst neglecting the good, occasionally (albeit rarely) at soporific length. Logan thinks that the majority of writers are praised too highly and expect too much, and the last line of the volume (which annoyingly lacks a full index) reads: 'Most writers get more than their due'. With varying degrees of success and necessity, *Our Savage Art* continues this critic's quest to redress the balance.

The Dark Horse and *Poetry Daily* (2010)

A MONUMENTAL TASK

An Anthology of Modern Irish Poetry, ed. Wes Davis
(Harvard University Press, 2010)

Spare a thought for the effort Wes Davis must have put into editing this anthology: it contains about nine hundred pages of poetry by more than fifty poets, chronologically arranged by date of birth, the oldest born in 1881, and the youngest ninety-one years later. The extreme length of Davis's book arises from his wish to give each poet plenty of page-space, and the poems – particularly those by more recent authors – have apparently been selected with the greatest attention to detail. As he notes in the preface:

> The earliest poets in the collection [...] are represented primarily by the kinds of poems that have stuck in the minds of later writers. On the other hand, my goal in selecting work from poets who are still writing – the bulk of the collection – was to show the range of their styles and interests. This meant including greatest hits where appropriate, but favoring less familiar poems when those reveal unexpected sides of well-known poets.

Moreover, the section for each poet is introduced with a short and well-informed biographical-critical essay. Researching and compiling this book as conscientiously as Davis has undoubtedly done must have been a monumental task, and as a feat of scholarship crossed with editorial attentiveness and acumen it would seem hard to beat. Indeed, there is no other volume of modern Irish poetry to match it either for bulk or erudition.

In terms of Irish nationalism, a topic that is rarely more than a few pages away, the anthology runs from the momentous events that led directly to the founding of the Irish Free State to the era of the 'Tiger Economy', from the Easter Rising to after the Good Friday Agreement. As such, the book spans a broad and sometimes brutal historical era, and there is a certain unity to it as a poetic record of an island in political flux. The first overt mention of the nationalist cause is Padraic Colum's rousing 'Roger Casement', about the nationalist leader hanged by the British for his role in orchestrating the Easter Rising (but for those who require it, Davis glosses such references):

> They have hanged Roger Casement to the tolling of a bell,
> *Ochone, och, ochone, ochone!*
> And their Smiths, and their Murrays, and their Cecils say it's well,
>
> *Ochone, och, ochone, ochone!*
> But there are outcast peoples to lift that spirit high,
> Flayed men and breastless women who laboured fearfully,
> And they will lift him, lift him, for the eyes of God to see,
> And it's well, after all, Roger Casement!

The earliest poets in the book – Colum, Austin Clarke, Cecil Day Lewis (who was born in Ireland, even though he hardly spent any of his life there; those incredulous about his credentials for inclusion beyond the limitations of his talent – including the present reviewer – might usefully be reminded of the granny rule that put John Aldridge in an Ireland shirt), Patrick Kavanagh, Louis MacNeice – are all significant, or at least notable. But from the outset there is an elephant in the room, and Davis knows it:

> Together Yeats and Joyce [...] had called a native Irish literature to life in the English language. Their extraordinary accomplishments established modern Ireland's place in the world's imagination.

Yeats was only sixteen years older than Colum, and wrote contemporaneously with eight or nine of the poets included in this anthology. The omission of this giant of modern Irish literature is regrettable in a breezeblock-sized book that purports to be a broad anthology of modern Irish poetry. Many of Yeats's greatest poems – 'A Second Coming' 'Sailing to Byzantium' 'The Tower', 'Among School Children' – postdate a lot of the earlier poems in this anthology, and for all the interest of Colum's 'Roger Casement', Yeats's 'Easter 1916' (for example) is a far more nuanced and fascinating work. The counter-argument, of course, is that the inclusion of Yeats would have necessitated also the inclusion of more of his contemporaries, stretched the anthology, and led to the subsequent omission of work by interesting if lesser poets later in the book. Readers must make their own minds up. Davis has made a brave editorial decision, at any rate.

The shadow of Yeats's influence falls across many of the pages in this book, one way or another. The poetry of the Romantic revival spearheaded by Yeats produced a plethora of poems about noble peasants and so forth, thoroughly undermined in the 1930s and 1940s by the likes of Clarke and, in particular, Kavanagh, whose rural peasants in 'The Great Hunger' (1942) were something different altogether:

> Clay is the word and clay is the flesh
> Where the potato-gatherers like mechanised scare-crows move
> Along the side-fall of the hill – Maguire and his men.
> If we watch them an hour is there anything we can prove
> Of life as it is broken-backed over the Book
> Of Death? Here crows gabble over worms and frogs
> And the gulls like old newspapers are blown clear of the hedges, luckily.
> Is there some light of imagination in these wet clods?

Probably not. It might have seemed hard, in the mid- to late 1940s, to conceive of the emergence of a new and distinctly Irish poetry, and it took the likes of Richard Murphy and Thomas Kinsella paradoxically to reassert one by keeping their sights beyond Ireland and displaying an eagerness to belong outside the Irish tradition. The proliferation of poets that emerged during the 1960s and 1970s, among them Derek Mahon, Seamus Heaney, Eiléan Ní Chuilleanáin, James Simmons, Frank Ormsby, Ciaran

Carson, Desmond O'Grady, Michael Longley, Eavan Boland and Bernard O'Donoghue – a disproportionate number from the then-conflict-dogged North – is testament to the significance of the Irish and Northern Irish in the English-language poetry of the past fifty years. It is also indicative, perhaps, of the influence a national crisis of identity can have on that nation's writers, or at least the interest of publishing houses in the work of poets from a region made sexy by its place in the public consciousness.

Some of these poets (Mahon, Heaney, Longley, perhaps a few others) could not possibly have been omitted, but beyond a few big names the anthologist is charged with picking wisely from an overwhelming number of notable contemporaries. Davis makes sensible choices most of the time, though an uninitiated reader might be forgiven for thinking that many modern Irish poets are overwhelmingly preoccupied with bombs and guns and balaclavas, and the book is unlikely to be endorsed by the Northern Irish Tourist Board. It is natural that the politics of Northern Ireland is something of a leitmotif, not least in the work of poets such as Ciaran Carson and Tom Paulin, but there is a higher proportion of political unrest in this book than there is even in the works of these two writers. Nonetheless, this unrest has inspired some of the finest modern poetry in English. The following is from Carson's 'Belfast Confetti', the phrase itself a morbidly tongue-in-cheek vernacular euphemism:

> Suddenly as the riot squad moved in, it was raining exclamation marks,
> Nuts, bolts, nails, car-keys. A fount of broken type. And the explosion
> Itself – an asterisk on the map.

A major cost of this sort of conflict is hate by rote, or ignorance, portrayed with poignancy in Padraic Fiacc's 'Enemies', which ends with frightened five-year-old Protestant girls yelling 'When are yez go'n to git married?' at some nuns. Other poems in the book, such as Michael Longley's 'Wounds', put this sort of all-too-human banality in a wider context:

> First, the Ulster Division at the Somme
> Going over the top with 'Fuck the Pope!'
> 'No surrender!': a boy about to die,
> Screaming 'Give 'em one for the Shankill!'

A different sort of Belfast and Northern Ireland is at the heart of Louis MacNeice's poetry, of course, as MacNeice died several years before the British Army rolled into the six counties in 1969. But he saw the gathering storm: Northern Ireland is a 'country of cowled and haunted faces', where 'The sun goes down with a banging of Orange drums', as he puts it in 'Belfast'. It is a shame Davis only finds room for twelve pages of MacNeice's poetry, and perhaps strange that he picks, by his own admission, almost exclusively from 'not his best known poems': other poets whose places in the canon are equally secure are not given this treatment. An explanation might be that in MacNeice's case the overwhelming majority of his 'best-known poems' have themes that are nothing to do with Ireland. It is not a very satisfying explanation, of course, but I can think of no other. Davis's selection of MacNeice is weighted disproportionately towards work that takes Ireland for its subject matter, and I see no reason why well-known poems such as 'Taxis', 'Soap-Suds' and 'Snow' do not have every claim to be in this anthology alongside 'Belfast', 'Carrickfergus', 'Train to Dublin' and 'Carrick Revisited'.

Two modern Irish poetries have emerged in the last century. There has been something of a renaissance for Irish-language poetry, and several poets writing in Irish are included, albeit in translation. Poetry in translation is always in one sense unsatisfactory, but Davis has done the best thing possible, because some of these poets deserve the wider attention of English-language readers. Consider, for example, Michael O'Loughlin's careful translation of Michael Davitt's 'For Bobby Sands on the Eve of his Death':

> We hear on the radio
> the grieving voice of your people
> sorrow surmounting hatred:
> our prayer for you
> is that it prevail.

Many of the translations in this book are by poets included in their own right. The fifteen pages of poetry from Nuala Ní Dhomhnaill, for instance, have been rendered in English by Michael Hartnett, Paul Muldoon, Derek Mahon, Ciaran Carson, Peter Fallon, Michael Longley, Medbh McGuckian, Eiléan Ní Chuilleanáin, and the author herself. This not only provides readers with a different perspective on these predominantly English-language poets, it also indicates the importance of Ní Dhomhnaill (and similar things might be said about Michael Davitt or Cathal Ó Searcaigh) on recent Irish poetry as a whole, and more than justifies her inclusion in this English-language volume.

This *is* the 'significant' anthology its blurb professes it to be, if only because there is nothing to match it in terms of scope and scale. As such, the inclusion particularly of certain of the most recent poets in the book will inevitably do no harm to the reputations of those poets. Davis perhaps does as well as anyone could at choosing from the recent crop, and what a pleasure it is to see handsome selections from poets such as Enda Wyley (born 1966), Justin Quinn (born 1968) and above all Sinéad Morrissey (born 1972), whose work draws the anthology to a close. There is no other poet quite like Morrissey, the most recent in a longish line of celebrated poets from Belfast. Yet her poems can sum up a generation. 'Tourism' could only be the product of a new era of tentative peace and relative goodwill in the poet's fractured industrial home city:

we buy them a pint with a Bushmills chaser
and then on to the festering gap in the shipyard
the Titanic made when it sank.

Our talent for holes that are bigger
than the things themselves
resurfaces at Stormont, our weak-kneed parliament,

which, unlike Rome, we gained in a day
and then lost, spectacularly, several days later
in a shower of badly-played cards. Another instance, we say,
of our off-beat, headstrong, suicidal charm.

Morrissey's often remarkable poems constitute a fitting end to the book, and Davis's selection from her four collections to date, ending with 'Through the Square Window' from the 2009 collection of the same name, is a fairly good and representative one.

Davis's policy of including a dozen or more pages for each poet almost always allows a reader to get a strong sense of the of the range of a poet's work, but this comes at a cost. For all of the anthology's considerable bulk, the list of notable absentees is a glittering one. There is no room for the 'peasant poet' Francis Ledwidge, Ireland's only prominent poet of the Great War. Or F. R. Higgins, a noted follower of Yeats. Or most of Ireland's 'second generation' Modernists, among them Brian Coffey, Denis Devlin and Blanaid Salkeld (though there is, of course, a slot for Samuel Beckett). The truth is that there have been more than fifty or so fairly significant Irish poets born since the 1880s, and some of Davis's omissions – and therefore also some of his inclusions – are bound to seem unfortunate. All anthologies are destined to have weaknesses, and this particular weakness is largely the inevitable consequence of a notable strength. Such is the lot of the anthologist: he is the football referee of literary taste (or, to make another Aldridge analogy, perhaps the fourth official).

A notable benefit of Davis's method, beside the scope it affords for each poet, is that it enables the inclusion of important long poems, such as the full twenty pages of Patrick Kavanagh's 'The Great Hunger' and Anthony Cronin's remarkable if flawed 'RMS Titanic', alongside selections of these poets' other works. But Davis's willingness to find space for long poems does not leave him blind to the merits of more obviously slight ones, such as Peter Fallon's 'Birches':

> Shadows cross
> the road;
> a row of birches:
> barcode.

And another virtue of this anthology, naturally, is that it allows readers to discover the work of poets with whom they are not familiar. This is likely to be particularly true in the latter third book, where younger poets jostle for the reader's attention. Never mind, for a minute, the absentees or few suspect inclusions: the more recent and less widely familiar poets Davis includes all seem to deserve their place, or at least one can see why Davis thinks they do. Whether or not (say) Conor O'Callaghan, Justin Quinn and Sara Berkeley are going to stand out as complete unknowns in Davis's anthology in a few decades' time is another matter, but when it comes to the tricky issue of selecting from writers presumably at the greener end of their careers in an anthology that includes the likes of Kinsella, Beckett and MacNeice, Davis has taken to the task with gusto and done so as proficiently as anyone could expect. Whilst posterity makes up her mind, this book deserves a space on your shelf.

PN Review, 2010

SELF'S THE MAN

Philip Larkin, *Letters to Monica*, ed. Anthony Thwaite (Faber, 2010)

Philip Larkin's relationship with his exact contemporary Monica Jones began in 1946 when she was a very young lecturer in English at University College, Leicester, he being on the college library staff, and it lasted until his death in 1985. Until near the end they lived apart – Monica in Leicester or at her cottage in Haydon Bridge, and Larkin mostly in Belfast, then Hull, with frequent stops visiting his sister and mother in Loughborough – and wrote to one another several times a week for years on end, often cross-posting in their enthusiasm to put something in the mail. However, when Anthony Thwaite edited Larkin's *Selected Letters* (1992), only a handful of letters to Monica were included, the rest having apparently gone missing. After Larkin died, she effectively became a version of Miss Havisham: disorganised, ailing, in perpetual mourning for the man who had spent a lifetime refusing to marry her. So it was perhaps not much of a surprise that, following her death in 2001, a vast cache of almost 2000 letters and postcards from Larkin should be discovered among her belongings, dating from the year they met until the year before he died (though with an inexplicable gap from 1973 to 1982). This was a major discovery, for as Thwaite notes in his introduction to the present volume: 'they form the most important correspondence of his life. Certainly they mark his most important relationship'.

Their author certainly regarded Monica as his most important correspondent, and perhaps he even had a weather-eye on posterity when he wrote to her in May 1956:

> I was reading about the Carlyles tonight [...]. 'Their greatest
> agonies seem to have come from [...] not getting letters on the day

they were expected when they were separated.' Do you think people will write like that about us when we are dead?

It might seem a fitting quirk of fate, then, that *Letters to Monica* should exist as an independent volume. This book includes nearly 450 pages of letters, so is approximately two thirds the length of its 1992 counterpart. Thwaite includes a few facsimiles of cards, drawings, and the infrequent hand-written letters sent by Larkin (though no photographs of the pair apart from on the dust-jacket, which is unfortunate), and while *Letters to Monica* constitutes a fairly narrow selection from approximately 7,500 extant posted pages, it is nonetheless a much roomier one than Thwaite could make for any of the extensive correspondence represented in the *Selected Letters* – with mixed results. Taken as a whole, these letters to Jones present a private man who is self-aware, flawed and troubled, grindingly saturnine, repetitive – and not infrequently admirable for all that. If Larkin can sound forthright about his self-diagnosed 'selfishness' in the poems – 'My life is for me. / As well ignore gravity', for example – a number of these loving letters reveal a fragile and tormented man constantly torn to shreds by his own self-doubt and sense of failure:

> I show such poor return: I reel onwards, day in day out, living entirely off the surface of my reactions, spending too long chattering & so on, immersed entirely in the present – then when I am at last alone, I rake about among the ashes of the day and find a very meagre personality left. You are nothing like this, & in contrast I find myself superficial, insensitive, somewhat vulgar. […] I am cowardly, fleeing not only others but myself too.

He could not write like this to anyone else. He wrote like this to Monica all the time.

The *Selected Letters* is in many places a very funny book, apart from anything else. Like most of us, Larkin adapted his writing style and topic of conversation to reflect the nature of the relationship between himself and his correspondent. With his life-long friends Kingsley Amis and Robert Conquest, for example, Larkin could be a brash and even offensive wit among wits, but with Monica he was less showy than to his male literary friends, and more intimate, both emotionally and intellectually. This volume of letters, then, is neither as various nor as entertaining as its predecessor, but in a way that is its strength, for it was to Monica that Larkin poured out not only his many insecurities, but also his opinions about life, work and most of the people around him, for almost all of his adult life, and generally unhampered by any impulse to save face or play up to others' expectations.

It was also to Monica, above all of his other correspondents, that Larkin wrote about literature, not least the work of Katharine Mansfield, D. H. Lawrence and Thomas Hardy. A few sections of this collection deserve to be read just for Larkin's thoughtful, idiosyncratic comments on poetry and fiction:

> I've come upon *An ancient to ancients* (658): this is the kind of success Hardy has, isn't it; the quite-original form that could never be used again by anyone, but can be used once well by him. How the reiterated 'Gentlemen' calls up a group of game old birds sitting round a table!

But perhaps the greatest value of this book lies in the occasional insights it affords into Larkin's own work. His first collection of poems, *The North Ship*, published when the poet was in his early twenties, is largely forgettable and emphatically sub-Yeatsean. His next, *The Less Deceived*, established his reputation and his distinctive 'voice', influenced peripherally by poets such as A. E. Housman, W. H. Auden, John Betjeman, and above all Hardy. Two years after the publication of *The Less Deceived*, Larkin writes to Monica with a thorough refutation of the value of Yeats:

I've been thinking about Yeats rejecting Milton in favour of Shakespeare, & how Yeats and Hardy are the two comparable poles today, and how I at any rate reject Yeats. No doubt people wd say that you can have both, but they seem opposites to me, like Disraeli & Gladstone. Yeats seems to me an utterly artificial poet, dealing in make-believe, arid, ultimately stifling. And so dull! I doubt if another poet has ever had such dull subject-matter, often none at all.

Monica was Larkin's most trusted sounding board, not least when he was putting together the contents of *The Less Deceived* in 1955. He asks her if she can 'suggest' a title for the collection, and, startlingly, wonders whether 'Church Going' deserves to be included: 'I'm not sure. What do you think?' A few weeks later he writes that his publisher 'wants to put in *Spring* & *Since we agreed*, both of wch I'd left out', and again asks: 'What do you think?' It is Monica we have to thank for Larkin's use of 'lozels' in 'Toads', and 'liturgy' in 'Water': 'I'm sure you're right about *liturgy*, and now you mention it I believe you mentioned it on Sark, but I didn't take it in. *Litany sounds* nicer – a nicer word – but sense should take precedence, I suppose'. Monica also received the brunt of the poet's frequent fears about his often-meagre poetic output. On 5 March 1956 he writes: 'I'm scared stiff. Whatever am I to do? Not a single idea on the subject of poetry occurs to me, or not constructive, repeatable ones at least'. He had finished the slight 'First Sight' only two days beforehand, but would not complete another poem ('Love Songs in Age') for ten months. In May 1962 – one of his more productive years, as it happens, in which he had already written 'Wild Oats' and was to write 'Essential Beauty', 'Send No Money', 'Toads Revisited' and 'Sunny Prestatyn' – he exclaims desperately: 'I am no good, all washed up, can't even write a bad poem, let alone a good one'.

In the early 1950s Larkin was ambitious, but a number of his friends and contemporaries were extremely *successful*, not least Kingsley Amis. About Amis, Larkin can be biting and jealous, as well as extremely boring. Monica knew that she was the model for the grotesque Margaret Peel in Amis's *Lucky Jim* (1954), a novel Larkin essentially edited, and which propelled its author to stardom when Larkin was still a relative unknown. His attacks on his friend in these letters, centred on the publication of Amis's second novel, *That Uncertain Feeling*, in 1955, must be read with these things in mind. But they are still, to use Larkin's own description, 'stupid jealous talk': 'I was interested to hear the book had gone to Gollancz – oh please God, make them return it, with a suggestion he "rewrites certain passages"! Nothing would delight me more. And I refuse to believe he can write a book on his own – at least a good one'. When the novel was published, Larkin hoped it would get 'a good scragging' in the press, and lamented that 'Anything clever or funny one says is liable to be jotted down to be passed off as his [Amis's] own in future'.

Larkin's private bashing of contemporaries broadened, if anything, after his literary stock had skyrocketed. John Wain, another friend, writes 'Terrible Novels'. There is nothing wrong with the poems of Thom Gunn 'except that they're dull', and similar charges are made against Elizabeth Jennings: 'what a lot she writes! And how sort of conventional it is!' Others get biffed rather harder. Edith Sitwell is a 'Silly old cow', and F. R. Leavis is a 'Stupid little sod, the ideas rattling in him like peas', and is 'full of tricks to make the students laugh, and venomous enough to make A. L. Rowse sound like Hotspur'. Larkin feels 'sure' that George Barker is 'a shit, a real layabout cadging ponce'. In 1971, as he was editing the *Oxford Book of Twentieth-Century English Verse* (1973), Larkin writes:

> I'm pegging away at the bloody OxBo. Trouble is I can't see any worth, or *hardly* any worth, in people like Roy Fuller, Day Lewis, Grigson, Gascoyne, Barker & the like, and want to leave them out. Secondly, I think everybody born after 1930 is no good.

Even Betjeman gets a thump: 'I'm *sick* of Betjeman: cosy secret

Tory weapon, for all I care, nostalgic & snobbish'. Elsewhere, Larkin describes him as 'easily the best English poet today': he loved Betjeman, but also loved venting his spleen to Monica. Readers and critics should be sure to take a lot of Larkin's comments about other writers in these letters with a fat pinch of salt.

In the same year that *That Uncertain Feeling* was published, Larkin writes: 'I've grown tired of all my friends except you – all my close friends, that is [...]. [W]hen I met Kingsley in Cheltenham, & the Strangs on Boar Hill, & Bruce in Abingdon, I thought on each occasion: I'm through with this. Basically. You have shown me better things!' Naturally, their bond led not infrequently to talk of marriage. As Thwaite puts it in his slight introduction, 'Monica would have been glad to marry him; Larkin, with many guilty twinges, always drew back'. Anyone who has read poems such as 'Self's the Man' or 'Talking in Bed' knows how Larkin felt about marriage, or even cohabitation, and he is very direct when discussing the subject with Monica:

> I hate leaving you at the end of a holiday, as if all that was over now and the toys were being put back in the box, yet the impulse to make it real and permanent doesn't seem strong enough to shift me off the sandbanks – or if it is then I'm too feeble to obey it – and all this absurd havering revolts me too.

He was afraid of 'the bigness, the awfulness of marriage – "till death do us part"', and nothing Monica could do would change his mind. Still, it is surprising just how close they evidently did come to marrying. In October 1957, Monica was offered a visiting appointment at Queen's, New York, and it seems she used this invitation as a racquet with which to smash the ball squarely into Larkin's court:

> I can't say 'Don't go' unless I'm prepared to marry you; and [...] if I'm prepared to marry you it shouldn't need an American invitation

> to precipitate the proposal. I wish I could describe how I feel without going on & on. I am simply terrified at the prospect of us going on year after year & not getting married – so terrified that it may almost be something else I'm terrified of but don't recognise: but equally there is something missing in me – or in the way we get on – that wd precipitate it.

In the same letter he admits: 'I should hate to think of you […] being "dated" by octagonal-spectacled PhDs who were in Rome last year, and think W. S. Merwin a real pawut', but also suggests that 'a year apart might prove to be just what the doctor ordered' – not the response Monica might have hoped for. She stayed in Leicester, where Larkin wanted her: within range, though barely.

Considering the length and intensity of their relationship, it is strange how infrequently matters of the flesh are mentioned, and how tame Larkin tends to be when they are:

> I lay in bed one morning last week remembering one after-breakfast time when you were looking out of my kitchen window, and let me tuck your skirt up round your waist to be admired. You were wearing the black nylon panties with the small hole in! In consequence of this memory I was guilty of what I believe the Confirmation Books call 'impure thoughts', and, worse, late for work.

Saucy. That was in 1954, eight years after they had met. By 1962 he is brave enough to sign off a letter with: 'I'd like to kiss you all over and give you a good mauling'. It appears, however, that 'mauling' was not a speciality of Larkin's, and his honest appraisals of sexual performances make awkward reading. Larkin did not have a readership broader than Monica Jones in mind when he wrote 'I should think I am as incompetent at sex as at algebra, dancing the galliard or talking the lingo in *Roma*', or 'I'm sorry that our lovemaking fizzled out in Devon, as you rightly noticed. […] I'm sorry to have failed you! That is what always depresses me: the enormous harvest-homes you deserve, the few stale, shabby crumbs you get'.

When Monica discovered the extent of Larkin's relationship with his colleague Maeve Brennan, in 1964, it made her physically sick with anguish. His perpetual unwillingness to marry Monica, coupled with her discovery of this other relationship, drove her into a deep and grinding state of anxiety and depression, and this makes some of the later parts of the book harrowing. It is clear that her letter following the revelation was full of self-reproach as well as anger, and his response is typically forthright, but hardly comforting:

> I am tempted to say how much I'm affected by sex fear & auto-erotic fantasies, & how I feel normal emotional relations & responsibilities a terrible strain, I mean a big tiring strain. I don't want to bore you with such things – only don't assume that I'm wise & 'mature' compared with you: I'm infantile & cowardly & selfish.

More innocent than Monica, less literary, less demanding, Maeve appealed to different things in Larkin, and about this he was candid:

> About love, if I could have said last September 'I'm in love with Maeve, goodbye', I wd: as it was, I couldn't – perhaps too fond of you, perhaps not fond enough of her, perhaps just too cowardly all round. So don't go thinking I am skipping like a young ram in a rosy haze, 'in love' – I think I get some of the emotions with her. But I get some of them with you.

Until he parted from Maeve more than a decade later, Monica's love for Larkin, the man to whom she had effectively dedicated her life, was painfully half-requited. She never forced him to choose, perhaps through fear or her sense of inadequacy, though it is hard not to feel that had she done so it would have concluded the affair with Maeve and perhaps even resulted in the marriage she wanted so badly: Larkin needed Monica in his life. As he put it, in unusually syrupy language, 'our spirits are joined, I think, in a way it wd be impossible to separate'.

Not wanting to marry and falling in love with two women did not in itself make Larkin a bad person. As he wrote in 1957, before his relationship with Maeve had developed, 'I hate causing people distress', adding modestly: 'I don't claim any virtue for it: it's rather like avoiding arguments'. This honest desire to avoid causing distress – ironic, considering the broken woman he left behind – is evident throughout these letters. For example, he worries inordinately about having hurt the feelings of his mother. In 1951, a couple of years after his father's early death, he muses:

> If I had said: Mother, come & live with me in Belfast, or told my father the nature & hopelessness of his disease, this facing of the facts would surely have lessened what I feel at present. I don't know. Of course it is no use worrying about these things, nor is it seemly to do the wrong thing & then claim credit for worrying about it – but that's me all over.

In fact, Larkin wrote to his mother even more frequently than he wrote to Monica, and visited her often, even though he found her very difficult to be around, forever moaning and worrying. He did far more for his mother than most adult sons, but gave himself next to no credit for it. When in 1958 the successful librarian and writer of *The Less Deceived*, half-way through completing the poems that would make up *The Whitsun Weddings*, dutifully writing a long letter to his sweetheart, bemoans ad nauseam that he is 'completely selfish without achieving anything', it is hard not to feel that he is selling himself pitifully short.

However, though it is intriguing as an insight into the most complicated and nourishing relationship of Larkin's life, there is no getting away from the fact that, had Thwaite been able to access the bulk of these letters for the 1992 book, the present volume would not exist, and most of its contents would have remained unpublished without negative consequences for literature or literary research. Thwaite has provided a helpful biographical glossary and reasonably detailed footnotes, many containing sizeable quotations from Monica's letters to Larkin. But beyond the wrangle for a ring, a smattering of literary talk, flashes of wit and vitriol, and a few fascinating insights into the poems, a lot of these letters are in fact fairly dull, and often sloppily written: the tender day-to-day musings of a man who has posthumously been bled for all of the writing we can get out of him.

Essays in Criticism, 2011

'I WOULD SOONER MARRY YOU THAN ANYONE ELSE I KNOW': PHILIP LARKIN, MONICA JONES AND MARRIAGE

Philip Larkin and Monica Jones were exact contemporaries, and both were English undergraduates at Oxford in wartime. However, they met in 1946, when she was a very young lecturer in English at University College, Leicester, and he was on the College library staff. A few years later, just as Larkin broke off his engagement to Ruth Bowman and it looked as though he and Monica might be developing a love affair, Larkin moved to Belfast, and for most of his life they lived apart – Monica in Leicester or in later life at her cottage in Northumberland, and Larkin mostly in Belfast and then Hull, with frequent stops visiting his sister and mother in Loughborough. They seem to have written to one another several times a week for years on end. However, when Anthony Thwaite edited Larkin's *Selected Letters* (1992), only a handful of letters to Monica were included, the rest having apparently gone missing. After Larkin died in 1985, she spent the rest of her life living in his house. So it was perhaps unsurprising that following her death in 2001, a vast cache of almost 2000 letters and postcards from Larkin should 'emerge', dating from December 1946 until near the end of his life.

A selection of these letters has just been published as *Letters to Monica*, also edited by Anthony Thwaite, containing some 450 pages of correspondence – approximately ten percent of the total. The volume also gives us an impression of Monica's writing, in short but often revealing footnote quotations. A pervasive theme throughout much of their correspondence, as one might expect, is marriage, and in this article I will consider certain exchanges from these letters and how they relate to a few of Larkin's poems on the subjects of love and matrimony.

Larkin first achieved fame with *The Less Deceived*, his second collection, published in 1955. On 7 July 1953, a recording of Larkin reading 'If, My Darling', written in May 1950 but at that time unpublished in book form, was broadcast nationwide on BBC radio, as part of the show *First Reading*. This should have been a significant event for the young poet, but he didn't even listen to it: 'This', he wrote to Monica, 'isn't affectation (if it matters whether it is or not): it wd cause me severe embarrassment to hear any of those lines'. The poem begins:

> If my darling were once to decide
> Not to stop at my eyes,
> But to jump, like Alice, with floating skirt into my head,
>
> She would find no table and chairs,
> No mahogany claw-footed sideboards,
> No undisturbed embers;
>
> The tantalus would not be filled, nor the fender-seat cosy,
> Nor the shelves stuffed with small-printed books for the Sabbath,
> Nor the butler bibulous, the housemaids lazy:
>
> She would find herself looped with the creep of varying light,
> Monkey-brown, fish-grey, a string of infected circles
> Loitering like bullies, about to coagulate […].

The speaker's 'darling' evidently does not understand him – but the fault is his, the onus is on him: she is merely naïve whereas, beneath a subdued exterior, he is nothing better than a complicated grotesque. The poem was clearly of concern to Monica, and was debated on a few occasions around the time of the broadcast. Larkin foresaw her qualms, and wrote the following to her on the night of the programme:

> I don't know if you wondered whether it is addressed to anyone in particular: as it isn't, I don't mind saying it isn't, though I was a good deal exercised in my mind at that time about my ex-fiancée.

This evidently failed to alleviate her concerns. A year later he writes, with a hint of impatience, 'I really don't see where the agony comes in, if you mean people wd take it as applying to you'.

It didn't, of course. By 1953, Larkin's complicated love life had already started to centre on Monica; when he had written the poem three years earlier, they had been close friends, only becoming occasional sexual partners months later. The 'darling' of the poem is likely modelled on Ruth Bowman, whose relationship with Larkin ended abruptly not long after he recounted the following 'disaster' to his friend Jim Sutton, in a letter dated 18 June 1950, the month after he had completed 'If, My Darling':

> I came home thinking how Ruth and I could start life afresh in a far countrie (I hadn't seen her in ages), which led me when I did see her last night to stumble along a high road of platitudes that led me to a garbled proposal of marriage. She demurred at this: but as the evening went on and we drank more and more she grew more enthusiastic, I more gloomy. Now today I cannot think what maggot was in my brain to produce such a monstrous egg. Or rather I *can* think: several maggots: – the maggot of loneliness, the maggot of romantic illusion, the maggot of sexual desire. I am not engaged, but heaven knows how I can get out of it now, decently or indecently.

But get out of it he did, and their relationship ended shortly afterwards. His next poem, 'Wants', finished on the 1 June 1950, celebrates, or at least acknowledges, 'the wish to be alone', in spite of the lures of love and company – or, as he less alluringly puts it, 'the printed directions of sex' and a shower of 'invitation cards'. Larkin and Ruth were temperamentally ill-suited, but his aversion to marrying wasn't only about Ruth. At the age of twenty-seven, his close shave with matrimony served as a reminder that 'My life is for me. / As well ignore gravity', as he would put it in 'Love' more than a decade later.

'My Wife', a sonnet written the year after Larkin's separation from Ruth, is unequivocal in its iteration that marriage obliterates choice and estranges one from one's true nature. The speaker might be Larkin's imagined alter-ego, who went ahead with his offer to marry Ruth Bowman; he relentlessly laments that 'Choice of you shuts up that peacock fan / The future was', and that 'Simply to choose stopped all ways up but one', and in the sestet notes without any joy in sacrifice that:

> [...] for your face I have exchanged all faces,
> for your few properties bargained the brisk
> baggage, the mask-and-magic-man's regalia.
> Now you become my boredom and my failure,
> Another way of suffering, a risk,
> A heavier-than-air hypostasis.

It is natural to be tempted by the false but mystical lure of happiness, promising as it does to squish 'the maggot of loneliness, the maggot of romantic illusion, the maggot of sexual desire', and symbolised here by 'the mask-and-magic-man's regalia'. But the 'magic-man' deals in illusions that distract from the dull truth, and it is the latter that stands out in the last line of the octave: 'No future now. I and you now. Alone'. The three stunted sentences in this line, and its emphasis on flat monosyllables, impart a sense of morbid dismay, of a blunt and unalterable fact, as do the two disyllables that stand out so boldly like a coded message: marriage, rather than signalling togetherness, heralds a 'future [...] [a]lone' – but alone as part of a couple, accountable to someone else.

As time went on, Larkin found that he needed Monica in his life. For one thing, she knew all about the 'creep of varying light' and the 'string of infected circles / loitering like bullies' in Larkin's 'head', for she had similar tendencies to fret unnecessarily and interminably, and an inclination towards self-deprecation that matched his. As he told her, in language that almost mimics a wedding vow: 'our spirits are joined, I think, in a way it wd be impossible to separate'. With Monica, Larkin could discuss his literary passions and his frequent fears about not being able to write; he could spew vitriol without having to worry about what his correspondent thought of him; he could share private jokes (often involving rabbits, for the woman he called his 'dear Bun'); and could moan interminably. For example, several of the letters in *Letters to Monica* revolve around his landlady's tendency to put the radio on too loud, and his futile attempts to blot it out with cotton wool, a phenomenon that would make its way into his poem 'Mr Bleaney'. Monica seems to have put up with all of this unquestioningly, becoming an essential sounding board for him, and an emotional comfort. There is no reason to doubt his sincerity when he writes: 'I've grown tired of all my friends except you'. Nor is there more than a slight whiff of hyperbole when he signs off the same letter by declaring: 'When I stop writing to you I feel bereft'.

Naturally, their talk turned not infrequently to marriage, but the animus that had informed 'To My Wife' years before had not evaporated under Monica's influence. It is clear that she would have married in an instant, and most of Larkin's remarks on the subject in *Letters to Monica* are careful responses, him deflecting the matrimonial advances of his love with deftness and, sometimes, subtlety. In reply to her asking, in 1955, 'would you rather marry me than anybody else?', he is candid and loving, and ultimately demurs:

> [I]f we were going to get married this would be a good point to do so. I have a living wage, you want to pack up your job, we both want – or think we want – the same kind of life, we know each other well enough, etc. And we are ageing! I would sooner marry you than *anyone* else I know, and in any case I don't want to lose you. The sort of thing that gives me pause (paws) is wondering whether I do more than just like you very, very much and find it flattering and easy to stay with you instead of, well, behaving as

folks do, rushing after other people who take their fancy […]. Is it fair to marry without feeling 'quite sure'?

A week later he gets to the heart of the problem: 'I think what frightens me most about marriage is the passing-a-law-never-to-be-alone-again side of it'. We are back to 'Wants' again, the 'wish to be alone' running 'beneath' everything else, underlining it. Marriage means not only choosing one person above all others, more importantly it is a threat to glorious isolation that must be fended off at all costs.

For most of his adult life, until very near the end, Larkin's relationship with Monica really was an epistolary one above all else. In September 1959, Monica's mother was dying. On learning this – by letter – Larkin wrote back at once: 'If you wanted to ring me up (41719) you cd always reverse the charges. I'm usually in my sitting room after 8p.m. (before that I shouldn't hear the telephone)'. Between many friends, this would seem nothing more or less than a considerate gesture. But Larkin and Monica had known one another for fourteen years, wrote almost daily, and were embroiled in a complex, long-term love affair. It seems odd, then, that she apparently did not know his telephone number.

It would appear, in fact, that their verbal communication could be somewhat strained, at least in contrast to their outpourings on paper. They had never been natural talkers on the telephone, and were together infrequently – and on balance, Larkin seems to have liked it that way. In another bout of marriage-musing in October 1955, he expresses sorrow at their parting, but not only sorrow:

> I hate leaving you at the end of a holiday, as if all that was over now and the toys were being put back in the box, yet the impulse to make it real and permanent doesn't seem strong enough to shift me off the sandbanks […].

There is an important virtue to this sadness: it means their relationship has not become insipid, and Larkin does not feel as though his 'wish to be alone' has been compromised for long enough to cause resentment. After too long in one another's company, Larkin's need for solitude could cause him to 'grow stiff and silent', as he put it in April 1955, and he often deeply regretted it. On this occasion, they had just returned from a weekend in York:

> I shall never forget you being so solicitous when I was cold & sulky on Sunday night, instead of hoofing me out in a dungeon. There's something makes me less good than I ought to be, and I wish it didn't.

He loved his Bun dearly, but each time they met for a holiday or weekend she did not necessarily bring the best out of him after a while. Nobody could have done. But he was desperate not to let their relationship ossify. Moreover, he could talk to her about such matters with a directness that might seem callous, and the very fact that he felt able be open with her about his need for time alone was part of why she was so important to him in the first place:

> I know I can't be said to present a consistent front to you on the subject of visits, holidays, etc., & I don't at all resent yr questioning what I mean, or what I feel. [...] Recently I've felt that we have grown slightly stale, like a good show that needs a break or a rest – does this sound very rude? – I mean myself as much as you: same jokes, same attitudes, same prejudices.

That was in July 1957. Three months later, Monica was offered a year-long visiting appointment at Queen's, New York, which instigated another careful parrying of the marriage question: 'If I'm prepared to marry you it shouldn't need an American invitation to precipitate the proposal.' He proceeds to suggest that a year apart might prove to be just what the doctor ordered'. She never went to New York.

He must have his solitude and the 'show' must not grow 'stale'. 'Talking in Bed', written just three years later in August 1960, seems to ring out a very personal warning – for all of the poem's universality – against the pitfalls of overdosing on intimacy. Nowhere is it stated that the relationship described in the poem is a marriage, after all, though it is clearly a cohabitational relationship. Understandably, Monica felt uneasy about the poem's inclusion in *The Whitsun Weddings* in 1964: 'it will cause so much talking here, in & out of beds, & indeed elsewhere – what do you think yr mother & relatives will make of it?' However, Monica did not seem angry about Larkin's intention with this poem, and it wasn't about their relationship, at least not as it existed. Rather, 'Talking in Bed' can be seen as a poem about what their relationship might become, if the poet was not careful. It presents two people lying together in bed, an enduring 'emblem' of honesty, and one in which it 'ought to be' easy to talk, 'Yet more and more time passes silently'. In the process of looking in on the private world of this couple, we are at once invited to look back outside again. There are huge and significant contrasts between the narrowly delimited room that they occupy and the vastness and fullness of the world 'Outside', which mocks the limitations of the former with enigmatically 'dark towns' that 'heap up' like unfulfilled dreams, out of reach 'on the horizon'. But the first thing the speaker notices beyond the window-pane is the overwhelming sky, and the pathetic fallacy of its 'incomplete unrest' is the emotional driving force of the poem. However, the speaker and his companion remain virtually inert in their bed. As in 'If, My Darling', with its comparison of what the 'darling' can see in the male speaker and the demons that lurk in his mind, 'Talking in Bed' explores the stark contrast between latent and manifest emotions: what can be shown on the surface, and what is going on under it. But in 'Talking in Bed', the domestic situation has developed beyond the youthful revelations of emotional awkwardness in 'If, My Darling', where a couple are emotionally estranged from one another because any revelation of the speaker's emotions 'Might knock my darling off her unpriceable pivot', to a dour, bed-ridden, overwhelming familiarity, unsettled by boredom and fear, in which there is (as 'To My Wife' has it) 'No future now. You and I now. Alone'. Like kissing at the altar, talking in bed is 'An emblem of two people being honest'. To Larkin, it is also a symbol of grinding personal constraint.

Being one half of this couple, who are emphatically not talking in bed, is the epitome of isolation, as it pitches both partners at a 'unique distance' where no-one else can quite reach or understand them, and where sharing their deepest feelings with one another would be too painful, even impossible. Thus, they remain quiet and 'more and more time passes silently'. Any 'dialogue' that exists between them is unvoiced, unpleasant and unhelpful, but also unrelenting and impossible to ignore. They are estranged from their essential selves, from one another, and from all the human possibilities that exist beyond their unsatisfactory, 'unique', private world. Marriage or no, choice has resolutely shut and bound the peacock-fan that was the future. It is a situation Larkin was determined to prevent in his relationship with Monica. There is little point in avoiding the registrar if you are going to slip into a virtual marriage anyway.

Only, that is exactly what they did do, in the end. In 1972, Larkin's mother went into a nursing home in Leicestershire, meaning that he visited Monica more frequently, and in 1978 he finally ended his seventeen-year affair with Maeve Brennan (albeit replacing it, briefly, with an affair with his secretary). In October 1982, Monica had a fall and required hospital treatment, and convalesced in Hull, at the large, modern house Larkin had moved to in 1974. The next spring, she developed shingles, and moved in with him permanently. Thus, two decades after Larkin had written 'Talking in Bed', they settled into what Thwaite describes as 'something close to marriage': monogamous cohabitation in suburbia.

Letters to Monica is not, sadly, full of previously-undiscovered poetic gems hidden away in letters, though it has its minor moments in this regard. One of these, titled 'Bun's Outing' and evidently from the inside of Larkin's Christmas card for 1984, ends the book:

> Saturday morning
> I go for the meat,
> Body all aching
> Likewise the feet.
> Fools at my elbow
> Gormlessly greet,
> Shopping is hell
> In Stupidity Street.

The joke in this Christmas squib is a private one. Rather than celebrating the season, his 'Bun' focuses on the awfulness of Christmas shopping: she is as peevish as the poet, and the eight short lines could equally (albeit less humorously, for Monica) bear the title 'My Outing'. In spite of everything their temperaments had thrown at them, fate and a wish in later life not to be alone meant that their relationship developed into a de facto marriage that neither of them would have changed, and that continued till death did them part. Larkin died days before they could commiserate their next Christmas together.

The Dark Horse, 2011

SUCH ABSENCES

Philip Larkin, *Poems: Selected by Martin Amis*
(Faber, 2011)

Larkin was a painstaking editor of his own work. His efforts were rendered futile with the publication, three years after his death, of *Collected Poems* (1988), edited by Anthony Thwaite. It included 242 poems, 135 more than Larkin had given us in his four very slim volumes. Many of these 135 were previously unpublished – several were even unfinished – but while some of them are atrocious, a few are superb or at least have superb elements. Thwaite also re-ordered Larkin's oeuvre to present the poems chronologically, and broke this chronology in two by putting all the 'early' poems, including the vast majority of the more Yeatsean ones, at the back. I have no idea whether Larkin would have approved, but it certainly made for a fascinating book.

It was apparently superseded in 2003 by a second *Collected Poems*. However, while the later book retained the order of Larkin's collections, and included poems that had been published elsewhere by the poet, it omitted everything that had not been chosen for publication during his lifetime – so some of the more intriguing pieces *that had already been published* were bumped off. Of course, it was a more consistent book than its predecessor, but at a mere two hundred pages it was also something of a regression.

Early in 2012 both *Collected*s are to be superseded in turn by a *Complete Poems*, edited by Archie Burnett. Last year I noted in *Essays in Criticism* that Larkin has been 'posthumously bled for all of the literature we can get out of him', and this volume, which will apparently – and somehow – have in the region of eight hundred pages, looks set to rubber-stamp the process. In addition to both versions of *Collected Poems*, we have had *Trouble at Willow Gables and Other Fictions* (2002), a book of previously unpublished Larkinalia edited by James Booth, which contains a number of poems by a young Larkin writing as one Brunette

Coleman. And then there was *Early Poems and Juvenilia* (2005), ed. A. T. Tolley: a tome larger than either *Collected*, and crammed full of tosh, albeit tosh of considerable interest to any Larkin enthusiast. A poet whose output had seemed, whilst he was alive, almost as meagre as A. E. Housman's or Ian Hamilton's has become, in death, as prolific as Hardy, and the bloated *Complete Poems* is certain to be as hit-and-miss as a game of Battleships.

So perhaps Faber has done enough to make room for *Poems*. And this is a very readable book. Omissions aside, Amis reverts to the order Larkin chose for his collections. He includes at the end only six poems uncollected by the poet – including, of course, the magnificent and terrifying 'Aubade' (which the editor's father Kingsley did not much care for, as it happens). Only two of the poems in the book ('Letter to a Friend About Girls' and 'Love Again') were not seen into print by Larkin, one way or another, and these were among the more worthwhile previously unpublished pieces included by Thwaite in 1988. So Amis's *modus operandi* seems sensible enough: conservative, necessary, an exercise in separating wheat and chaff.

No *Selected Poems* is ever so simple, of course – and, fittingly, in the front cover photograph of this book, a fifty-something Larkin gazes wryly through the top of thick-rimmed specs and seems to ask: 'What the bloody hell did you do that for, you silly boy?' As there are about 140 pages of Larkin's poetry with real literary merit – and there is a considerable gulf between that and the rest – it seems pertinent to ask what the point is of a selection that contains almost two thirds of these pages. Why not just include the others, too?

But that was presumably not Amis's commission. So how did he decide which third of the real Larkin would not make it – or, rather, which two-thirds *would* make it? The giveaway is in his introductory essay, in which the novelist son of Larkin's novelist best mate remarks that whilst Larkin is 'a people's poet', he is 'also, definingly, a novelist's poet':

> Larkin is a scene-setting phrasemaker of the first echelon. What novelist, reading 'Show Saturday', could fail to covet 'mugfaced middleaged wives/Glaring at jellies' and 'husbands on leave from the garden/Watchful as weasels' and 'car-tuning curt-haired sons'?

Amis goes on to praise Larkin's simultaneously terse and novelistic sensibility: 'Many poems, many individual stanzas, read like distilled short stories, as if quickened by the pressure of a larger story, a larger life.' 'Mr Bleaney' has the 'amplitude of a novella', and 'Livings I' 'begins "I deal with farmers, things like dips and feed". And after a single pentameter the reader is lucidly present in another life'.

Amis has nailed one of Larkin's traits, and has set out his stall in the process, for it is the poems of a more novelistic kind that tend to prevail here. I do not wish to criticise the editor for making an honest selection; though it is as well to remark, for example, that only one poem of six lines makes the cut from Larkin's overlooked and overly impressionistic first collection, *The North Ship* (1945). That is probably a fair reflection on the worth of that volume, actually. But it seems odd that he includes just over a third of *The Less Deceived* (1955), leaving out almost all of the pithier poems, and finds no room for 'Myxomatosis', though he does include among the handful of 'uncollected' pieces the clearly inferior kill-an-animal-and-ponder poem 'The Mower'. And though Amis does not deny us the handful of poems that really *had* to be in this book ('Church Going', 'The Whitsun Weddings', 'Dockery and Son', 'The Building', 'This Be the Verse', 'Aubade'), it is hard not to feel that Larkin's more beautiful poems are often overlooked in favour of his meaner, wittier ones. 'Reference Back', 'First Sight', 'Water' and – alarmingly – 'Love Songs in Age' are all missing from the poems selected from *The Whitsun Weddings* (1964); it is strange that all but two of the poems from *High Windows* (1974) are included and yet that book's beautiful and mystical closer, 'The Explosion', is not among them. And how bizarre that the back cover quotes 'Absences':

> Above the sea, the yet more shoreless day,
> Riddled by wind, trails lit-up galleries:
> They shift to giant ribbing, sift away.
>
> Such attics cleared of me! Such absences!

'Absences' is not included in the book; its tone is singular among Larkin's poems (he thought it sounded like a French formalist and once said he wished he could 'write like this more often'); and it is poles apart from the Larkin Amis wants to give us. 'Larkin', the editor writes, 'is most definitely *this* novelist's poet.' And make no mistake about it: this is the best of Larkin in Amis's image more than it is an attempt at representing the people's 'people's poet'.

So: this is an intriguing volume, but one even more flawed than its *Collected* predecessors – for reasons both beyond and within Amis's control. If I wanted to present a Larkin book to a friend unacquainted with the poet's work (someone who has spent all of life in a cork-lined room, for instance), I would root around for the (out of print) book Thwaite put together all those years ago. And anyone with a fuller interest in Larkin is surely better off waiting for the *Complete Poems*.

PN Review, 2011

R. S. THOMAS, *THE STONES OF THE FIELD* (CARMARTHEN: THE DRUID PRESS, 1946)

Whether *The Stones of the Field* is or is not a first collection depends on your definition. It was published by a vanity press, as was *An Acre of Land* (1952); most of the poems in both were then included, along with newer work, in *Song at the Year's Turning* (1955), published more salubriously by Rupert Hart-Davis. This later book bore an introduction by John Betjeman, which ended: 'The "name" which has the honour to introduce this fine poet to a wider public will be forgotten long before that of R. S. Thomas'. But I'm going to focus on the original debut, a book once printed by an outfit tucked in a room above a chippy in Carmarthen, which sold pitifully at the time and cost the author £60 – roughly two months' wages – to print, and which would now set you back something close to £1500.

Thomas turned thirty-three in 1946, so it wasn't an especially early debut, but perhaps we should be thankful that this relative benchmark didn't come along earlier. His juvenilia, some of it printed in the Bangor college magazine under the pseudonym Curtis Langdon and in *The Dublin Magazine* in 1939–40, had been almost uniformly wistful and lightweight, the poems of someone who has not yet developed a voice of his own or found anything original to say, and who therefore sticks to generalities:

> I know no clouds
> More beautiful than they
> That the far hills shroud
> At the end of the day.

Good for you, Ronald. However, this is painfully trite and equally painfully contrived; the inversion 'That the far hills shroud' creates confusion about which is the subject, which the object, and has obviously been perpetrated to get a rhyme.

It is a far cry from the stark impressions of local and personal life that were to make Thomas's name a few years later. By the end of the war this man, used to life in Holyhead and Bangor and at least passingly familiar with the company of scholars and theologians, was working as a priest in the tiny mid-Wales village of Manafon, and trying to fall in love with his country in the flesh as he had in theory. The villages of mid-Wales had a profound and deeply invigorating effect on the poems he wrote, and this is immediately apparent in *The Stones of the Field*: when the *Times Literary Supplement* gave it brief notice, the reviewer described not a navel-gazing fop, but 'a Welshman steeped in the customs, traditions and feelings of his country', and a new poetic voice with 'a fearful intensity and reality'. None of the stuff in that earlier, faux-Georgian mode infiltrates the 1946 book.

The most famous poem in this collection is perhaps the best-known poem Thomas would ever write: 'A Peasant'. Here he begins his two-decade poetic relationship with Iago Prytherch, a 'prototype' hill-farmer somewhat akin to Patrick Kavanagh's Maguire in 'The Great Hunger'. At the start of the poem, Prytherch is presented in achingly bucolic fashion as 'an ordinary man of the bald Welsh hills, / Who pens a few sheep in a gap of cloud'. But there is a hint of what is to come in the pun on 'pens': in very different senses Thomas and Prytherch both 'pen' these sheep, but neither seems to know much about the working life of the other. Thomas is paving the way for a shocking close-up, for Prytherch does not remain a distant symbol but a reality like Maguire, and at close quarters any shadowy romanticism is suddenly and surprisingly blotted out by stark reality. This is a long way from the world of study, intellectual rigour, writing poetry:

> [A]t night see him fixed in his chair
> Motionless, except when he leans to gob in the fire.
> There is something frightening in the vacancy of his mind.
> His clothes, sour with years of sweat
> And animal contact [...].

At least he 'gobs at the fire', unlike Maguire, who 'spreads his legs over the impotent cinders'. Just as Philip Larkin's 'The Card-Players' presents the comically unsavoury Jan van Hogspeuw, who 'Gobs at the grate' and simultaneously seems eternal and truthful, so Prytherch appears to be (to borrow Charles Causley's phrase) in his 'fixed place in God's universe'. '[S]eason by season / Against siege of rain and the wind's attrition', he 'Preserves his stock', and being suddenly at close quarters with him we are forced to recognise both the depth of his bond to his environment and the shallowness of his mind – as though the two are necessary counterparts. It is a giddying juxtaposition and near-epiphany. Then, in the last line of the poem, after zooming so far in on the apparently uncouth existence of the peasant, the poem gratefully zooms back out to leave him once more a symbol of fortitude, 'Enduring like a tree under the curious stars', as fascinatingly strange to the poet as are celestial bodies – and in a sense equally far away.

In 'A Peasant', the farmer's rancid clothes 'shock the refined, / But affected sense'; there can be little doubt that they shock the speaker, and the enjambment immediately makes the two words that follow it seem bathetic on the part of those thus affected. In attacking this false etiquette and propriety, Thomas turns the tide of opprobrium on himself (and probably on the reader, too) in an instant. And what is more, Prytherch 'is your prototype': we have no right to our proud condemnation. Thomas is echoing Part IV of Eliot's *The Waste Land*, 'Death by Water', which recalls the demise of Phlebas the Phoenician, and ends:

Gentile or Jew
O you who turn the wheel and look to windward,
Consider Phlebas, who was once handsome and tall as you.

Though an uncouth idiot, Iago Prytherch is simultaneously an embodiment of belonging and endurance and, like Phlebas, a warning against hubris.

But while 'A Peasant' challenges readers (and the poet) to assess their own smug positions, as well as the true nature of the rustic hill-farmer, this is taken to a new level in 'An Airy Tomb'. This poem, easily the longest thing in the book, describes in some detail the 'long life alone' on the moor of another named farmer, Twm, full of yearnings and failures that again call to mind Kavanagh's Maguire. Near the end, however, the narrative voice sours abruptly, as the poem turns to attack the reader's artistic proclivities and presumed sense of social superiority:

> And you, hypocrite reader, at ease in your chair,
> Do not mock their conduct, for are you not also weary
> Of this odd tale, preferring the usual climax?

How dare he!

Thomas in his early thirties, then, is nothing like the same poet as Thomas in his mid-twenties. What on earth happened? It is hard not to feel that he must have read Kavanagh's book when it came out in 1942, and that it had a profound effect on him; but the presentation of Prytherch is far more confused than that of Maguire, as well as being much more protracted. As Thomas moved farther into the heart of Wales, following his curacies, there fermented in him a means for exploring the ensuing hurt, hope and discomfort he felt in his new environment. As he fell deeply in love with his small country and simultaneously found himself for the first time at close quarters with his rural countryfolk, the ideal and reality did not always match up, and this antagonism invigorates the poetry, full as it is of naked love and loathing, despair and admiration. Nowhere is this truer than in 'A Priest to His People'. Here, Thomas writes what, in spite of the poem's title, he would never have proclaimed from the pulpit – perhaps safe in the knowledge that the considerable majority of 'his people' would not read it:

> Men of the hills, wantoners, men of Wales
> With your sheep and your pigs and your ponies, your sweaty females,
> How I have hated you for your irreverence, your scorn even
> Of the refinements of art and the mysteries of the Church [...].

'Wantoners' are impervious to moral teaching. But 'hate', at least when misplaced, is a deeply irreverent and un-Christian emotion, and the irony of this is not lost on Thomas. Moreover, his powerful distaste raises serious concerns for the priest about his own earthly purpose. These 'hated' (default) men and 'sweaty females' are in fact the people who *belong* in this environment: they are '*of* the hills', '*of* Wales' (my italics), and the speaker is an intruder in their midst. Thomas's scorn is therefore rooted not only in disgust, but also in the jealous fear that he might be obsolete, that those he addresses are not 'his people' at all, and seem to be getting by quite well without more than perfunctory recourse to their local intermediary with God. His vocational and Godly duty is to serve 'his' people, but priest and people repel one another.

The recognition of this results in a sequence of thoughts that leads to an extraordinary volte-face, an unholy epiphany. The lives of the priest's 'people' are not unhappy: though 'curt and graceless', their 'sudden laughter / Is sharp and bright as a whipped pool', and noticing this laughter and realising what it means alters utterly the priest-speaker's perception. Suddenly he understands their lack of interest in the Church, their inability to see its relevance to their lives:

> [...] your strength is a mockery
> Of the pale words in the black Book,
> And why should you come like sparrows for prayer crumbs [...]?

What need have they for God, who have already in a sense inherited the earth and who live in harmony with their environment? Why should they be anything other than 'indifferent to all that [the priest] can offer'? The poet is torn between feelings of admiring jealousy and loathing for these enigmatic beings that will, regardless of his influence, 'continue to unwind [their] days / In a crude tapestry under the jealous heavens', and who are, unwittingly, his muses, able to 'affront, bewilder, *yet compel* my gaze' (my italics again). Indeed, 'jealous' God seems to need them more than they need Him – and certainly the poet does. They might not be aware of the artistic flame they have ignited (or the 'artistry' of their dwellings 'on the bare hill') but they are illuminated by it nonetheless.

Thomas rarely names specific locations in these poems, as though doing so might have compromised the relative universality of his message about life in rural Wales. 'Country Church (Manafon)' is the only exception, and here the location is significant:

> The church stands, built from the river stone,
> Brittle with light, as though a breath could shatter
> Its slender frame, or spill the limpid water,
> Quiet as sunlight, cupped within the bone.
>
> It stands yet. But though soft flowers break
> In delicate waves round limbs the river fashioned
> With so smooth care, no friendly God has cautioned
> The brimming tides of fescue for its sake.

The churchyard is wild with fescue grass and flowers; the building's stones have been fashioned by an almost anthropomorphised caring river; the verse is couched in an ABBA rhyme scheme with feminine central half-rhymes, enacting a sort of gentle prosodic encasement. This is a romantic scene in which animate and inanimate intertwine organically, but more than that it commemorates a building in which sanctuary can be sought from the 'brimming tides' without: a metaphor for more than just the natural environment. The poem could describe any of scores of village churches in Britain, though, were it not for the bracketed subtitle; Thomas is reclaiming the village, or the part of it he is most attuned to, and tacitly commemorating its historic social and spiritual hub as a personal place of refuge from those without, whom he found so inscrutable. The repetition of 'stands' is a quietly emphatic celebration of the church's permanence and the sense of spiritual belonging it enables in this village community from which he feels estranged. This is not a poem of belonging to Manafon, but of surviving in spite of it – a leitmotif for the book as a whole.

There are none of Thomas's ostensibly nationalist poems in this tiny book. Here, we experience a poet fraught with uncertainties, decades before he became so sure-footed. *The Stones of the Field* presents one of the greatest modern poets at his finest and most volatile, writing poems that, at the time of their initial publication, nobody wanted to print on their author's behalf. To open it is to be confronted by a threshold.

The Dark Horse, 2012

N.B. This article was written for a feature on first collections.

A MULTIPLICITY OF BELONGING

Justin Quinn, *Close Quarters* (Gallery, 2011); Bernard O'Donoghue, *Farmers Cross* (Faber, 2011)

Justin Quinn's 'close quarters' are various. Quinn is from County Dublin, but has taught American literature in Prague since 1995, arriving 'in the wreck / of central Europe', as he puts it in 'The City Gates', a few years after the fall of the Iron Curtain. His younger self turned up in Prague speculatively, one feels, knowing 'a girl, some words in Czech', and since then he has raised a family in his adopted homeland; an experience that initially was 'like being dead' has transmuted into a fully-supported life.

His seems to be an identity refracted, not fractured: many of the poems speak of a consciousness that knows where it belongs, and appreciates the multiplicity of that belonging – in literary as well as geographical and familial terms. There are poems here beginning with lines by Edward Thomas, with the Czech food and travel writer Evan Rail, the American folk-rock band Fleet Foxes; others proudly take inspiration from Horace, Ernest Hilbert, Folgóre da San Gimignano. It is a sense of multiplicity imparted and encouraged in hopeful and spirited poems such as 'Seminar', which is rooted in Quinn's teaching life: 'I carry America into these young heads, / at least some parts of it that haven't yet got there'. They lap it up; he celebrates them for this, and for, at the end of class, readying themselves 'for their daily trek / across a continent and ocean home'.

Most of *Close Quarters* is metrical verse, much of it in rhymed quatrains of pentameters. Quinn's tone and method are sometimes reminiscent of Tony Harrison and, as Harrison did in his early poems, Quinn gets away with the occasional pat rhyme because at his finest he achieves a rare poignancy, as in these lines from 'Musílkova':

> Named for a local doctor, executed
> in 1940 for his work in resistance.
> Whether he was recruiter or recruited,
> whether he placed bombs or just gave assistance,
>
> is hard to find out now, or why he joined
> when most other people were dragging their feet.
> Suddenly no options left. A single point.
> Led out into a yard. Became a street.

Quinn's wide-eyed but intelligent fascination with his environments, coupled with his talent for getting at the universal through the local and personal, has much to do with why this collection is so enjoyable to read. He is a realist, with a strong social conscience and sense of history, but a realist can keep faith too. Even his poem about yelling 'Fuck' when his small child punches him in the balls while playing Batman turns to a frank meditation on what love is, and perhaps isn't, and is at once a startling warning and a tribute:

> Your mother
> and I embrace you more
> than we do one another.
> You are now where we store
> our fun, and like a parable
> we've lately turned to marble.

The close quarters in *Close Quarters*, then, are undoubtedly the poet's. But we might see something of ourselves in even his most personal poems.

Farmers Cross, Bernard O'Donoghue's sixth collection, is another book full of displacements, often of a highly suggestive kind: 'battalions / of unknown children, speaking in accents / different from their parents'; watching 'the Americans spray shaving foam' to bring out the inscriptions of ancestors, thoughtlessly leaving behind a 'aromatic blear' when they have gone back to 'their duties in New England or Chicago'; holidaying in Bavaria and being 'pulled up short by a sudden smell / I hadn't breathed for years. Chaff', before stopping at Dachau, now 'closed on Monday'. Like Quinn, O'Donoghue ranges for his allusions and comparisons – mostly into a strange medieval world that he seeks to refresh, to make startlingly relevant. (O'Donoghue, born in County Cork, teaches medieval English literature at Oxford.) The collection contains an emotionally faithful translation of the 'Prologue' from *Piers Plowman* (the speaker of which is appositely itinerant, of course), a translation of part of Dante's *Purgatorio*, and a superb modern retelling of 'The Wanderer', updated with the flotsam of modern life but expressing the universal concerns of the Anglo-Saxon original. There are several other references to medieval sources: Ælfric's *The Life of King Edmund*, Chaucer, Petrarch. O'Donoghue's preoccupation with place and displacement, belonging and estrangement, leads him, like Seamus Heaney in *North*, to consider Gunnar, the chieftain in Njál's saga who refused to flee the land of his fathers: 'it also meant / he'd chosen to remain where death closed in'.

O'Donoghue's shift of homeland, from the west of Ireland to Oxford via Manchester as a teenager, is on the face of it a little less dramatic than Quinn's. But, as Charles Causley pointed out, 'sometimes the shortest-seeming journey takes us furthest from what we think of as home'. O'Donoghue expresses no anxiety about his mixed identity – a mixed identity many of us share, in one way or another. Nevertheless, 'Emigration', a poem for the Oxford-based Palestinian poet Yousif Qasmiyeh, exudes a kind of gentle wisdom that smacks of empathy, at least insofar as it concerns what is at stake and what must be remembered:

Unhappy the man that has lacked the occasion
to return to the village on a sun-struck May morning,
to shake the hands of the neighbours he'd left

a lifetime ago and tell the world's wonders,
before settling down by his hearth once again.

The poems in *Farmers Cross* tend to be pragmatic, albeit keenly observed: not for O'Donoghue the beautiful lyricism of Quinn's finest poems. There is an emotional reticence at the heart of some of them, which is to say that O'Donoghue never lets emotion get in the way of reason, even when he writes about how

> I myself, in a desperate state,
> years from home and friends,
> and sick with misery,
> must chain my wretched tongue
> as I watch them burying
> my dear friends in the cold earth.

Farmers Cross communicates with assurance, modesty, level-headedness. The poems are often quiet, but they repay close listening.

Times Literary Supplement, 2012

TO ME IT WAS DILUTION

Philip Larkin, *Complete Poems*, ed. Archie Burnett
(Faber, 2012)

Larkin died in 1985 with four very short collections of poetry to his name. There was also a smattering of other published poems, such as 'Aubade', included in the Christmas 1977 edition of the *Times Literary Supplement*, and brimming with tidings of comfort and joy:

> I work all day, and get half drunk at night.
> Waking at four to soundless dark, I stare.
> In time the curtain-edges will grow light.
> Till then I see what's really always there:
> Unresting death, a whole day nearer now [...].

Collected Poems was published three years after unresting death caught up with him. It was surprisingly thick, the editor Anthony Thwaite including a lot of poems Larkin had chosen not to publish or hadn't even finished. Some were superb, or at least illuminating; others were neither. A slimmer *Collected* then appeared in 2003, followed a couple of years later by an unfeasibly fat volume of juvenilia, this time edited by A. T. Tolley.

Now these books have potentially been superseded in turn by the present, altogether more substantial tome. The poems in *Complete Poems* are apportioned to seven categories: the four collections plus 'Other Poems Published in the Poet's Lifetime', 'Poems Not Published in the Poet's Lifetime' and 'Undated or Approximately Dated Poems' – the latter three categories filling 230 pages, considerably more than twice the space of the first four. Such a book needs justifying, in the light of its predecessors, and Burnett gets straight to task. 'An accurate text is, and always must be, the chief justification', he writes in his often sandpaper-dry introduction, and '*Collected Poems* (1988) contains a scattering of errors, some of which were subsequently corrected.' (He lists them.) Tolley's volume added many more, containing '72 errors of wording, 47 of punctuation, 8 of letter-case, 5 of word-division, 4 of font and 3 of format'. Moreover, the notes on completion dates in *Collected Poems* are also apparently vague or misleading in places. For example, as Burnett explains:

> A 'completion date' of 12 October 1944 is given for Night-Music (poem XI in TNS [*The North Ship*]) in both editions of *Collected Poems* and in Tolley's edition of *Early Poems and Juvenilia* (2005), and one of the drafts in Workbook I does indeed bear the date '12. x. 44'. But the drafts, beginning after '8. x. 44', continue substantially after 12 October 1944 and before the next date in the workbook, 23 October 1944. The drafts fall, therefore, between 8 and 23 October 1944, the latter being the date by which the poet stopped drafting the poem in the workbook.

And so forth. How ironic that Larkin is noted for compression of feeling, for being memorable.

That said, it is of course pleasing to have such a diligently edited volume. Perhaps the biggest value of this edition is its *apparatus criticus*, which fills almost half the book and is crammed with elucidating comments from various sources, as well as variant wordings, completion dates and first publication information. On the other hand – and unsurprisingly – quite a few of the previously unpublished 'poems' test the boundaries of what we might decently think a poem to be. In addition to the handful of recently uncovered longer pieces, these include numerous squibs from workbooks, letters and the like, which Thwaite did not see before publishing (or did not see fit to include in) the 1988 book. They are, by turns, sidelined versions of things done better elsewhere, witty ditties, self-consciously narrow-minded quips, nonsensical blatherings, kitsch amusements in pat verse, and so forth: as varied in tone as the letters from which many of them have been pilfered. Some are memorable for obvious and not always the same reasons. Here Larkin conflates at least three of his poems in a quatrain that does not appear to have been subjected to his famously stringent artistic scrutiny:

> This was Mr Bleaney's bungalow,
> Standing in the concrete jungle, o-
> ver-looking an arterial road –
> Here I live with old Toad.

And here he makes an unusual foray into Orientalism:

> Outside, a dog barks
> Swinging from your prick, I muse
> On Wang-Lei's lyrics.

And in this couplet Dr Larkin offers medical advice:

> Sherry does more than Bovril can,
> To stop you feeling like puking in the lavatory pan.

No poet in his or her senses would contemplate publishing these and their ilk; I can't see how they have any justification for inclusion in a *Collected Poems* beyond our voracious appetite for Larkinalia. Moreover, the vast majority of Larkin's squibs are already accessible, in their proper contexts, in the Larkin archive at Hull or in published letters. I have spent time looking at the Larkin archives myself, and therefore many of the post-Tolley additions should not have been new to me, but most are wholly forgettable. I did, however, notice a few curious omissions from Burnett's book, including one squib about Loyalist Sandy Row in Belfast that makes an interesting counterpart to Larkin's poem about living in that city, 'The Importance of Elsewhere'. An omission many others are more likely to notice is 'The Winter Palace', included in the 1988 *Collected* and anthologised in popular volumes such as *Short and Sweet* (Faber, 2002), edited by Simon Armitage. Burnett has his reasons, though, of course:

> 'It is on grounds that the poet left only cancelled and incomplete versions of lines 3–4 of 'The Winter Palace' that – not without regret – the poem has been removed from the canon in the present edition [...]. [I]t seemed best to acknowledge that Larkin did not finish work on the poem, and leave it at that.'

Burnett has an eye for detail that makes me positively giddy, but the fact that so much dross is included in a book called *Complete Poems*, and a real, well, *poem* is not, suggests that his method is less than perfect. Nonetheless, even when the newly-published pieces are trite they can be worth having. For instance, it is hard, at least for me, not both to smile and wince upon learning that Larkin broke off in the middle of working at the profoundly serious 'Faith Healing' to jot this:

> Great baying groans burst from my lips
> Looking at women's breasts and hips.

What is *Complete Poems* trying to be: a book for the specialist, for the general reader, or for both? We should judge a book on its aims as well as its merits, and as far as the former is concerned it is in many ways a triumph, scrupulously edited and crammed full of information and more poems than even the poet himself probably knew he'd written. But this book is also cumbersome, packing its verses into all of the available page space and even cracking stanzas in two to fit everything in. By the same token, the slew of abbreviations in the notes can be forbidding. It just isn't a very nice book to read, and most of the 'poems' are rubbish. Still, I wouldn't be without it.

PN Review, 2012

ALMOST INSTINCTS ALMOST TRUE: PHILIP LARKIN'S 'STATEMENT' OF 1955

Like Philip Larkin in 1955, I was asked to write a short statement on my poetry for an anthology at what I rather hope was an early stage of my writing career – in my case for *New Poetries V* (Carcanet, 2011). Larkin had no idea his 'Statement' for *Poets of the 1950s* would be printed in its submitted form, whereas I was all too aware that mine would be, and fretted over it with farcical fastidiousness, rather too concerned that anything foolish I said might come back to haunt me. In 1983, when his reputation as one of our most significant post-war writers was secure, Larkin allowed his 'Statement' to be reprinted in *Required Writing*, but included a footnote making clear that he had initially submitted it on the assumption that it would be no more than 'raw material for an introduction' to be written by D. J. Enright, the editor of the 1950s book, and was 'rather dashed' to find it instead printed there *verbatim*. Larkin's 'Statement' has been taken by some as evidence, straight from the horse's mouth, of painful narrow-mindedness and lowered artistic ambition. But I don't think he meant much of what he wrote there – not wholly, anyway.

'I write poems to preserve things I have seen/thought/felt', he claims. This seems fair enough, though it also suggests one necessary order of production: eureka moment followed by preservation of eureka moment in poetic form. Of course, it isn't like this at all. At least part of finding out must be in the writing, surely – or, as E. M. Forster put it, 'How can I know what I think till I see what I say?' Larkin's claim is an oversimplification, then, but it is one loaded with modesty. I am reminded of something he said about the inspiration for his great poem 'The Whitsun Weddings': 'It was just a transcription of a very happy afternoon. I didn't change a thing, it was just there to be written down'. This just *isn't true*, and if it were true the poem would be nothing but a vivid diary entry. Larkin's method of composition was often to spend a long time rewriting the same poem, occasionally dropping it for months or even years before resuming, as the thoughts proliferated and could be harnessed and moulded. It is this drawn-out process of development, indeed, that led to the creation of the seemingly effortless 'The Whitsun Weddings', which was started several years before it was completed. More was going on than the simple preservation of what had been seen and thought and felt on a train one sunny Whitsun: the thinking and feeling were ongoing preoccupations that enabled an idea to become a poem independent of the event that inspired it. But obviously things either seen, thought or felt must be at the heart of any poem, to some extent.

Of course, Modernist masterpieces such as T. S. Eliot's *The Waste Land* or Ezra Pound's *The Cantos* are concerned as much as anything else with the atmosphere in a particular epoch: things thought and felt and, to varying extents, seen. This isn't negated by any perceived or actual Modernist attempt at impersonality. But, according to Larkin in his 'Statement', the light a poem shines on experience must be pure, not refracted:

> As a guiding principle I believe that every poem must be its own sole freshly created universe, and therefore have no belief in 'tradition' or a common myth-kitty or casual allusions in poems to other poems or poets, which last I find unpleasantly like the talk of literary understrappers letting you see they know the right people.

Ouch. Here Larkin was presumably railing against what he saw as the insidious influence of the Modernist 'mad lads', as he called them elsewhere, whom he accused of taking poetry from the general to the specialised readership.

But the attack is ham-fisted; his comment is bile and nonsense. First of all: good luck, Philip. A poem cannot exist in a vacuum, cannot be 'its own sole freshly created universe' – which is not to say that it is by necessity beholden to the strong gravitational pulls of other bodies. Secondly, and more significantly, Larkin is simply being disingenuous to his own aims, both as they had been before

1955 (the same year that his second collection, *The Less Deceived*, had been published) and as they would continue to be. A few years later, in 1962, he was happy to note that the last lines of 'Absences', which is included in *The Less Deceived* and which ends 'Such attics cleared of me! Such absences!', sounds like a 'translation from a French formalist. I wish I could write like this more often'. This is a resonance, of course, not an allusion – much less a dip into the Classical 'myth-kitty'. But while he tends to leave the myth-kitty closed, a surprising number of 'casual allusions' to other poems or poets *are* scattered throughout his work, not least in sardonic or ironic poem titles. For example, 'I Remember, I Remember', a poem about forgotten youth written just a few months before the 'Statement', is named after either Thomas Hood's or Winthrop Mackworth Praed's poems of the same name, both of which celebrate memories of youth much more than Larkin's poem does. The title 'Sad Steps' is provided by Philip Sidney's *Astrophel and Stella*, giving an ironic twist to Larkin's speaker's own sky-gazing and the reference to 'the strength and pain / Of being young'. 'This Be the Verse' ('They fuck you up, your mum and dad') takes its title with comparable irony from Robert Louis Stevenson's 'Requiem'. 'Annus Mirabilis' is a moniker shared with Dryden's poem about a year in the seventeenth century. 'Toads', another poem written just months before the 'Statement', includes the phrase 'that's the stuff / That dreams are made on', an archaic construction (modern English would need 'made of') consciously echoing Prospero in Shakespeare's *The Tempest*, right down to the positioning of the line-break: 'We are such stuff / As dreams are made on'. This list could go on. One can understand and enjoy these poems without picking up on the references, but they are nonetheless there to be noticed by, and to add a wry extra layer of meaning for, certain readers. Each of these poems isn't 'its own sole freshly created universe', but it can be enjoyed on its own terms without requiring the reader to work beyond its most obvious limits – in a way that just isn't the case with, say, Eliot's or Pound's works mentioned above.

In his 'Statement' Larkin makes one point I agree with unreservedly: 'It is fatal to decide, intellectually, what good poetry is because you are then in honour bound to try to write it, instead of the poems that only you can write.' This is in the first paragraph, before he provides what is in effect a sort of assessment by means of negation of what constitutes 'good poetry', with its own silly rules. But this should not blind us to the fact that Larkin broke these rules as often as he stuck to them. Throughout his life he said or wrote quite a lot of silly things about his writing, and in different ways some people are wont to put these things in the way of the appreciation of his poetry, as if to prove him a narrow-minded provincial and 'essentially a minor poet', in the unsubstantiated words of Peter Ackroyd. Go back to his poems, which provide evidence to the contrary.

A Poet's Sourcebook, ed. Dawn Potter (Autumn House, 2012)

JOHN AGARD, *TRAVEL LIGHT, TRAVEL DARK* (BLOODAXE, 2013)

John Agard's first book since he finally won the Queen's Gold Medal for Poetry is typically cosmopolitan, with one eye on the past and the other on the present. Many of the poems concentrate one way or another on British imperialism and its corollaries. A Congolese boy about to be transported to Wales asks 'How far that place from Congo?' Sugar cane tells its own tale of global conquest: 'In Spain I invaded the quince's meat. / In England I blackened a fair queen's teeth.' In modern Britain 'little Brits' (a play on 'little shits'?) whizz around on skateboards, 'diasporas in their skin'. Agard also likes getting inside people or objects: Columbus sails his 'interior seas'; an oak becomes a ship of imperial conquest, deracinated and sent 'a world away from acorns'. The poems are allusive – 'Severus, that Libyan bloke' one minute, Tupaia, Cook's Tahitian navigator and translator the next – but they are also very direct: he wants us to think about what they say, not wonder what they might mean.

Many of these poems are also typically playful. In some, the metre jerks around violently and the rhymes flail for one another, and the poet embraces their flailing. This can add lustre to such original and entertaining poems as 'Prospero Caliban Cricket', in which Caliban thrashes Prospero at the noble game, the latter 'wishing Shakespeare was de umpire'. Often it is less successful:

> Look out for a pub called the Lamb of God.
> They do brilliant chips with mushy peas and cod.
> But things have changed. Not like in ancient time
> When on Friday nights the bards battled in rhyme.

There's nothing McGonagallian about this, really: Agard knows what he's doing even if he doesn't seem to care. But the poignancy and gravity of some of the less humorous poems do not necessarily save those from charges of sloppiness, either: when a certain fleshy fruit in 'Slip of a Riddle' becomes 'a mindless missile / hurled at a football pitch', one wonders what missiles *do* have minds. Smart bombs, perhaps?

Discussing Kipling, Orwell concluded that he wrote 'good bad poems': 'graceful monuments to the obvious'. Agard certainly can be a good bad poet, and a bad bad poet for that matter, but here he is often something of a bad good one instead:

> I'm a grand ole piano mama
> Insides of steel, yet sweet of tone.
> Eighty-eight teeth, and all my own.
> Tonight I'm in the mood for flesh and bone

But readers – often schoolteachers and their pupils – tend to love his work, perhaps not noticing (to make an example of these lines) that the rhyme is firmly in the driving seat, or the phrasing is stiff ('sweet of tone'?), but relishing the boldly mischievous conceits, the ease with which Agard shows them things they wouldn't have imagined and enables them to talk about anything but poetry. This thought-provoking, puckish, tender book will not disappoint them, and I'll continue to love him too.

Times Literary Supplement, 2013

THOUGHTS TRAINED TO ONE FURROW

R. S. Thomas, *Uncollected Poems*, ed. Tony Brown and Jason Walford Davies (Bloodaxe, 2013); R. S. Thomas, *Poems to Elsi*, ed. Damian Walford Davies (Seren, 2013)

This year is the centenary of the Welsh poet R. S. Thomas's birth. But Tony Brown and Jason Walford Davies, the editors of his *Uncollected Poems*, stress that their incentive is far greater than a desire to capitalise on that. Having studied 'Thomas's uncollected poems – that is, those published in magazines, newspapers, journals, pamphlets etc., but not included in any of his collections – it immediately became apparent that there were in fact a significant number of poems [...] that deserved to be reclaimed'. And here they are, in chronological order.

It is an intriguing assertion. Thomas published too much of his poetry, even in his collections – to the extent that, for *Collected Poems* (1993), he threw out a fifth of them without anyone noticing. His was always a poetry of accretion: themes were circumnavigated, reiterated, returned to from new and not-so-new angles; the less successful book-published poems discarded from the *Collected* were mostly weaker counterparts of things done better (and sometimes extraordinarily well) elsewhere. On the face of it, then, the prospects for what amount to the initial leftovers are pretty slim.

But Thomas is a major poet of the twentieth century, and we should welcome this book for the wider insights it affords us, if not for the quality of much of the work itself. *Uncollected Poems* brings us, for example, the earliest of Thomas's many poems for his first wife, a sonnet from 1939, which begins:

> I never thought in this poor world to find
> Another who had loved the things I love,
> The wind, the trees, the cloud-swept sky above [...].

Rather than the cloud-swept sky below, presumably. It might surprise some to find the author of famous poems such as 'Death of a Peasant' and 'Welsh Landscape' writing rhyme-driven, utterly predictable and sub-Georgian poesy (guess what happens in the sestet), but he even assembled a typescript collection of this sort of thing in the late 1930s. (Brown and Walford Davies spare us most of the others.) It is in stark contrast to all that follows. Next, there is a slew of the 'peasant' farmers of Wales, such as 'Gideon Pugh', 'his thoughts trained to one furrow'. There are the poems expressing a barbed love for his 'beloved country' and a loathing of its ruination – 'beauty was responsible / for your prostitution' – that prompts nationalist rhetoric of an occasionally wearisome and vulgar variety, as when he claims artists and lecturers are 'ineffectual' because 'None of them will ever set a bomb / alight or bring disaster / on England'. And later still, we get the priest-poet's fragile, violently enjambed poems about the *deus absconditus* and *via negativa*: 'We address you / in silence. / You answer / us with the echo / that never dies'. Then, concentrated towards the end of the book, are more internationally conscious, if not always unmuddled, poems, such as 'Insularities', in which 'Trident surfaces / amid the tears of the poor', and 'Oil': 'smelling of corruption, of which / the whole world thinks itself in need'.

Uncollected Poems, then, offers us a shadow of the full range of Thomas's mature work. Not many of the poems are extraordinary in themselves, but this collection shows more than any other just how his preoccupations and his poetics continued to develop after that sudden early shift from painting by numbers to bold expressionism. What caused that shift? In a sense, Thomas was never a great original: in later life he learned from, among others, Ted Hughes and William Carlos Williams, adapting their rhythms and notions to his own, often startling purposes. It seems likely that in 1942 he procured a copy of Patrick Kavanagh's *The Great Hunger*, with its labourer Maguire, and that this fed into his own freshly pragmatic style and his preoccupation with the loneliness and steadfastness of those working the 'bold' Welsh hill country. Thomas's 'Maguires', Iago Prytherch most famous among them, recur obsessively in the two decades after this – one almost wonders why 2013 isn't also seeing the publication of *Iago Prytherch Poems* – but it turns out he wrote quite a few more than those we have come to know. Some, like 'Gideon Pugh', are little more than imitation Kavanagh; others are more intriguing, such as 'Welsh Shepherd', which comes to us now sounding more like imitation Thomas:

> There he stands, counting his phantom flock
> Carefully as his money, while the ravens mock
> Each dream picture of a swollen fold.
> A theme for sentiment? Yet spare your tears […].

And that exemplifies a saving grace of this book. In it, we can see Thomas, a poet who rarely tackled topics once if he could tackle them thirty times from thirty slightly different angles, tackling them instead from forty, working out what he needs to say, and sometimes doing away with (or believing he was doing away with) a fine poem in the ultimate service of an even finer one. And, moreover, the editors are correct, though they rather overstate the point, that some of these poems really do deserve our attention in their own right, among them simple, affecting pieces such as 'Dimensions', first published in 1972, the same year as Thomas's notoriously bleak, *Crow*-inspired *H'm*:

> The sea turns over
> In its sleep. It dreams
> Of ships, ports, empires
> It will devour.
>
> The child takes a shell,
> Listens; is tuned in
> To an immense world the sea
> Knows nothing about.

Despite opening with 'I never thought in this poor world to find', *Poems to Elsi* is a far more consistent volume. Thomas's fifty-one-year marriage to Mildred E. Eldridge – 'Elsi' – inspired some of the greatest modern poems about matrimony in English. Here, they are presented in a loosely biographical order of the editor, Damian Walford Davies's choosing, starting with a few pieces of courtship juvenilia, and ending with elegies. It is a generally sympathetic and unobtrusive order, though there are a few exceptions. 'For Instance', for example ('I loved her? That is how / I saw things. But not she') appears right near the end, looking for all the world like another elegy for Thomas's dead wife, though it first appeared a quarter of a century before her death in the collection called *Pietà*.

The uninitiated reader might be surprised by the astringent tone of many of these poems. There isn't much here to borrow for your next Valentine's Day card. In 'Nineteen', written to mark their nineteenth wedding anniversary, looking at one another 'thaws suspicion'; in 'Golden Wedding', finally 'the heart has become warm'. For some years – though the slight, albeit highly illuminating introduction does not mention it – Elsi and Ronald lived in separate ends of the same cottage, apparently happily. Too close a comparison to Hardy is inimical: as Rowan Williams points out in his astute foreword, 'R.S. was not another Thomas Hardy, making amends to a departed wife by reconstructing a relationship that in reality had failed'. This couple were not estranged, just strange, and good for them. But as with Hardy, the death of Thomas's wife precipitated a flurry of sad, moving, often self-questioning elegies, most written after he had remarried, such as 'No Time':

> She left me. What voice
> colder than the wind
> out of the grave said:
> 'It is over'? Impalpable,
> invisible, she comes

do, and I at my reading.

Poems to Elsi contains only two (relatively weak) poems that have not been printed elsewhere. And it is a shame that the edition alters the lineation of 'A Marriage', one of the finest elegies written by Thomas or anyone: elsewhere it is printed with indented alternate lines, but not here. All the same, this is a handsome and moving book, bringing together sixty years' worth of mainly remarkable poems that belong between one set of covers.

Times Literary Supplement, 2013

BATTERED, BUT NOT AT EL ALAMEIN

James Andrew Taylor, *Walking Wounded: The Life & Poetry of Vernon Scannell* (OUP, 2013)

Few literary biographies have a more intriguing, maddening subject than the writer Vernon Scannell – as he came to be known. John Vernon Bain was born in 1922, the second of three children who spent an itinerant childhood in England and Ireland as their father, a portrait photographer, sought steady work. Their mother appears to have been emotionally wooden, and the 'Old Man', as the children called him, brutal and addicted to wielding a leather strap: 'a sadistic man' whose 'sadism took both physical and mental forms', in the poet's words some decades later. Scannell's older brother taught him to read, and then guided his reading; among the books shared was a *Methuen Anthology of Modern Verse*, and soon the younger boy was writing his own poems, 'like parodies of the worst poems in the anthology'. Reading was an act of rebellion: the 'Old Man' regarded coveting books – along with wearing underpants – as 'the mark of a sissy'. A passion for boxing appears to have been his sole positive influence on the boys: 'Vernon boxed as a schoolboy, as a student, as a successful amateur and briefly as a less successful professional'.

Boxing was a subject the son would return to in his fiction. His sporting career, though, culminated in low-level ignominy, with a stint as a fairground boxer-performer, paid to lose in faux-dramatic fashion. But that was all ahead of him when he left school at fifteen with dreams of being a poet and a champion pugilist, and instead embarked on a career as an accounts clerk. Three years later, he found out that his girlfriend Barbara – one of several women entirely written out of Scannell's own memoirs – was pregnant, prompting him first to marry and then to abandon her. (He would have only 'a couple of brief meetings' with his first son, and none for decades.) The War was under way, and he signed up for the Army as an allegedly unmarried man with no dependants. He proved a terrible soldier, incompetent with weapons and prone to going AWOL for weeks at a time. Scannell implies in his memoirs, and 'would tell his friends', that, like Keith Douglas, he had taken part in the Battle of El Alamein, but James Andrew Taylor reveals he cannot have been there. He was, however, involved in some other operations, and they traumatised him. The final straw seems to have been the sight of fellow British soldiers looting corpses at Wadi Akarit – 'like fucking flies' – which prompted another desertion and eventually landed him in a military prison. He was cannily released in time for the invasion of Normandy, however, where his closest friend in the platoon was killed, and where he received a gunshot wound bad enough to send him home: Scannell had accidentally left his gun's safety catch on and so had not defended himself.

Soon he deserted again, hobbling out of hospital without having been discharged, and finally turned up on his sister's doorstep. An underworld contact of her boyfriend (an anarchist and conscientious objector) secured some identity papers for one 'Vernon Scannell' – perhaps a dead man, or a pickpocketed visitor to the contact's brothel – giving the would-be poet a gift he would keep, one which apparently distanced him both from his abusive parents and the family he had abandoned. Soon he met Ella Cope, a medical student at Leeds University, and moved to Leeds with her, then used his new identity to enter into a bigamous marriage – something he never spoke about (Taylor notes that 'his children were astonished to hear about [it] after his death'). This false marriage, too, disintegrated almost instantly, but at the same time Scannell fell under the influence of academic staff at Leeds, who encouraged his passion for literature.

Desertion and bigamy seemed to have caught up with him when he was inevitably arrested a few years later. First, he was hauled before the military authorities, declared to be suffering from 'anxiety neurosis', and discharged as 'permanently unfit for any form of Military Service'. Then a trial for bigamy also ended with unexpected leniency. By now, Scannell's poems were being published. A debut collection appeared from the Fortune Press in 1948, although, like Philip Larkin's *The North Ship* from the same imprint, it quickly came to be seen by its author as an embarrassment. Soon, with the help of G. Wilson Knight at Leeds, Scannell landed a job teaching at a private school in Ealing – 'teaching is the soundest basis for anyone wanting to write', Knight told him – where he espoused left-wing ideas in 'slightly throaty voiced, officer-class Received Pronunciation'. He had an instinctive sympathy for the vulnerable, and loathed what he called the 'smug, lying, hypocritical, mean, greedy, materialistic bunch of shitbags' in the Conservative Party; though evidently a passionate teacher, he left the job at the first opportunity, on receiving an advance of £50 for his first novel, *The Fight*.

The next and last woman he would marry was Jo Higson, 'so precious to me that I was in a fever of apprehension in case I should lose her'. They had several children (one of whom died in infancy) and their marriage lasted for twenty years, taking Scannell to beautiful homes and short-lived jobs in Dorset and Kent, as his literary reputation continued to grow. And all the while, on numerous occasions, 'this literate, friendly and sensitive man would stagger home drunk and beat his wife until she bled'.

Scannell's drinking would slip in and out of control for the rest of his life. Even a spell in prison for drink-driving and the death of a female drinking companion in his house did nothing to curtail his thirst. The violence and jealousy would also persist: *Walking Wounded* reveals a man unable to learn from his mistakes or overcome his impulses. He got on well with many fellow-poets, though, and Taylor includes several juicy morsels of gossip – such as the tale of Scannell and Ted Hughes sneaking out of Lumb Bank, where they were teaching an Arvon course, and meeting up with women in a nearby town before sneaking back into the 'retreat' at dawn. Scannell was still with Jo, but their estrangement was becoming inevitable.

There followed a few more declarations of love for women who soon became old flames. Then, in his late fifties, Scannell met 'a strikingly pretty twenty-year-old girl' called Angela Beese, and returned with her to Leeds. He couldn't believe his luck, suddenly having a beautiful, intelligent and impressionable lover whom he could instruct in English poetry – 'an introduction for A and a reappraisal for me', was how he put it. 'Overshadowing everything', however, was 'Vernon's uncontrollable jealousy', including an obsession with whether she had, three years previously, told a boy she loved him. She too soon found herself being beaten up until she left. Finally, in his seventieth year, Scannell met a schoolteacher called Jo Peters, and began a relationship that would endure until his death in 2007. She found him 'very easy to be close to', though like the other women in his life she experienced 'nights of "awfulness"', with Vernon punching [her] in the face'. By now, his heavy smoking was beginning to catch up with him. He suffered emphysema, wheezing, shaking and feeling like a 'poor old crock' – and dished out the beatings a little less frequently. He survived throat cancer, and lived out his last years writing some of his finest poems – 'not at all the poems you might expect from a sick man', as his final publisher, John Lucas, put it.

Though often well received by critics, Scannell's poetry was never especially popular. He did not fit easily into any of the literary bundles of his day, and generally disliked those who did: the Movement poets he professed to find 'unadventurous, decorous'; J. H. Prynne wrote 'nonsensical gibberish'; the 'Liverpool pop poets' were 'the direct antithesis of poetry', guilty of 'the slackest use of language'. He incessantly worried about his own poetry being dismissed, though, and about being viewed as 'a representative of the rear-guard bumbling stick-in-the-muds'. Uninitiated readers can make up their own minds, to some extent, since this book helpfully includes a pamphlet-length appendix of poems that are discussed in the text, very much weighted towards Scannell's later work but including earlier and more famous pieces such as the 'war poem' 'Walking Wounded', and 'A Case of Murder', about a child purposely killing a cat then suffering remorse and emotional torment.

This appendix is a valuable extra; though since most of Scannell's poems are, as the prefatory note puts it, 'not easily available', it is a shame a wider selection has not been provided, or that a new *Collected* isn't in print. The foreword by John Carey, which concentrates on whetting one's appetite for the poems rather than the life, would have served such a volume well. Scannell could be a superb poet, moving and technically masterful without a hint of fustiness. Carey – no pushover, and a man who once described *Not Without Glory*, Scannell's survey of Second World War poetry, as a work of 'mechanical obtuseness' – is right to praise his 'ability to transform the ordinary with a single word', and to note that 'empathy' is his 'great gift'. But when Carey claims that one poem is 'in subject and treatment far beyond Larkin's scope', it is an unfairly lofty comparison, serving as much as anything to highlight Scannell's limitations. It is in keeping with Taylor's approach to the poems, however, which often seems to suffer from what we might call biographer's overstatement. After a lively discussion of 'Walking Wounded', he concludes rather unhelpfully that it is 'a dream-poem of universal relevance that bears comparison with Wilfred Owen's "Strange Meeting"'. It doesn't, and Taylor's matching of these two poems inadvertently encourages us not to enjoy Scannell's for what it is, but to dwell on its slight prolixity, the awkwardness and flatness of some of its phrasing, and especially the comparative ordinariness of its transcendence ('a sour sadness stirs; / Imagination pauses and returns / To see them walking still') in comparison to what might be Owen's greatest achievement.

Though intermittently insightful in his literary analyses, and justifiably dismissive of some of Scannell's novels, Taylor appears loath to treat the poems with anything less than a reverence they do not always deserve. Almost everything is swooned over as 'deeply imaginative', or 'remarkable', or a work of 'emotional sensitivity and craftsmanship'. The occasional bad rhymes and wooden stanzas go unmentioned or receive praise anyway. Moreover, while Taylor likes to remind us that 'It is, of course, important to avoid facile identifications of the "I" of this or any of Scannell's poems', or that 'it's important to be cautious before forcing a directly autobiographical interpretation', he doesn't always follow his own advice – as when he writes that a senior psychiatrist claims Scannell's 'story [i.e. his life] and specifically "A Case of Murder", represent a classic case of post-traumatic stress disorder'.

It is a pity Taylor was not able to interview his subject, but his investigative work is nonetheless consistently impressive. He is particularly good at piecing together this evasive man's stories from two published memoirs (*The Tiger and the Rose*, 1971; *A Proper Gentleman*, 1977) and over half a century's worth of diaries, official documents, and interviews, then testing the authenticity of Scannell's versions of events. Thus we learn all about Ella, whom Scannell wrote 'ruthlessly out of his life'; and that one of his desertions from the army, far from being the tale of 'a hapless and semi-comic Just William figure', as he presented it, was that of a victim of trauma experiencing 'the beginnings of alcoholism'. Even here, though, Taylor can be a little too diplomatic. Discussing the impression Scannell repeatedly gave in his second memoir that he had fought at El Alamein, Taylor suggests that 'perhaps, more than forty years on, false memories of battle had persuaded him that he really *was* there'. And while he is prepared to suggest that Scannell's violence was a legacy of his wartime experience, he never affords that generosity to the 'Old Man' (Taylor quickly drops the quotation marks), who had served in the trenches during the First World War, and who comes across here as straightforwardly ghoulish.

Taylor also has a cheesy penchant for leaving chapters on cheap cliff-hangers – 'And that was a quality he was going to need', and so forth – and for fictionalising scenes rather unnecessarily: as Scannell slips off on one of his desertions, 'Bare-legged girls in summer dresses strolled down the street without a care in the world; the doors of the pubs were wide and welcoming; on the street the traffic moved freely', etc. More irritating is an occasional tendency to banal generalisation: 'Poets may be entertaining companions, even easy people to fall in love with, but they are not necessarily a good bet as a life-long partner'. The same might be said about biographers, or marriage counsellors. And for all Taylor's investigative vigour and rigour, there are also some gaps in the story which might have been filled without any loss of space had all of this unnecessary padding been removed. We never learn much about Scannell's relationships with his children when they were adults, or what happened when he met his first child all those years later. Scannell's later life, as presented here, is generally characterised by love affairs turning, with one last partial exception, from sickly romance to sickening abuse and ultimate failure, against a backdrop of binge drinking, gradually declining health and even more gradually declining literary standing. It can all get a bit repetitive. For all that, *Walking Wounded: The Life and Poetry of Vernon Scannell* remains a revealing, troubling, often gripping, occasionally funny and surprisingly heart-warming biography, a flawed but noble monument to an undervalued poet, shedding light not only on his life but also on British literary and poetic culture in the late twentieth century from the perspective of one of its less celebrated but still significant figures.

Times Literary Supplement, 2014

REFLECTIONS ON THE UNDERSIDE

Maurice Riordan, *The Water Stealer* (Faber, 2013)

Maurice Riordan's fourth collection of poems is typically quiet, acute and personal, its infrequent leitmotif a rural childhood in County Cork. But this is no gentle pastoral: Riordan often begins a poem by promising us, in unforced and conversational four- or five-stress lines, a simple tale, which transmutes into a haunting, even macabre, study of human behaviour and incipient understanding. In 'The Hare' – a particularly successful example – a boy crosses fields to a ringfort, and comes upon the eponymous creature in a snare:

> and she jumps, outstretched in air and free
> for a second, but held in the frame of her leap
> by the rusted teeth sunk into her hind leg.
>
> So the boy finds a stone, as he must […].

Indeed, several of the poems here are elegies for a lost childhood, or for other human losses: 'the hissing thumping piston […] of grief', as he puts it in 'The Age of Steam'. Flirting dangerously with syrup and sentimentality, 'The Flight' begins:

> For a good half hour this morning, from five
> till the mobile's ringtone woke me in a sweat,
> I was young again and mammy was alive'.

I won't spoil its conclusion; the poem then twists hauntingly, eschewing the obvious ending – but never forsaking feeling for cleverness, as so many other poets would.

There are, perhaps inevitably, a few stumbles. Riordan's less successful poems are often too sure of themselves or – like 'The Water Spider', a depiction of a creature who 'builds a chamber to hatch her eggs / and lives off prey in easy reach' – do not do enough to transcend mere description, however precise and pleasing that description might be. Moreover, for a poet of such control and grace, it is surprising how awkward Riordan's phrasing can be on occasion. 'The Poacher' begins with the speaker's father hunting: 'he shoots the duck – the drake, that is. / Tonight he'll grace our father's plate'. The slight confusion over pronouns is not, it turns out, a fruitful one. But the poem remains affecting and taut in spite of that, a kind of unnerving counterpart to Yeats's 'The Wild Swans at Coole', which also ends by directing our attention to different fowl apparently doing the same thing on the same lake after a long period of change for the observer. Indeed, this often sad, wry collection is full of comings and goings – normally with the speaker coming and other life going: 'As I step into the dun light, an owl slips / dream-quick from the corner of my eye', he writes in 'The Barn'. It is an image that comes as close as anything to typifying the book.

The theme of water recurs a few times, too, in very different contexts. 'Irish', another poem of confused belonging, begins with a vision of

> That gleam the sand has before the tide,
> Its fish-skin-wet and soft-cement texture,
> So it stands out as if above the strand
> – is there a word for it in Irish?

There apparently isn't one in English. The poem then muses that 'In English, there's a word I've forgotten / for those reflections on the underside / of the prow'. The collection's more ostensibly playful title poem begins in waterless confusion, with someone apparently having come 'to the pond in the night and emptied it' – eventually calling to mind 'our old pond back in Lisgoold / and heat-struck hours with my cousins'.

For such a habitually meditative poet, Riordan can be rather funny, in his dry and often self-deprecating way. 'Faun

Whistling to a Blackbird' hits us squarely with the groan of a terrible pun: perhaps a blackbird mistook his notebook for bread because the pages contained 'some crumbs about growing old and sex'. 'The Noughties', a four-line, older man's quizzical look at 'every nutcase' of 'the electronic age', who spends 'nights locked up in chatrooms', was of course just a few years out of date by the time this book came to print. It is hard to work out precisely where Riordan stands in such poems: the irony is palpable, but who exactly is being ironised? Rather less ambiguous is 'Habits', a poem not about wearing purple clothes and red hats in (relative) age, but about showing one's boundless virility all the same by feeding toenail clippings to a cactus and mouthing 'asshole' (why the Americanism?) at an 'unsuspecting youth'. Indeed, many of these poems, even the less showy ones, are saved from being little scowls of poetical contemplation by the poet's refusal to take himself too seriously. For all its small faults and inconsistencies, then, this is a moving, lively book of poems, not infrequently distinctive, serious but never boring, and full of wit and feeling.

Times Literary Supplement, 2014

KEVIN POWERS, *LETTER COMPOSED DURING A LULL IN THE FIGHTING* (SCEPTRE, 2014)

As the centenary of the First World War heaves into view, and anthologies of its poetry fill bookshop windows, it is natural to think also about the anglophone poetry has emerged from the recent wars in Iraq and Afghanistan. Some poets – Owen Sheers, Andrew Motion and Tony Harrison among them – have written about them from afar; in 2003 an anthology brought together '100 poets against the war'. But Kevin Powers, who served with the US Army in Iraq from 2004–5, is one of the few English-language poets (Brian Turner being another) who was actually there.

Powers has written about the Iraq War already, in his debut novel, *The Yellow Birds* (2012). Those familiar with the novel should have a good idea what to expect from his first collection of poems, which again largely focuses on what it was like to be involved. There are flashes of horror, but the tone is more frequently inquisitive and even pensive: 'Think almost reaching grief, but / not quite getting there', as 'Field Manual' puts it. Powers certainly tries to give some sense of what being a soldier in that war was like, though, from 'some cutouts from / a *Maxim* magazine and / a Polaroid of my girlfriend's tits' to seeing a 'little boy' as 'the possibilities of shooting him or not extend out from me / like the spokes of a wheel', to the woman 'so brutalized by bullets it was hard to tell her sex', to being enraged, back home, by a group of Young Republicans in a bar: 'I want to rub their clean / bodies in blood'. 'Photographing the Suddenly Dead' is honest in a way that is hardly likely to endear Powers to his former paymasters, describing as it does the sort of thing that became a hideous leitmotif of that war: 'three young men whose crime / was an unwillingness / to apply the brakes in time' at a checkpoint are being photographed after the fact:

Someone laughed as it was taken.
Everyone wave good-bye,
we said and laughed again
when our relief arrived.

The book ends with poems mainly set back in Powers's native Virginia, and the flavour of these later pieces is somewhat augmented by their context. 'Nominally', for example, describes 'a parking lot, which covers up a grave, / a name we give in singular for the hundred slaves / they buried there back then'. But frankness provides no guarantee of quality. Consider the title poem, which reads as though it was composed during a very short lull in the fighting indeed, and which ends in a pedestrian observation conveyed in undistinctive lines:

I tell her how Private Bartle says, offhand,
that war is just us
making little pieces of metal
pass through each other.

The awkward truth is that the circumstances surrounding Kevin Powers's poetry are often rather more fascinating than the poetry itself. If he hasn't exhausted his subject and failed to find another, I doubt his next book will be a collection of poems.

Times Literary Supplement, 2014

PATIENCE AGBABI, *TELLING TALES* (CANONGATE, 2014)

'Fynde wordes newe', wrote Geoffrey Chaucer, in lines quoted as an epigraph and taken as a challenge by Patience Agbabi in this, her fourth collection. *Telling Tales* is a *Canterbury Tales* for and about twenty-first-century England – a fast-paced, modern equivalent with a contemporary cast (whose biographical notes appear at the back). After all, as Agbabi's host puts it in this version's 'Prologue', 'reminisce this: / Chaucer Tales were an unfinished business'.

Some of Agbabi's narratives are rather closer to the originals than others, with mixed results. Our updated 'Miller's Tale' is presented not by Robyn the drunken Miller but by 'part-time barmaid, full-time motormouth' Robyn Miller, whose story is set in a world of hard drugs and social media. Much else is the same as the fourteenth-century version – in the tale, if not in its telling:

> Window's open, total geared
> he's tongueing me but something's weird:
> too right, cos I ain't got no beard,
> stead of my lips, he got my rear!

Not infrequently, as here, the rhyme seems to take control. In places, the poems are further undermined, and in various ways. For example, in the 'Prologue', our host, Harry 'Bells' Bailey, who apparently holds a monthly storytelling night in his pub, proves himself a proud and impertinent man indeed:

> see my jaw dropping neat Anglo-Saxon,
> I got ink in my veins more than Caxton
> and it flows hand to mouth, here's a mouthfeast,
> verbal feats from the streets of the South-East
>
> No, I can't (this is a book); no, it isn't (by 'Anglo-Saxon' Agbabi

probably means Old English – Chaucer wrote in Middle English, and patently the host is using neither); no, you haven't. The boast rattles by sheer force of rhyming words from nonsensical to banal, and who cares anyway? Still, there is a joyous force to the rhythm that encourages you not to care about such things.

Other tales differ rather more conclusively from their precursors, such as the version of 'The Tale of Sir Thopas' – a self-deprecating joke in Chaucer's original, with the host interrupting the poet's own ridiculous and dire tale of 'love-longynge' to exclaim 'Thy drasty rymyng is nat worth a toord!' Agbabi, whose version is a rap battle between 'Sir Topaz and Da Elephant', finds no need for such an interjection, though 'mad applause' and 'booing' attend sentiments such as 'your trunk's defunct, her cunt's mine' (Topaz) and 'your dick's a Bic, a biro' (Elephant). It is 'love-longynge' of a kind. Agbabi's 'Prioress's Tale' eschews another difficulty, losing the problematically gleeful anti-Semitism of the original, the child-murdering Jews being replaced by a more easily vilified switchblade-wielding gang and the murdered child being given his own voice, 'chattin on a mix made / in heaven' to his mother back on Earth.

There are numerous glowing endorsements on the dust jacket from Jackie Kay, Andrew Motion and others, including Helen Cooper, Professor of Medieval Literature at the University of Cambridge, who authoritatively tells us the Father of English literature 'would have been proud', so there you have it.

Times Literary Supplement, 2014

THE LAST GASP OF INSPIRATION

James Booth, *Philip Larkin: Life, Art and Love* (Bloomsbury, 2014); John Osborne, *Radical Larkin: Seven Types of Technical Mastery* (Palgrave Macmillan, 2014)

James Booth's *Philip Larkin: Life, Art and Love* is the third biography of Larkin. Each one has been – like Larkin's collections of poems – published about a decade after the last. Andrew Motion's *Philip Larkin: A Writer's Life* (1993) is comprehensive but at times prissy, and of course has nothing to say about what has come to light since, such as the numerous recently-discovered poems and letters; and Richard Bradford's short *First Boredom, Then Fear: The Life of Philip Larkin* (2005) is the academic equivalent of a potboiler. On the face of it, then, there appears to be just about enough room for this third retelling of Larkin's life story.

Such as it is. Larkin was born in Coventry in 1922, to middle-class parents. He attended Oxford, where he befriended Kingsley Amis among others, and avoided serving in the war because of his poor eyesight. By his mid-twenties he had published two novels and a passable poetry collection that bears a heavy stamp of W. B. Yeats. His first real literary success was *The Less Deceived* (1955), in his distinctive mature poetic style, and two further collections would follow in his lifetime. After Oxford, he worked as a librarian in Wellington, Leicester and Belfast, before being appointed University Librarian at Hull in his early thirties, a job he stayed in until his death. He never married, but had a number of awkward youthful romances – the longest of which was with Ruth Bowman, whom he met in Wellington – and two more long-term and largely concurrent partners, one the opinionated and intellectual Monica Jones, and the other Maeve Brennan, a kind and devout Catholic on his library staff. Larkin's later years, of which he had too few, were marked by growing literary acclaim and failing health and poetic inspiration. He died of cancer at sixty-three, the same age as his father, one of his final acts being to ensure the destruction of his diaries.

None of this is inherently the stuff of legend, and his would be no more than a moderately successful and relatively uneventful life story were it not for his remarkable, epoch-defining poems. A biography of this man cannot, then, rely on relaying the broader details of his life, which are anyway very well known indeed. It has to do rather more, offering fresh insights into the poems and their relationship to the life (or vice versa), both of which have by now been discussed ad nauseam in both the popular and academic press. Larkin's third biographer has a tough job on his hands.

Booth knows his subject – he has already published two monographs on Larkin and co-edits the journal *About Larkin*, among numerous other Larkin-related activities. His painstaking documentation shows that the transition from Larkin's Yeatsean style to his 'mature' poetry was rather gradual, which is not normally supposed to be the case. Booth is probably more familiar with the poet's archive than anyone else alive, which enables some sprightly allusions to, for example, Larkin's letters to his mother (excluded from the *Selected Letters* of 1992). Moreover, he complicates the easy answers provided elsewhere regarding Larkin's politics, concluding after some fair and well-researched analysis that 'his shallower instincts […] gave him, at least in his earlier years, a "prejudice for the left"'. Booth also provides some factual correctives to the myths surrounding Larkin's upbringing and attitudes: the apparently foot-high bust of Hitler that Richard Bradford describes Larkin's father owning, for example, which apparently sprang into a Nazi salute at the push of a button, was in fact a tourist figurine three inches tall; and, regarding those destroyed diaries, 'there is no evidence that they were as utterly disgusting as Andrew Motion imagines'.

However, too often Booth's discussions of the poems are little more than brief synopses, and these are sometimes bolted on to the life story with insufficient justification. Discussing 'Deceptions', a poem about a Victorian servant-girl who has been raped, for example, Booth notes the central allusion in the poem to a line of Ophelia's in *Hamlet*, and concludes: 'The biographical parallel with Philip's relationship with Ruth is clear. Both Hamlet and Larkin have lost their fathers and both are tormenting their beloveds with antisocial moodiness.' This is perhaps excessive; but Booth's claim that the poem is 'an indirect apology' to Bowman is complete fantasy, which he supports with no evidence whatsoever. It is one of several such fantasies in the book.

Booth's prose is prolix but serviceable, albeit occasionally resonant with clangers ('its classic status was recognised at once'; 'her perfection is spoiled by fingering'). Moreover, the book is underwritten by a generally noble aim: the continued restoration of the reputation of Larkin the man – which, since the grim revelations of the early 1990s and the gleefully sanctimonious furore that ensued, has taken a turn for the worse and has for some overshadowed the work. Unfortunately, weaknesses in Booth's capacity for analysis rather undermine his aim. The introduction is as much a lengthy defence of the poet's character against charges of racism, sexism and snobbery as it is a paean to the poetry – a defence that in fact draws attention to the charges without persuasively countering them: 'Larkin the racist' is written off as a 'fiction' because 'his handful of racist comments [...] are confined to private letters written to prejudiced correspondents', though the same might equally (and equally bizarrely) be said about the recipients. When Booth writes that 'For all his verbal transgressiveness, it is impossible to imagine Larkin ever acting with racist motives' he is correct insofar as Larkin was certainly no far-right activist. He is equally correct when he notes (though it has been noted hundreds of times before) how 'unfair' it is that 'Larkin has suffered so disproportionately for the flashes of performative racism in correspondence' when other writers have not. But when, in typically over-emphatic and under-nuanced fashion, he calls the poem 'Sympathy in White Major' for the defence, Booth does not reinforce his argument: 'He was not a racist, either "casual" and "habitual" or, for that matter, consistent and systematic. The speaker of "Sympathy in White Major" declares, "White is not my favourite colour"'. And when Booth states that Larkin 'could speak of "the paki next door" in a letter to a friend without the slightest implication that he lacked respect for his neighbour', he blithely risks sounding worse than silly.

Part of the problem with Booth's analysis is that he holds too resolutely to contradictory statements depending on the point he is trying to make. So, for example, we are told that 'Nationalism was alien to Larkin's sensibility' one minute, then, a few pages later, 'It is dispiriting to see his [...] narrow defensive nationalism'. (Both are listed next to one another in the index, under 'Larkin, Philip and nationalism'.) His desire to identify directly biographical links to Larkin's poems and other writing can lead to some rather po-faced absurdities, too, as when he discusses the young Larkin's jealous reworking of some lines by Sidney Keyes, in which 'it is a year again since they poured / The dumb ground into your mouth' is regurgitated as 'August again, and it is a year again / Since I poured the hot toss into your arse'. Booth extrapolates: 'The image of buggery [...] may perhaps express self-disgust at his clumsy advance to [a young woman] a year earlier'. Well, useful to get that learnt. Other conclusions Booth reaches are equally fantastic, for all of the straightforward assertiveness with which they are delivered – as when he proclaims that the three words 'and fucking piss', which Larkin added to a typed draft of 'High Windows', have 'now become an inextricable part of the poem' and make it 'a more profound work'.

There are some odd choices of focus, too. Larkin's two published novels are covered in eleven pages, Booth referring to the second of them by its author's preferred title (*The Kingdom of Winter*) rather than the one (*A Girl in Winter*) foisted on him by Faber. But twenty-five pages are lavished on the awful schoolgirl fiction Larkin wrote as a young man, for his own amusement and that of his friends, and did not intend to publish (*Trouble at Willow Gables*, Booth's edition of them, appeared in 2002). Reading the many excerpts and synopses Booth provides here is an act of sheer willpower. He might instead have provided a small flavour of this material and some solid discussion of why Larkin felt such a compulsion to write it.

At times, the literary analysis is based rather relentlessly on careful and unimaginative counting. Booth's discussion of the *Oxford Book of Twentieth-Century English Verse*, which Larkin edited, confines itself largely to totting up the lines of poetry apportioned to several of the included poets and using that statistic to draw broad conclusions (Eliot comes out on top, in case you were wondering). On many occasions Booth highlights words that Larkin has used only once in his poetry, leading to some eyebrow-raising assertions. For example, he humorously (one hopes) identifies one of Larkin's final poems, 'Love Again', which describes masturbating while imagining an ex-lover in bed with someone else, as 'a blues anti-aubade of the small hours', before going on to re-flog the dead donkey of scrupulous word-counting. Here are:

> the only appearances in Larkin's poetry of 'cunt' and 'wanking'. He seems to have been aware, at this last gasp of inspiration, that these key words, with the unique quality they would bring, remained to be used. Without them his oeuvre would be incomplete.

Wanking completed him, as it were.

So, despite the limited successes of *Philip Larkin: Life, Art and Love*, the wait goes on for the definitive successor to Motion's biography that Larkin deserves. Surely there will be no further attempt until 2035 when the embargo is lifted on his letters to his Oxford friend Bruce Montgomery; perhaps by then the world will be ready for another overhauling of the life story.

Booth's frequent and untroubled conflation of speaker and poet puts his criticism strikingly at odds with that of John Osborne, his colleague at the University of Hull. *Radical Larkin: Seven Types of Technical Mastery* breaks from the overly biographical orthodoxy, offering 'a text-centred alternative' to the 'author-centred formula', and professes to concentrate on Larkin's techniques rather than his life – though it in fact dedicates a great deal of space to sledgehammering criticism that favours the latter. 'Until very recently', Osborne writes,

> the *doxa* in Larkin studies was, in Andrew Motion's words, that 'the poems *are* autobiographical'. As Larkin's biographer he would say that, wouldn't he? But so did the other three authorities who dominated the field: Anthony Thwaite, Trevor Tolley, James Booth.

But Osborne would say that, wouldn't he? Because by 'until very recently' he is referring to his own book, *Larkin, Ideology and Critical Violence* (2008), to which this is something of a sequel. As in that book, a principal bugbear in *Radical Larkin* concerns 'Larkin's commentators knowing much more about the narrator than the poem does'.

Osborne's penchant is for tackling poems and other texts at considerable length and from numerous angles. The blurb claims that this is 'the first critical monograph to benefit from […] *The Complete Poems* (2012)', but it in fact concentrates on eleven of what are dubbed Larkin's 'greatest hits' from 'across his career span' – a slightly unusual set including 'March Past', which Larkin did not publish, and *A Girl in Winter*, in addition to some major poems. Osborne is thus able to home in on precisely what he thinks is being missed or manipulated by critics such as Booth, in a style that is ostensibly far more forensic than Booth's. Indeed, his introduction is a work of fastidious myth-debunking and loud space-clearing for his second addition to the bloated canon of Larkin studies. He is not afraid to go to war, either, with what he regards as the critical 'old guard' of the subgenre. Tolley, whose three books on Larkin 'all begin by thanking Larkin for his help – as though [he] were receiving spirit-message endorsements from beyond the grave', is guilty of 'outright negligence', and proves himself 'a master of thinking *inside* the box'. Booth, who is rightly found guilty of giving way too readily to 'the fundamental predicate that author and narrator are one', is also (and also rightly) found guilty of a willingness to 'mislay [the] obvious truth' about a poem if it is inconvenient to his point.

Osborne's book is littered with often persuasive refutations of the casual biographical links Booth and others have made to certain of Larkin's poems – such as 'Aubade', which Osborne identifies as having a universalised, ungendered speaker. Considering Booth's readings alongside Osborne's can be diverting, but more often leaves one feeling (perhaps in deference to one of Larkin's speakers) dissatisfied with both. For example, discussing the famous poem 'Church Going', Booth readily conflates speaker and poet, and resorts to a quotation from one of Larkin's letters to assert flatly that the much-debated donation of an Irish sixpence in the poem is a slightly dismissive act. Osborne gives pages to a discussion of this half line, and the assumptions of critics regarding both the location and denomination of the poem's speaker are shown to be ungrounded.

Some of Osborne's criticisms founder on the rocks of inconsequence. In accordance with the veiled homage to Empson in his subtitle, he makes something of a fetish of ambiguity, such as when he highlights the apparently 'polysemic phrase "at one another's throats"' in 'This Be the Verse', and then suggests this might plausibly be 'out of voracious sexual hunger'. And to think they say the best way to kill a joke is to try explaining it. A central argument regarding 'An Arundel Tomb' is that critics have jumped to conclusions about its setting that are not in the poem. For all that they highlight a slight laziness on the part of some critics, the kernels of such exegeses are often rather small, considering the effort required to reach them. Osborne also likes the clarity of tables, though the rewards of reading them vary significantly. In some, the narrative of a poem is presented alongside (out-of-sequence) matching quotations from Larkin's novels. In one table, 'Larkin's titular binaries' are presented in two columns: 'Coming' and 'Going', 'Arrivals' and 'Poetry of Departures', and so on. There are lots of them, their number bolstered by pairings that are not binaries (oppositions) at all, such as 'At Grass' and 'Cut Grass'; and in most cases Osborne does nothing to indicate whether the 'binaries' are echoed in the poems themselves.

Certainly this book is immaculately researched in a manner that, Osborne is at pains to point out, many books on Larkin are not. Moreover, it is impressive in its hunting down of allusions and intertextual connections – if at times excessive in its claims for their influence on Larkin's poems. There are lots of real if minor insights hidden behind the jargon and long-windedness and jostling for position. For example, Osborne's tables indicating where poems might be broken into three-act or four-act structures and how they fit the Aristotelian plot devices are both convincing and elucidating. Surely there can be no third instalment, but this is another flawed but worthwhile addition to the canon, and Osborne is a largely entertaining, erudite cat among the pigeons.

Times Literary Supplement, 2014

THE ART OF NON-CRITICISM, OR THE SWORD IS MIGHTIER THAN THE PEN

Norman Mailer, writer and boxing fan, once famously punched Gore Vidal at a party, after receiving a negative review from him. But it wasn't a knockout: 'Once again words fail Norman Mailer', Vidal is said to have retorted – proving that, though he couldn't dance like a butterfly, he could certainly sting like a wasp. And after Vidal's cutman pressed a bag of frozen peas to his cheek for half an hour or so (possibly), there was, in fact, a clear winner. Like George Foreman in the Rumble in the Jungle, the harder hitter had punched himself out all too early in the contest.

There are morals to this story, of greater and lesser kinds. Moral 1: reviewers and reviewees are bound to cross paths, and both should probably be careful as well as honest. Moral 2: reviewers might want to have a *bon mot* ready for when the displeased subject of a not wholly positive article decides to turn a literary bun-fight into a literal fist-fight. Moral 3: the wounded author is probably best off making a bonfire of his (I'll stick with 'his') grievances. A writer has no right to expect lavish, untempered praise just because he has the privilege of seeing his name on the cover of a book. The most interesting books have often tended to flummox or peeve reviewers anyway.

I've reviewed for as long as I've been publishing poems, and can't imagine doing one without sometimes also doing the other. Being a poet as well as a reviewer has probably reminded me not to be unkind unless I really can't help it, or help myself, and turning in a less than praising review always makes me feel anxious, even though I've previously pretended it doesn't. I'm also the co-editor of the poetry magazine *New Walk*, which has its own reviews section, so I edit other people's reviews and therefore sometimes please or displease authors indirectly as well. My debut collection was published in November 2013, and has been quite widely reviewed, so for the past year and a bit I've been a review subject too. I'm sure thinking about poetry books and books of criticism as a reviewer helps me not to accept my less successful poems, and maybe to write poems too, even if it might also ensure they get ridiculed one day. And luckily, I've learned that, no matter the temptation and unless it is to say thank you, going after reviewers is almost never a good idea. Let them have their moments.

Having said that, reviewing has led to some wonderful – and occasionally weirdly wonderful – correspondences: a warm and fascinating letter from an old friend of Vernon Scannell; a friendship with the art critic David Whiting, a pal of R. S. Thomas's, after I'd written on that poet's *Uncollected Poems*. I've had beguiling, supportive and sometimes moving letters and emails, gifts of books and records, invitations. Someone recently thanked me for a 'great review' and said it had 'inspired' a poem beginning 'Love again: wanking at half past three / This is Philip Larkin and not me,' which I puzzled over merrily for a while until the same review inspired something even stranger and more amusing shortly afterwards (but more about that later). I've had the odd come-back in letters pages, too. John Lucas wrote a letter to this magazine after my review of his last collection, though it was only really to point out a factual error. (Guilty.) Little did either of us then know that I'd soon be living a few miles from John, working at Nottingham Trent University where he is a rightly revered emeritus professor, and regularly attending many of the same events as him (see Moral 1, above). John then demonstrated his integrity by writing a highly engaged review of my collection for *The Dark Horse* when some others would no doubt have trashed it or passed on it. Whether John is the exception or the rule I don't know, but I do know my reviews have also cost me invitations to take part in events. (I was told that someone's suggestion I attend their university department was vetoed by a senior colleague whose book I'd reviewed less than wholly favourably.) They have also made me look gauche, apparently: a self-professed 'ex-friend' of a poet I'd reviewed once emailed me to say that she knows her ex-friend will be hurt by my criticism of his poetry – which amounted to something very mild indeed. This was less worrying than the American poet who told me to 'crawl back under your rock and die', though luckily he didn't also present me with the rock under which I might crawl. But most of the direct contact I've had with writers I've reviewed has been cordial, even thankful: like me, when reviews of my own collection have appeared, they are grateful to have been given serious consideration.

You shouldn't review a book unless you are prepared to be honest about it. I've long felt strongly that, as Maurice Riordan put it in a *Poetry Review* editorial, 'the writing of poetry needs to be attended by a scrupulous criticism, by those who set the bar according to the measure of tradition', and that critics should strike 'an honest contract with their readers' – which is difficult for more reasons than may at first be apparent in the small greenhouse that is British poetry. Poetry criticism is a difficult art, not least because the best critics make judgements they must then stand my, and everyone remembers the critics down the ages who got everything so awfully and obviously wrong. The best reviews at least attempt to demonstrate more than they profess, and the best reviewers are not more or less kind to different books in their pursuit of 'truth' in a field that is, ultimately, subjective: when John Mole read in Nottingham a few months ago, and said to me, 'your review of my book was kind', I took it that he was being modest, rather than implying disingenuousness on my part. William Logan claims a reviewer has to be a good hater if he is to be a good lover; I wouldn't put it that strongly, and I'd rather love, man, but he does have a point. Sometimes it's best for a reviewer just to pass, anyway: it is so much nicer to be in love, for all concerned. But when a book receives undue limelight, or is positively obnoxious, it almost feels an obligation *not* to pass.

Last year, I found myself pushing on through James Booth's biography of Philip Larkin, commissioned to write a long review of it. I had so wanted the book to be good, not least because its appearance means there is no room for another biography of

Larkin for a generation. And there was a slight personal connection complicating matters, too: the magazine Booth edits, *About Larkin*, published my undergraduate dissertation in 2005, which at the time made me feel rather more special than I was – and then, a year later, part of my MA dissertation as well. Anyway, whether that author's disapproval of my review is or is not related to the following story, it is probably the oddest one I have about the fallout from reviewing. When the piece appeared, he responded by emailing me on several occasions, with titbits: an explanation of why the phrase 'the Paki next door' is not, in his view, inherently offensive; a link to a more positive review; the location of a typo. His riposte to Helen Vendler's *LRB* review had just appeared in that publication, delightfully titled 'How to write about Larkin', and naturally I expected something similar to follow. I was wrong. However, a letter lambasting my 'outrageous' review did appear shortly afterwards in the publication where my review had been, undersigned with a name I couldn't trace and an address that doesn't exist – though the author of the letter did have a similar name to one of Booth's former colleagues, who has in fact written up an event for *About Larkin* (in the same issue in which that chunk of my MA dissertation appears, as it happens). So, would Edward McAlindon of 28 The Quays, Carrickfergus like me to make him a 'missing persons' poster? Please let me know, Edward.

'No fisticuffs this year', one host of a literary do I attended a couple of years ago noted, with world-weary nonchalance, at the end of the evening. Well maybe it is because I am only thirty-three, but I've certainly never seen raised fists at a literary do – just warm embraces and occasional cold shoulders, along with a far greater slew of people who don't have a clue who I am and who have no reason to care. Perhaps literary barnies just aren't what they used to be. I'm yet to be 'Mailered' myself, anyway, but reviewing has shown me that some authors think they have every right to be praised, and when they're not, sorry skulduggery is not out of the question. And, well, some wounded reviewees might just stop at nothing. I have occasional nightmares about a crowbar-wielding nutter ringing the doorbell and whispering 'Ello, yer bastard' at me through a balaclava. After which, all goes dark...

PN Review, 2015

COME COME COME AND GULL ME

Samuel Beckett, *Collected Poems*, ed. Seán Lawlor and John Pilling (Faber, 2015)

Most of Samuel Beckett's admirers are well aware that he wrote poems as well as plays and fiction, but not many people seem actually to have read many of them, and the canon of Beckett studies includes only one monograph concentrating on the poetry. However, it was as a poet that Beckett initially tried to establish a literary reputation, and writing poetry remained important to him throughout his life. This book is an attempt to bring that work together, definitively, and to support it with the necessary scholarly apparatus.

Following a fairly perfunctory preface, we begin with Beckett's first collection, *Echo's Bones and Other Precipitates*, published in 1935 by the grandly named but unglamorous Europa Press, and then move on to the early poems he omitted from it, before finally getting to the later work. It is a baptism of fire. On the whole, the poems in *Echo's Bones* are densely allusive and inventive but often unsatisfyingly unintelligible – especially the longer and more inchoate ones: they are the poems of a young man with little concern for the footing of his reader and not necessarily much to say, but a nascent genius for saying it. Many are phantasmagorical, apparently autobiographical straggles of verse grounded in real urban or semi-urban settings around Dublin. 'Enueg I', for example, is certainly vivid and atmospheric in snatches:

> Blotches of domed yellow in the pit of the Liffey;
> the fingers of the ladders hooked over the parapet,
> soliciting;
> a slush of vigilant gulls in the grey spew of the sewer.

'Eneug' apparently means 'ennui' in Provençal, which seems

fitting. But most of these early poems offer few footholds for further elucidation on their own, rich as they are in image and allusion: as the editors put it in their introduction, Beckett 'perhaps presumed too much upon the ability of his readers to follow the twists and turns, and the exceptional allusiveness, of a quicksilver mind'.

The same can be said of Beckett's first published poem, the 118-line 'Whoroscope' (1930), which he initially wrote for a poetry competition on the theme of time. (He won.) Beckett claimed to have written 'Whoroscope' in one night, and it is tempting to believe him, stacked to the brim though the poem is with learned posturing. It begins:

What's that?
An egg?
By the brothers Boot it stinks fresh.
Give it to Gillot.

As is made clear by Beckett's notes to 'Whoroscope', included in an appendix, these are references to the life and associates of Descartes, who is the speaker of the poem. Beckett glosses line 4 thus: 'Descartes passed on the easier problems in analytical geometry to his valet Gillot'. It is possible to make quite a lot of this absurd, flagrantly Modernist monologue if you give it the time, and the editors do as much as possible to help you in that aim, but 'Prufrock' it ain't. Beckett, the poet of the 1930s, certainly knew his stuff, but he hadn't worked out how to write a completely successful poem yet, and I must admit that when I reached page 15 of this 500-page volume – sub-Joyce one minute, sub-Pound the next, sub-Eliot the next – and read 'Lord have mercy upon us', I felt a grim pang of empathy.

There are, of course, hints in his poetry of what Beckett was up to in his fiction, and what he would get up to in his drama. Beckett the young poet certainly demonstrates a predilection for meshing high- and lowbrow rhetoric, for instance, or for crude playfulness. For example, as the editors note, the prose poem 'Text 1' uses an edition of John Ford's plays as an intertext, but gives 'hard words' (sic) borrowed from that volume 'a suggestive sexual flavour which they do not have in Ford':

> oh and I dreamed he would come and come come come and cull
> me bonny bony double-bed cony swiftly my springal and my thin
> Wicklow twingle-twangler [...]

This is plainly stupid, and though I enjoyed it, I'm not especially proud of myself. Lawlor and Pilling diligently gloss every reference – so we learn, for example, that 'twingle-twangler' is from *Perkin Warbeck* and is nothing less innocuous than a Gaelic harp. Elsewhere, Beckett lances highbrow rhetoric and esoteric allusions with slapsticky images and toilet humour: 'the Barfrau makes a big impression with her mighty bottom / Dante and blissful Beatrice are there'; 'a Ritter with a pommelled scrotum'. The cumulative effect of these poems is not, however, very satisfying. Beckett's early poetry often resembles his early fiction in its characteristics and defects: in *More Pricks than Kicks* (1934) his prose glisters with stylistic pyrotechnics, but the stories rarely succeed. Almost none of the early poems do.

The small number of these earlier poems that do not eschew direct statement, most of which he did not collect, are often – and perhaps surprisingly – rather too simple for anyone's good. 'Gnome' is a sudden attack on learning, in four tightly-rhymed and well-turned lines that lack the wit and wisdom to comprise the epigram the author clearly intended:

> Spend the years of learning squandering
> Courage for the years of wandering
> Through the world politely turning
> From the loutishness of learning.

Thankfully, the editors' note is, typically, an elucidatory bit of scholarship, deepening our appreciation of Beckett's poetics:

> The '-ing' ending upon which this poem depends is part of a prevailing participial tendency in SB's pre-war poems in English, which contain more than 150 examples of the form. It seems likely that Beckett favoured the form because it leavened his 'statemental' tendency, and left the greater precision of more specific tenses suspended in a kind of limbo.

The back half of the book is given over to these editors' notes, full of such observations, and they often reward more than the poems, in addition to providing contextual information and variants.

Around this time, Beckett completed many translations of poems from French. They are all here – and many (not least Beckett's version of Rimbaud's famous 'Le Bateau ivre', the only copy of which was rediscovered in the 1970s folded in another book which had survived a fire) are exceptional for their linguistic dexterity. In the later 1930s, in addition to continuing to translate poems from French and some other languages, Beckett turned his attention to writing in French. Lawlor and Pilling include his French poems without translating them. However, they do tell us that 'The recondite manner of the *EBOP* collection was well within SB's compass on switching to French [...] but he chose instead to adopt a deliberate simplification and refinement of means and method'. This seems to have informed most of his subsequent, and often infrequent, poetry in English. Moreover, if the younger Beckett sometimes seems to have lacked a poetic subject, he had certainly found one by the time he reached middle age, not least because of his activities in the Second World War with the French Resistance and the Irish Red Cross. The enigmatic 'Saint-Lô', named after a French town devastated during the Battle of Normandy in 1944, is considered by some to be Beckett's poetic masterpiece:

> Vire will wind in other shadows
> unborn through the bright ways tremble
> and the old mind ghost-forsaken
> sink into its havoc

Lawlor's and Pilling's two full pages of context, parsing, cross-references, and line-by-line identification of allusions and near-allusions, constitute an impressive and sustained feat, and help us to reach our own conclusions about this troubling miniature, so lucid yet so elusive.

Of course, Beckett's style underwent significant change after this time, in all of his writing. The poetry is no exception, though he turned to writing it a little less frequently. Some of the stark later poems are reminiscent of Beckett's 'dramaticules' and later fictions, with apparent dialogues – or internal, dialogic monologues – in anxious stasis:

> something there
> where
> out there
> out where
> outside
> what
> the head what else
> something there something outside
> the head

It is hardly surprising that in later life Beckett would be drawn to the roundelay, a French repeating form (Beckett's example is terse, even minimalist) and the subject and concision of epitaphs, such as: 'Hereunder lies the above who up below / So hourly died that he lived on till now'. Beckett's later poetry also includes a number of what he called 'mirlitonnades', written in the late 1970s. ('Vers de mirliton' means 'trashy verse' in French, a mirliton being a toy flute.) Most are in French, though some are easy enough even for an English-speaking monoglot to unpack:

> aller
> absent
> absent
> arrêter

A few poems of the same kind are in English, and most of these are equally difficult to regard as especially significant, impeccably alert though they often are to language and line-break:

> let ill alone
> let ill
> alone

The poetry portion of the book ends with Beckett's final work, which he wrote first in French as 'Comment dire' and then in English as 'what is the word', while recovering in hospital from a series of falls. It is one of the most moving, simple and bleak poems in the volume – the author's minimalist masterpiece, and the culmination of his later style. In his poetry, as in his work in other genres, this late style was inherently entropic, diminishing, vivifying, unostentatious:

> folly –
> folly for to –
> for to –
> what is the word –
> folly from this –
> all this –
> folly from all this –
> given –
> folly given all this –
> seeing –

fully seeing all this
this –

The poem staggers down the page, clutching after the answer to what its lack of question-mark denies is a question, slicing at the air with those dashes at each line-ending, until it eventually culminates with the unpunctuated repetition of the title. We'll never know – unless *what*, itself a vague question, is the word.

This is an impressive book, and it will surely remain definitive. Though slender by the standards of most volumes of collected poems, it is bulkier than the Grove Press *Collected Poems in English and French* (1977), and considerably more informative – though that book did contain all of the best poems. But it is also an unwieldy one for anything but the specialist reader, with Beckett's better poems buried under the slurry of some of his least worthwhile published writing. Many readers might be just as well off with the 2009 *Selected Poems*, edited and exquisitely introduced by David Wheatley, though it lacks the exhaustive scholarly apparatus of this volume.

PN Review, 2015

LINE FOR LINE

Michael Cullup, *W. H. Davies: Man and Poet – A Reassessment* (Greenwich Exchange, 2014)

W. H. Davies was an oddity. Born in Newport, Wales, in 1871, he fled drudgery in his early twenties and spent several years living mainly as a tramp in North America, stowing away clandestinely on trains and bedding down at beggars' camps, with the occasional spot of temporary work on canals, farms, cattle boats. Chasing the Klondike gold rush in 1899, he jumped a train in Ontario, slipped, and lost a foot beneath the wheel – an accident that nearly killed him and led to some concentrated soul-searching back home.

Now dedicated to becoming a poet, Davies worked tirelessly, ingeniously and completely unsuccessfully at his aim, and lived in doss-houses. Eventually, a collection of poems, *The Soul's Destroyer*, was published at his own expense, and met with further silence until it was discovered by a journalist looking for a story; before long, Davies was a minor literary celebrity. His new friends included Edward Thomas (who gave him use of a cottage), and in 1908 he wrote his most successful prose book, *The Autobiography of a Super-Tramp*, which recounted his unique story. Further memoirs followed, and many poetry books; when Edward Marsh picked him up for all five of his successful *Georgian Poetry* anthologies between 1912 and 1922, his reputation seemed secure. In middle age, he enjoyed London's literary society before retiring to Gloucestershire with his young wife, whom he had met at a bus stop. He died in 1940.

W. H. Davies: Man and Poet – A Reassessment is more critical introduction than literary biography, and while Davies's life story is traced, the emphasis is on his memoirs and poems. Callup is, fortunately, aware of his subject's flaws, as well as his idiosyncratic gifts. 'Davies was no stylist. […] He progresses from incident to incident with the same inflexibility', but, perhaps paradoxically,

'Davies can tell a tale' and after all 'there is, simply, nothing quite like it'. *Young Emma*, Davies's candid account of finding and marrying his wife Helen, is regarded as especially important for revealing 'much of the real Davies behind the mask', though Cullup's discussion of that book essentially comprises a dry synopsis missing a spoiler warning.

Callup makes some astute points about the poems. Davies is now perhaps most famous for his poem 'Leisure', beginning 'What is this life if full of care'. But, as Cullup notes, though Davies had 'nothing of the technical virtuosity of de la Mare, nothing of the learning and sense of tradition of Blunden, nothing of the careful seriousness of Edward Thomas', his best poetry does not fit comfily in the mould of the worst Georgian nature poesy, either. Having achieved his aim of writing for a living, Davies had to keep it up by writing, and writing far too much, in the style for which he had been rewarded; 'he didn't have the courage (and could not afford) to discard those poems which he must have known failed to ignite'. But his best poems, Cullup asserts with justification, are poems of 'exact statement, spare diction, and fine technical and emotional control', and when his inimitable life gets into them, they can 'have a power and depth which stirs and disturbs'. The book closes with twenty-five pages of such poems.

Unfortunately, Cullup's book is simply too short – yet often repetitive – for its own good, and rarely gets to grips with Davies's work in sufficient detail. For example, there is no significant mention of *The True Travellers*, one of Davies's more intriguing, bawdy prose books, and little close literary analysis of Davies's poems, though the book rightly shows that some of them deserve it. The text is also undermined by some shoddy research: Cullup locates Davies's accident in the wrong country, and claims Edward Thomas 'found a house for Davies' several years after Thomas had in fact been killed in action. Regarding *Young Emma*, which was not published until 1980, after Helen Davies had died, Cullup asks why Davies was 'keen for the public to know that he had suffered from venereal disease, that he had been in the fairly regular habit of sleeping with prostitutes'. But he hadn't been: Davies initially intended the book to be published anonymously, then withdrew it when his publisher pointed out that certain details might give away his and his wife's identities.

This study comes a decade after two short literary biographies: Lawrence Normand's brief and astute *W. H. Davies* (2003) and Barbara Hooper's engaging but under-researched *Time to Stand and Stare: A Life of W. H. Davies* (2004). Cullup's, which is shorter and less well researched than either, ends with the statement that 'a full reassessment of his work has long been overdue.' This isn't it, but we should thank Michael Cullup for making the point.

Times Literary Supplement, 2015

TOGARA MUZANENHAMO, *GUMIGURU* (CARCANET, 2014)

Togara Muzanenhamo's second collection, named for the hot and dry tenth month of the Shona calendar, is a harsh but heartfelt tribute to the people and landscapes of the author's native Zimbabwe. We encounter a varied cast of memorable folk, from a preacher who 'calls Herod a *cunt*' to a sixteen-year-old girl with 'sex in every stride' and many workmen – such as the wire gang, a 'workforce strumming pole and steel, laying wire, / squaring acres off; each labourer's hardened hands / knowing nothing but work, a wife's skin, and prayer'. Behind it all looms the colonial past: 'lanes with old English and Dutch names sophisticated with elision', or 'old colonial names – faded / but blocked out in concrete – / speak[ing] like scripts'.

Many of the poems are slow affairs – in some cases, slower than they need to be. The moving fifty-six-line 'The Chronicles' stands out, for all that on the face of things it does little to transcend straightforward description:

> They still drew the old roller over the cricket pitches with men
> yoked like a team of oxen to the stubborn iron wheel.
> The grass smelt as the grass did, all rich beneath the afternoon sun –
> the heat flashing off the ground like a blinding flick of steel.

It is an anecdote in verse, the long lines and regular stanzas measuring the narrative out steadily and surely. This approach allows Muzanenhamo to maintain a clarity that implies distance; what is more, he knows he is not quite the same as some of the people he documents. In 'Kubvumbi', which takes its name from the month furthest from Gumiguru:

> Neighbours wake to curse the weather, maize fields
> Sodden and dark. From dawn to dusk, the same grey
> Stare over the trudged hoof-suck of mud-trenched cattle

> Grieved by the trees. But here, the rhythm of drizzle
> Falls gently, filling our sleep with a layered peace […].

Muzanenhamo's matter-of-fact approach results in some poems that are imprecise or long-winded, or just too obvious and simple for their own good, and about a third the way into *Gumiguru*, one starts to come across poems that feel familiar from earlier on. There is just too much here. But this poet has a rare gift and should be admired for the risks he takes, which have enabled him to write some unusual, moving and yet understated poems of conflict, love and hard graft.

Times Literary Supplement, 2015

JAMES SUTHERLAND-SMITH, *MOUTH* (SHEARSMAN, 2014)

As James Sutherland-Smith writes in his introduction to *Mouth*, the central image of this sequence 'is the human mouth and its relationship to human utterances whether in speech or song and poetry'. This turns out to include allusions to Ruskin, Pound, Dante, Gottfried Benn, Ts'en Shen – for all that it is otherwise quite straightforward. The first of the 99 fifteen-line sections indicates something of Sutherland-Smith's meditative directness, though Gary Snyder's 'pissing / watching / a waterfall' takes us further quicker, and is more alert to line-breaks. A brook accelerates 'through / two lumpy boulders', swallows 'nip through trees / taking midges', and the speaker emerges from a cabin door, 'hair spiky, / for my early morning piss, / all of us a word forming / the moment a mouth opens'. The opening section of the book is a many-angled contemplation of the ineffable and the oral, and is set in Slovakia, where the author keeps a cabin. A mouth is seen to be 'like a flowerhead', 'a sepulchre / stone uprights topped / by stone lintel', and – of course! – a 'vagina'. Then, from section 26, we leap from North Africa to China by way of Arabia and Persia, where the speaker seems less sure of himself, and engages in some odd oral exchanges, such as when a dentist admires his teeth while giving him a crown.

Elsewhere, though, any doubt is replaced by bizarre self-congratulation. 'The sound of silence' is 'beloved of bad poets', but 'for those of us with better hearing' there is no silence: 'Even in outer space suited up / there is one's heartbeat and breathing'. Since the poet is here congratulating his perspicacity, the tired language is particularly unfortunate. This is followed by a poem after Laforgue – an attempt, we are told, to get 'the sequence out of the metaphysical fix it was drifting towards'. Sutherland-Smith has no interest in disguising his obviously intense struggle to keep the sequence keel-down, but it has a tendency to go belly-up, not least in the occasional rhymes: 'complexity within complexity /

into which truth passes and becomes perplexity' sounds like Leibniz speaking through the mouth of Vanilla Ice.

This is highly personal poetry, for all its apparent objectivity. The introduction explains that Sutherland-Smith is at various points describing his daughter, his first love Vera, his wife Viera: 'she and my wife signify the beginning and culmination of my passionate affections' – or, as 19 puts it, laced with ambiguity, 'Vera her name, a first love, / almost the same as my last, / Viera, meaning faith'. Then, in 21, Viera transforms into Sophia, divine woman of the Gnostics: '"I wish to give birth to God," you said'. And near the end of it all, Sutherland-Smith implores us to rejoice in life – by way of our mouths, naturally: 'Everything that has lived / from virus to Einstein is God', so 'creator, lift up your voice'.

Times Literary Supplement, 2015

I DIDN'T QUALIFY: IAN PARKS, MEXBOROUGH, AND THE QUEST FOR IDENTITY

Ian Parks was born in the town of Mexborough, South Yorkshire, in 1959, in the front room of a Victorian terraced house built for a miner's family. Mexborough had swelled during the Industrial Revolution, largely as a result of its six coal mines; Parks's family had been there for as long as anyone could remember, and the men had gone down the pit as soon as they came of age. As he has put it in a brief essay, 'A Poet's Yorkshire: A Place Where Poems Might Happen':

> Mexborough was and, to some extent, still is defined by its past; and that past is defined by mining. My father, both grandfathers, and all the male members of my family from as far back as anyone could remember had worked the mines.

Ian put a stop to that tradition. He grew up in an age of relative prosperity and increased social mobility, and had both the intelligence and ambition to choose his own career path to an extent his grandparents, and even his parents, would have found bewildering in their own time. He became both the first man in the family for generations not to go down the mines, and the first to attend university, swapping Mexborough for Sheffield (though his digs were only twenty minutes away by train) in order to study English and Philosophy from 1980 to 1983. He also became the family's first published author, when his poetry book *Gargoyles in Winter* appeared in 1986, and its first Doctor a decade later, when he completed a PhD in Chartist poetry at Oxford, supervised by Raphael Samuel. Like Tony Harrison, twenty-two years his senior, Parks took advantage of opportunities that had not been open to his forebears to 'better' himself, and became of all things that 'crude four-letter word', as Harrison's alter-ego put it in his poem 'v.': a poet. And in doing so, he inadvertently distanced himself from the people he had grown up among and had most loved.

This made returning to live in his hometown for the long term, which Parks did in 2008, all the more difficult – but also, as he wrote to me in August 2013, all the more essential:

> I came back to Mexborough in 2008 and found that the process of becoming a poet had distanced me from that community. But I feel very strongly that I want to write from it rather than about it.

And he really is writing 'from it': his new home is the one in which he was born, the terraced house he inherited from his mother. This return to Mexborough has coincided with a reinvigorated interest – even almost an artistic obsession – with reconnecting with the town, its history and his upbringing. It is the overarching theme, the leitmotif, of his most recent collection *The Exile's House* (Waterloo Press, 2012), particularly in the opening third of that book. I will concentrate on a few of those poems and try to explain why they move and encourage me.

The collection has a title poem, an elusive one about the home of an exile built 'on a cliff above the sea' and the man sheltering there who 'listens as the night dictates / words of resistance, lines of dissent.' This is a specific man, though we learn nothing more about him. But set free from this context – as all titles from short title poems are when they appear isolated on a book cover – it simply suggests the home of any exile. And this is intriguing when we consider that an unusually high proportion of the poems in this book are indeed quite personal ones written from the perspective of a man who has returned from elsewhere to a town outsiders rarely visit, and who, like the speaker of 'A Pool of Petrol', 'finds traces of the place where he was born / despite the evidence of other lives'. The exile's house of the title poem, and of the book title, is both a place of the imagination and the tiny house where the poet was born, from which he looks out on a 'sea' of other natives who never left. We might just about be reminded of Douglas Dunn, looking out, in the opening section of his first book, from his terraced house in Terry Street, Hull, at the apparently inscrutable goings on of the working class outside, and not feeling comfortable in the slightest. But Parks looks out from his exile's house not on a strange world, but on a native world made strange by experience. In a sense, he is an insider, a Mexborough man. But he is also an outsider, one who has chosen to return, who has lived extensively elsewhere, and who feels distanced from his fellow Mexborough people by the same artistic medium he relies on in order to reconnect emotionally to his innate environment.

There are lots of poems about childhood and coming of age in *The Exile's House*, and often they are also poems about mining. Normally, the life evoked seems to be that of the poet, or an imagined version of him in the wilderness, as in the two poems mentioned thus far. In 'The Cage', however, the focus is on his father instead. The poem begins by evoking the final part of a miner's journey to work, the short-lined poem racing down the page in a visual echo of the way the men it describes plummet through bedrock on a journey the poet had never needed to take:

> My father relinquished
> his claim on the light.
> At sixteen he went down
>
> to work the seams.
> The cage was lowered
> on a rusted thread;
>
> the men were crowded in
> behind steel bars.

Mining might have sustained Mexborough, until the pit closures of the 1980s at least, but Parks refuses to sentimentalise it much. There is a very good reason he didn't opt to follow his dad by going 'down' on 'a rusted thread', and he knows it. When we read that his 'father relinquished / his claim on the light', this is at once a literal drop into the dark and a metaphorical end to the 'light' of a childhood which has been foreshortened, a 'light' which he had no choice about relinquishing.

However, if there is one thing the father gains because of his job, other than his wage packet, it is solidarity with his workmates – something unavailable to those who have never taken the plunge, no matter how eloquently they write about what it must be like. The next poem in the book, on the facing page, is 'The Incident'. This recounts an event on the picket line on 'the coldest morning / of the strike' – that is, the nationwide Miners' Strike of 1984–1985. The speaker is present with his striking father when a snowstorm brings some cheer to the freezing men. For a while afterwards they build a snowman every morning, only for a 'growling cavalcade' to come along, scatter the men, and run the snowman down. One day, the speaker's father has had enough, and orchestrates the construction of a new snowman, 'bigger than before', around a bollard. The result is obvious enough; however, the poem does not end in that minor triumph, but in personal defeat, with the speaker remembering that because he 'couldn't move for laughing' he became the first to 'catch a gloved fist in the face'.

In this poem, as elsewhere in the collection, Parks writes about the life of his town from a periphery – but he keeps coming back to it. When I asked him why Mexborough and an upbringing there had become a particular concern in this book, more than in any of his others, he told me that he thought there might be two reasons:

> The painful experiences of the strike (my parents divorced as a result of it) made it difficult for me to gain any degree of objectivity. Only recently have I been able to explore it in poetry. Secondly, I felt for a long time that I didn't want to 'capitalise' on

the suffering and strife of people I knew. For a long time I felt I might be betraying them by making it a subject for poetry.

A generation on, and back living where it all happened, he has come to feel able to recount what is his story, too. 'The Incident' is a poem from the perspective of one enthusiastic and impassioned but somewhat dithering non-miner: it doesn't capitalise on the suffering of the miners, but on the principled hanger-on activities of the activist son, the returnee, deeply concerned for his family and the people among whom he grew up.

In the tale of us versus them recounted in 'The Incident', it is obvious which side the speaker is on; but his is a reasoned political stance more than one resulting from personal necessity. When the Miner's Strike was going on thirty years ago, Parks was in his mid-twenties, and had a degree from one of our most prestigious universities. He was back in Mexborough, but wouldn't stick around for long. He is implicitly and inextricably on the side of the miners, but he isn't one of them, either. He is instead one of the politicised but also highly educated Left. And in spite of all his qualifications,

> I didn't qualify.
> The nearest I'd been to the coal face
>
> was going to the pit head to pick up
> my father's sick pay when he did his leg.
>
> I'd learned it all from books
> which somehow made me suspect,
>
> set apart.

He ends up being punched in the face because he is laughing so much – more, it would seem, than anyone else – that he is incapacitated. But even his enthusiasm for their cause, thus conceived, sets him apart from those too wearied to laugh at all, and too good at dodging fists.

Another snowy poem, 'Sledge', also ends with an apparently positive action being undermined by uncertainty. The speaker happens upon his mother's battered, corroded sledge in the cellar of what had been the family home, a dark place where he 'never used to go'. She has died, it seems, and in a sense the sledge has too: with 'the frame intact / and all the rest decayed' it might be a skeleton in a grave, merely the subterranean remains of what was once a cared-for, mobile body. But it is still accessible, and she is not, which precipitates a meditation:

> Strange how things outlast us
> as they too
>
> outlast the limits
> of their usefulness.

Metrically, these four lines are two disguised pentameters, broken in two and so imperfected. Four lines of apparently free verse are in fact constrained by tradition – just as the speaker, free to come and go from this home, is actually constrained to this house and town because of an obligation to tradition, a sense of filial belonging. The poem ends with an attempt not to allow the sledge to have outlasted the limits of its usefulness, the speaker taking it upstairs and out to the snow. But we know already that it is decayed, spilling 'rust-flakes', so this is a purely sentimental act, a futile and sad attempt to reconnect to a vanished past – quite divorced from the thoughtless and unfettered joy of sledding.

'The Wheel' is another meditation on a disused hunk of metal. But here we move from a leisure item in the rarely visited cellar of a home, to a utilitarian machine-cum-monument representing a whole community: the 'great wheel' of a coal mine. This poem ties together several strands in the collection, and is central to a lot of Parks's present concerns, as poet and as editor. He recently edited an anthology and is currently putting together two more. These are, respectively, a book of contemporary Yorkshire poetry, one of poetry about coalmining, and an anthology of poetry by the mid-nineteenth-century Chartists. The mining and Yorkshire-related references and inferences in 'The Wheel' and elsewhere in much of the book are obvious enough, and that is emphasised here in the dedication of the poem to the Sheffield-based, Chesterfield-born young poet Helen Mort – a dedication Parks describes as an act of Yorkshire 'solidarity' – and the poem's pointed use of the second-person pronoun, which firmly establishes the addressee as a fellow northerner. The influence of Chartist poetry on the poem is perhaps less conspicuous, and I'll return to that shortly.

The poem splits quite neatly into four phases. First, we have a slightly rosy-eyed reminiscence of a mining community in full swing, generation after generation, extracting coal from the ground and being buried in turn. If we take this community to be Mexborough, we can say that the speaker is the poet – but the same story could be true of almost any mining town in South Wales, the North, the Midlands, southern Scotland, and so on:

> The pithead used to dominate the town.
> My dead forefathers came and went,
> were buried in the shadow cast by it.
> I passed it on my way to school,
> heard its revolutions in the night.
> If the pithead was the place's heart
> the great wheel was its soul.

The wheel was the 'soul' of this town. It was visible and audible above and at the centre of the community, a secular source of fortitude and togetherness to challenge or even supplant that of any house of God. But this is all in the past tense, begging a question that remains unanswered throughout the poem: what is the town's 'soul', and where is its 'heart', now that this revolving wheel has been taken down?

Next, we are presented with a recollection of this metaphorical 'heart' and 'soul' of the town being removed:

> And then there was the slow dismantling.
> The slagheap was grassed over: it became
> an innocent green mound where cattle graze.
> They hauled the winding gear away
> and sold the chain for scrap
> then took the giant wheel and clamped it down.

In time, the grassy slagheap is given over to farmers: often benefactors of the same Tory government that closed the mines, people commonly allied to the Conservative party. The wheel remains nearby as a sign of fortitude and remembrance, but is put beyond use, its 'revolutions' ended for the long term as it is 'clamped down', kept firmly in place. Following this, the poet muses on what is left for 'us' now, with this recycled monument in our midst:

> They did this to remind us of where we came from,
> what we did and who we were –
> a monument of rusting metal spokes
> that radiate from hub to rim
> for kids to climb on, point at questioning.

Again, the poem adopts the past tense, and here the choice of tense is especially intriguing. Earlier in the poem, Parks is merely being truthful when he describes the effect of the once-working wheel on the town: it has since gone. Now, however, the use of the past tense implies a loss of personal identity: the wheel does not represent what these people are, only what they have been. Strictly, though with figurative intent, we are told that the people was the wheel: it was their identity, and that identity has been taken from utility to artefact. This begs the question: what and who are we now? The poem doesn't have anything to say about this.

The town's twenty-first-century children don't even know what the wheel is, which would have been unthinkable to their parents, and the fact that the new generations might forget what has happened here only seems to strengthen the speaker's resolve: he does not want to let them. And here it is worth returning to the poem's dedicatee. Helen Mort was only 27 when the poem was published, is too young to remember the Strike, and is in fact barely old enough to recall the Thatcher years at all. The poem may well be written in 'solidarity' with her, but it is also a handing down of a torch, a reminder to her and others of younger generations that they also have an obligation to their heritage. (Mort's debut collection, *Division Street* (Chatto & Windus, 2013), demonstrates an emphatic, empathetic awareness of that.)

This sets up the end of the poem, and what amounts to an impossible, empty threat:

> Some day we'll come with picks and dynamite,
> dislodge it from its concrete plinth.
> We'll drag it from the valley floor,
> aim it at the cities of the south,
> set the wheel in motion, watch it roll.

They won't, of course – and a comparably sweeping sense of us and them, albeit with the boot on the other foot, was part of the problem in the first place. The poem ends with this futile dream of retribution, the wheel (and with it those it stands for) freed and turned to a newer, more destructive purpose. This is crude revolutionary rhetoric – and of course the notion of this kind of working-class 'revolution' has its counterpart in the homonym at the start of the poem, when the child hears other long-gone revolutions in the night.

And here I'll return to Chartism, an interest of Parks's so strong and abiding that he also made it the subject of his doctoral thesis two decades ago. Chartist poet rhetoric is central to this poem, which ends not in uncertainty or personal defeat but in the promise (however fanciful it is) of future glory – or at least glory of a kind. The Chartist newspaper, the *Northern Star*, was at one time the second most popular newspaper in Britain, and ran a poetry column in every issue. Chartist poetry wasn't always of the greatest literary value, but it was unmistakably popular: a Chartist poem was frequently a rallying cry, recited at meetings, in homes and halls, in the street. And Chartist poetry was commonly imbued with what we might think of as the language of menace: the poems often promised a time when those denied their birthright would rise and take what should have been theirs, knocking down their oppressors in the process – as in the anonymously-authored 'The Voice of the People', printed in the *Northern Star* on 4th December 1841:

> 'Tis the voice of the people I hear it on high,
> It peals o'er the mountains – it soars to the sky;
> Through wide fields of heather, it wings its swift flight;
> Like thunders of heaven arrayed in their might.
> It rushes still on, like the torrent's loud roar;
> And bears on its surges the wrongs of the poor.
> Its shock like the earthquake shall fill with dismay,
> The hearts of the tyrants and sweep them away.

'The people' no longer tend to read, recite or write much poetry. But it is this tradition that Parks seems intent to tap into at the end of his poem: a flight of fancy leads him to want to knock down the 'tyrants', all of whom are apparently safe at home down in merrie Middle England, guilty of ripping the heart and soul from the place he loves and which sustained his forebears.

There can be no doubt that Parks's recent poetry reveals a powerful sense of belonging in his hometown, then: he is in one sense an embittered insider, a native. He is part of the people for whom the wheel is a reminder of 'what we did', even though he never actually 'did' it himself. But in another sense, he can never be embittered by the town's demise in quite the same way as those who were left unemployed: he never relied on the pit for his pay, and his education and interests separated him almost as much as they sustained him. That these bookish interests setting him apart reach their apotheosis in doctorate-level research into Chartism, and poems of working-class struggle and occasionally Chartist-style revolutionary rhetoric, is a bitter irony that he cannot escape, and has instead chosen to embrace.

The Dark Horse, 2015

JUST LIKE THAT

Sean O'Brien, *The Beautiful Librarians* (Picador, 2015)

I suspect it is a strange feeling for a poet to publish a *Collected Poems* when he quite evidently still has plenty left in the tank. Sean O'Brien's handsome *Collected* (2012) included all eight of his slim volumes up to and including his best to date, the psychologically rich, witty, and historically aware *November* (2011). *The Beautiful Librarians* is another book preoccupied above all with the past, the way things alter, and our control or lack of control of these matters, though O'Brien is far too interesting and interested a poet to nosedive into sentimentality or to give us too often exactly what we expect from his tackling such topics. The first poem, 'Audiology', provides a ready example. Among many other things, O'Brien's speaker can hear 'logorrhoea / On the dreaded Quiet Coach', the verb transferred to what seems, at first sight, the wrong noun: is it the coach he 'dreads'? Well, yes, if that means the predictably noisy 'quiet' one. But really this is a poem about an altogether more significant lack of control:

> And I'm told that soon it will be easier
> To balance out the love-cry and the howl,
> To wear an aid and act my age, to hear the world
> Behind this world and not to crave amnesia.

And who is doing this telling?

O'Brien is frequently a poet of quotidian realities, and their inextricability from the big poetic themes of love and death, longing and fear. His poems are often laced with a wit that can be delightfully wry and only occasionally smacks a little too much of crowd-pleasing. 'Residential Brownjohnesque' (a nod to Alan Brownjohn's enjoyable line in disenchanted social comment) gathers the participants of a writers' retreat:

Euphemia Bandersnatch, Clive Overbite
And the indomitable Norman Shouty,
And someone who is always not there yet
But on a train [...].

Their hapless main human subject of the poem prepares to do his best with this motley crew: 'you have to talk to them. They're waiting'. One wonders what O'Brien's employers make of their Professor of Creative Writing penning this fairly easy attack on an aspect of the industry, but you have to admire his chutzpah, and the willingness to roll about like a loose cannon is one of O'Brien's charms, if you like that kind of thing. O'Brien likes fooling around with characterisation, and any readers not prepared to attune themselves to that might find the caricatures off-puttingly relentless. Another example is the subject of 'Protocols of the Superfluous Immortal', a rather sad 'god long since retired to the seaside', who reads the *Telegraph* and tuts to himself.

As this probably implies, O'Brien is not opposed to turning a poisoned quill in the direction of Toryism, and the past five years have given him plenty of material. 'Another Country' is a particularly rollicking diatribe, pounding along on its off-kilter mainly-fourteeners like a Pacer traversing the Pennines, its subject the north-south divide, the class divide, maybe even the '[uz] and them' of Tony Harrison at his finest, but three decades after Thatcherism:

> You stand for everything there was to loathe about the south –
> The avarice, the snobbery, the ever-sneering mouth,
>
> The lack of solidarity with any cause but *me*,
> The certainty that what you were was what the world should be.
>
> The North? Another country. No one you knew ever went.
> (Betteshanger, Snowdown, Tilmanstone: where were they? In Kent.)

'People' tell us nowadays these views are terribly unfair,
But these forgiving 'people' aren't the 'people' who were there.

That fifth line is a subtle and politically charged variation on L. P. Hartley's famous dictum that 'The past is a foreign country: they do things differently there'. For all its barely reined-in snarling, though, what does such a poem teach us? That we still agree or disagree with its point just as we did before we read it? Political poetry too often turns to simple grandstanding or simplistic sideswiping, nuance replaced by didacticism, as in Harrison's 'Kreig Anthology' – it is as hard to see the point as it is to disagree.

O'Brien's finest engagements with the politics of our times come instead in several of the book's more ambitious and multivalent poems. The title poem, for example, is a miniature masterpiece of memory and feeling, a piece of writing for our times and for all times. Recent swingeing cuts to Britain's public libraries are not explicitly mentioned in the poem, which is nonetheless an elegy on the passing of such public services. The speaker remembers his youthful visits to this world of

> The fairly recent graduates who sat
> Like Francoise Hardy's shampooed sisters
> With cardigans across their shoulders
> On quiet evenings at the issue desk,
> Stamping books and never looking up
> At where I stood in admiration.

Collective characterisation – even stereotyping – is dangerous, and in this context one of the risks is a charge of sexism. Even the metre joins in, with those delicately downshifting feminine endings to the second and third lines quoted above. Later in the poem, O'Brien gives us another stereotype: these women, surrounded by books all day, went home to fail at being writers themselves: 'The novels they were writing secretly' would turn, in time, 'to "Mum's old stuff"'. But this is a warm caricature, self-aware in its irony, and in any case the speaker never had access to the librarians' apparently clandestine world – would never 'even brush [them] in passing'. They are left to his memory as 'ice-queens in their realms of gold' (those last three words lifted straight from Keats's paean to reading, 'On First Looking into Chapman's Homer'), and he remained in thrall to them and faithful to their cause: 'Book after book I kept my word / Elsewhere, long after they were gone / And all the brilliant stock was sold'. That last word, rhyming with the Keats allusion five lines earlier, rings out in bathetic response: their metaphorical 'gold', a treasure trove of learning for all, has been, it is implied, superseded by financial profit for the few.

This poem in part succeeds because it doesn't tell us what to think, while shifting from the local and personal to take in a swathe of history. The irony, the subtle dipping into the myth kitty in a manner that won't alienate those who miss it, the wry characterisation that is at once perspicacious and generalising, the focus on commonplaces, the roomy yet taut stanzaic structure: all call to mind Philip Larkin – and, of course, even the subject evokes Larkin's career as a university librarian. O'Brien doesn't exactly do much to prevent us from thinking of Larkin as we read these poems, and at times he positively embraces the possibility. 'The Lost of England', which might even more suitably have given the book its title, has a distinctly Larkinesque/O'Brienesque air of loss and time torn off unused – 'somewhere at hand / Lay cities we would never visit' – and takes as its subject a train journey through the English Midlands, 'past nameless settlements and cooling towers, / Chains of ponds, canals where nothing moved, low hills'. Are these Larkin's 'nondescript' towns from 'The Whitsun Weddings'? Aren't those cooling towers – or one of them, at least – also straight from the list of things seen in Larkin's poem (as well as being outside the train window at beauty spots such as East Midlands Parkway)? Is what doesn't move on the canal Larkin's 'industrial froth', perhaps? This poet isn't Larkinising in mere deference, though, as too many poets seem to. O'Brien's ostensibly more beautiful and vaguer canal is tainted by Larkin's now-canonical, half-century-old images of despoliation, and we are reminded that it is still going on, all of it, still going on.

In fact, the poem has just as much in common with Donald Davie's 'In the Stopping Train', in which 'this journey will punish the bastard' speaker, left to his thoughts in a lethargic carriage. There are several trains in *The Beautiful Librarians*, as there are throughout O'Brien's work (he has even edited a book of poetical train journeys), and on most of them the speaker is a passenger, symbolically shunted back and forth as an observer to his own fortunes. Here, O'Brien's protagonist falls half-asleep, work papers on his lap, into a sort of quasi-anglophilic reverie of a 'railway bridge, more woods, a half-mown hillside, / Sheds, allotments, barrows propped on end – the whole misfigured / Fact of things that you can neither touch nor live without', only to wake at what 'looked like Crewe'. In the next poem, Passage for New Holland', we turn from a dream-state to full wakefulness, as 'The ragged pastoral grows picturesque / With too much looking'. New Holland is a Lincolnshire village and tiny port on the Humber, directly opposite the Yorkshire city of Kingston upon Hull, where O'Brien grew up. It is a lonely, flat and mysterious corner of England, somehow even less glamorous than the nothing-village of Sunk Island across the estuary in East Yorkshire, which was the subject of one of the most startling poems in *November*. Once again, with subtlety, nuance and no answers, O'Brien shifts delicately and purposefully beyond mere evocation:

The tide has risen, just like that.

Lovers and the dead will not
Persuade it to release a single anecdote,
And yet the craving for a sign
Converts the slightest pretext to a rite.

Be faithful, then. Here comes the night.

Some rather pointless squibs have made it through the editorial filter: 'Damn Right I Got the Blues: Ovid Live in Tomis' conflates Ovid's exile with the rhythms and language of blues, for reasons best known to Sean O'Brien; and the 'Three Frivolous Poems' really are that. But for the most part this book is a very considerable achievement.

Times Literary Supplement, 2015

IN PASSING

Blake Morrison, *Shingle Street* (Chatto & Windus, 2015)

In the 1980s, Blake Morrison established his reputation as a poet (with *Dark Glasses* and *The Ballad of the Yorkshire Ripper*) and influential editor (at the *TLS*, the *Observer* and, alongside Andrew Motion, with *The Penguin Book of Contemporary British Poetry*). Since then, his attention has mostly been focused on other genres: fiction (*South of the River*, *The Last Weekend*), drama, criticism, and, of course, memoir (the best-selling *And When Did You Last See Your Father?*). *Shingle Street*, his first full-length collection of poems in almost thirty years, begins boldly, with its near-title poem, 'The Ballad of Shingle Street', a magnificent 140-line evocation of a Suffolk fishing hamlet and its environs, in jauntily rhymed, otherwise calmly insistent dimeters and tetrameters that make effective use of repetition and refrain. Shingle Street was evacuated in 1940, and is predicted to succumb to coastal erosion within a few decades:

> From Shingle Street
> To Orford Ness
> The waves maraud,
> The winds oppress,
> The earth can't help
> But acquiesce
> For this is east, and east means loss,
> A lessening shore, receding ground,
> Three feet gone last year, four feet this,
> Where land runs out and nothing's sound.
> Nothing lasts long on Shingle Street.

Indeed, Suffolk's crumbling coast dominates the first half of the book. The setting of 'Covehithe' is a village (and glorious ruined church) adjacent to the most speedily eroding cliffs in Britain: 'The tides go in and out / but the cliffs are stuck in reverse', until they threaten the graveyard full of sailors and fishermen. Cue a sweetly fanciful conclusion: the dead, 'who long to be back at sea', are imagined enticing 'the sea to come to them'. In the next poem, 'Dunwich', such a reclamation has already taken place: 'the waves took him back / his slab disappearing in a cliff-fall'. (Dunwich was once the capital of the East Angles, and by the late medieval period its population rivalled that of London, though it has since mostly disappeared and is now a small village.) But there are poems of land and the living here, too. 'Remember the year the sandbank appeared?', begins 'Carissimo', a simple but affecting love poem – as is 'On the Beach', which might have been named after its near-namesake cocktail, and which straddles a line between bravado and what might be self-deprecation:

When you sat up afterwards
a row of pebbles stuck to your back
like medals awarded for bravery.

Similar themes are picked up in 'Flotsam', a gathering of shoreline miniatures. These are crisp, if inconsequential: 'White sand, white bone, the skull of a catfish / and an oystercatcher's skeleton, / the wind through them like a piccolo', reads one – which is a haunting image, though it also offers up the unintended suggestion that the *wind* is like a piccolo. Like many other poets' imagistic shorts, it also feels as though it hasn't quite been made into a poem yet. 'Flotsam' highlights an occasional failing in *Shingle Street*: some of the poems really don't amount to much, or (like 'Sea Walk', which also evokes coastal erosion), they repeat what has already been better said elsewhere in the book. 'Life Writing', a villanelle, flirts too much with unfruitful *ars poetica*: 'You're trying to bring to life what's in your head', and so on. Reading 'Wet' feels like stumbling across your mother's teenage diary: 'I lay in wait for him. / And I was wet for him'. Some poems are let down a little by cliché or dull abstraction: epitaphs are 'lovely'; 'we never saw a soul'. The sequence 'This Poem' is diverting if not exactly surprising, with its restrained anger in tackling subjects such as hacking, bankers' bonuses, government surveillance scandals. And if you are going to use two of Philip Larkin's most famous lines from which to launch a slightly laborious formal exercise, you should probably get them right.

It is in the more substantial poems, though, that *Shingle Street* is fully charged. 'Passing Places' is typically beautiful – and again finds us by water. A holiday alone in the Scottish islands, among 'Salmon farms, highland cattle, / lambs like schoolgirls in black and white socks, / oystercatchers patrolling a loch', turns to memento mori, as the speaker stumbles across graveyards displaying his surname:

> The words said nothing of their lives
> but sometimes the dates said it,
>
> 'aged 5', 'aged 10', 'aged 17',
> the rain flooding their chests,
> the snow clogging their lungs,
> and the futures awaiting them –
> nurse, farmer, architect, mother –
> swept away like a branch in burn.

The book culminates with several poignant, anecdotal poems, such as 'Old Men Sighing', in which the 'old men' are the speaker and his father, at the same stage of life:

> Now like him I've started sighing
> for no reason. *Just that time when…*
> *if only I'd…* all the haunting almosts
> and the one implacable was.

These are humane poems, often skilful, conversational, delicate and more complex than they at first appear.

Times Literary Supplement, 2015

Poetry, October 2014–September 2015

Two years ago, Don Share replaced Christian Wiman as the editor of America's longest-running poetry magazine, expressing a desire to take 'risks with unpredictable, difficult, and infuriating work'. He is especially keen for *Poetry* to appeal to readers from a diverse range of backgrounds, and to support the ambitions of younger writers: this year's eleven issues include the snapshot-anthologies 'Young Irish Poets' (September 2015; under forty-five, in case you were wondering) and 'Poets from the United Kingdom' (October 2014). Others have contained features dedicated to such schools and/or groups as BreakBeat poets (allied to Hip-Hop), and 'angsty teens'. On several occasions, the editorial reins have been handed over: Patrick Cotter introduced and assembled the cast of the wide-ranging Irish issue; a third of the material in the UK issue came from the British magazine *Poetry Review*; the BreakBeat feature is an excerpt from the recent anthology *The BreakBeat Poets*, and in his introduction Share quotes from that book: 'this is work "for people who love Hip-Hop ... for people who thought poems were only something done by dead white dudes who got lost in a forest, and for poetry heads." In other words, it is for everyone.'

Of course, some are bound to think: 'Well, that doesn't sound like it is for *me*'. Share has certainly taken his call to inclusivity seriously, though, and there have surely been more poets in recent issues of *Poetry*, from a greater range of social, ethnic and national backgrounds, than at any other time in its history. The UK issue naturally received considerable recognition here, and included a disparate sample, with a slight bias towards relatively young poets whose current collections are also their debuts (Frances Leviston, Liz Berry, James Brookes and Caleb Claces, among others, including me); but it also had room for David Harsent, Pascale Petit, Hugo Williams. It was perhaps less successful as a showcase of the range of our poetry criticism, which comprised Todd Swift's thirteen-page circumnavigation of four collections by (again) young poets, where we learn that, for example, Helen Mort is 'from Sheffield in the relatively impoverished North of England (home to the major indie band Arctic Monkeys)'. The proportion of critical prose at the back of *Poetry* has generally decreased since 2013, and its tone softened; in keeping with this, Swift's piece is a self-indulgent, *sui generis* celebration of work he believes in.

Some of the independently edited features are inclined to raise eyebrows – although saying as much about the obviously well-intentioned 'Las Chavas' segment (January 2015), edited by the Episcopalian priest Spencer Reece, feels gauche. This comprises poems by female Honduran orphans, to whom Reece taught poetry, and with whom he 'worked closely', helping them to 'improve their English and their understanding of English poetry and metre'. Poems that highlight circumstances we should not ignore, and which might normally end up in a community anthology, thus find a print audience of 30,000. Through Reece's translation, fifteen-year-old Ricci writes:

> This young
> rose, it represents all of us here.
> Careful! It is the prettiest young rose
> we have: life needs love,
> love needs life.

The project is complemented by smart photographs of children playing, an outstretched hand, a girl concentrating, Reece writing 'Poesía' on a whiteboard in apparent semi-darkness, and so forth. The 'Pathetic Little Thing' feature (July/August 2015), introduced by nineteen-year-old Tavi Gevinson with an essay she wrote at the age of fourteen, mainly consists of poems 'by self-proclaimed angsty teens'; reading through these, one begins to empathise with teachers marking A-Level Creative Writing assignments. Is this sort of egalitarianism, in which concerns about reaching out sometimes inevitably trump those about literary quality, a function of *Poetry* magazine? Well, yes, it is now.

Such features obviously attract attention, and tend to fire (or dampen) the heart. Mostly, though, *Poetry* under Share's editorship is a less predictable, slightly less substantial but more exuberant version of what it was under Wiman: it remains both indispensable and – yes – infuriating. The same issue that dedicates so much space to the rudiments of youthful anxiety also contains a superb long poem by Paul Batchelor, a not entirely coherent statement from Ai Weiwei on the necessity of poetry (his broad definition of which has room for 'poetic acts' that include a solution, or palliative, to existential angst), and a portfolio of ten typically tricksy poems by Alice Notley, a recipient of this year's Ruth Lilly Prize, perspicaciously introduced by Share. 'If at first you have trouble reading her work', he writes, 'bear in mind that she conceives of herself as disobeying even her own readership.' He then adds: 'Could there be anything more vitally important to our own time, than to let voices in, to listen?' Both statements can easily be reimagined as defences of his editorial practice.

Times Literary Supplement, 2015

MOODY EXCAVATIONS

Jack Clemo, *Selected Poems*, ed. Luke Thompson (Enitharmon, 2015)

This is the first selection from the poems of the Cornishman Jack Clemo (1916–1994) to appear since six years before his death, and it comes none to soon. Clemo was born to a staunch Nonconformist mother and a father who was a clay-kiln worker by trade and died in the First World War. As Rowan Williams notes in his short but useful introduction, in some ways Clemo's was 'a confined and unhappy childhood', which was followed by the onset of problems with his eyesight and hearing in his teens and early twenties. To the extent that he is known now, it is generally for his stark evocations of the Cornish scenes he knew best, his uncompromising Calvinism, his occasional but passionate eroticism – and his disability.

It is perhaps not surprising that the tone of the earlier poems is one of 'insistent ferocity', as Williams puts it; 'My faith and symbol shall be stark', Clemo writes in one early poem. His is the tourist-free Cornwall of 'the pit-head stain', and earth-plundering machines such as the 'grim excavator' that 'shields me / From lateral rain-gusts, its square body turned / To storm-lashed precipices it has churned'. He makes an emotive allegory for God's necessary devastation of the earth from this rutted and gutted land of 'moody excavations'. And he also finds intimations of salvation in it: 'A cross that lacks the symmetry / Of those in churches, but is more / Like His' – or, as he puts it in 'Christ in the Clay-Pit', 'I peer / Upon His footsteps in this quarried mud; / I see His blood / In rusty stains on pit-props'.

Much of this early work is energised formally by strict rhyme schemes and varied line lengths. 'A Calvinist in Love', for example, begins:

I will not kiss you, country fashion,
>   By hedgesides where
>   Weasel and hare
> Claim kinship with our passion.
>
> I care no more for fickle moonlight:
>   Would rather see
>   Your face touch me
> Under a claywork dune-light.

Unfortunately, many of these poems have a tendency to get to the point quickly and then outstay their welcome; once you've read those first two stanzas, you know almost everything the remaining nine have to tell you. In his later work, Clemo relaxes slowly into a freer style, his tone becomes more reflective, and his imagery loses some of its vigour, though his always remains 'a savage Cornwall' with 'earth-rind peeling', as he puts it in 'Wessex and Lyonesse'. 'Salvaged', written in 1977, demonstrates some of Clemo's pervasive virtues and flaws – which by then included a weakness for cliché – and also explains something of his life and motivations. He 'narrowly missed being born on a farm' because of his grandfather's death, and his 'parents had to migrate' to 'a cramped cottage near a sand-tip':

> As a young schoolboy I scanned the farmhouse
> With mild curiosity – then it vanished,
> Swallowed by a clay-pit; and for thirty years
> I saw the whole farm eaten away.

And the boy sat at home, his nose in 'Wesleyan and Puritan' books – not knowing that 'a girl then in London' was apparently simultaneously 'ransacking similar tomes'. Finally, we reach the rather worthy moral:

Showing that the land's peace can deceive, seduce,
That thunder and flash and devastation
May mean that heaven is working on a soul,
Shifting the deep fixations, intending kindness.

Another later poem, 'On the Prospect of Leaving my Birthplace', is a glad valediction to an old home and newly redundant ways of thinking about the world. A 'happy husband' has no need for images of 'clay-ravage': 'the man I am, the fulfilled believer, / Needs palms, sweet modest hills and gentle / Cleansing ripples on the unhacked beach'. As this book's editor Luke Thompson adds in a note, this was written in 1984, the year Clemo and his wife Ruth moved to her hometown of Weymouth, Dorset. (What Thompson doesn't mention, however, is that Clemo's Cornish cottage would eventually also be demolished, by the Goonvean China Clay company, in 2005.) Not infrequently, though, the later poems relax into prolix self-satisfaction. As Clemo writes in 'Sunset in Dorset', 'I have lost the tense, suffering sinew', and 'who / Caring for truth, would regret the transition?' Fair enough, but the poetry suffers when overly concerned with telling us as much.

Jack Clemo remains, though, an inspirational, stoical figure, and a unique if narrow talent whose poetry deserves to stay in print. And, while it leaves room for an authoritative, fully glossed *Complete Poems*, this is about as good a *Selected* as it could be. Thompson's notes are concise but useful, giving publication details and occasional contextual information, and though the book contains only eighty-two pages of poetry, there are no very obvious omissions, and the selection is drawn evenly from across his oeuvre, with the exception of the rhyme-driven earliest work. If *Selected Poems* doesn't win Clemo more readers, it is hard to see what will.

Times Literary Supplement, 2016

SONGS WE STILL SING

Stephen Burt, *The Poem is You: 60 Contemporary American Poems and How to Read Them* (Harvard University Press, 2016)

There is nothing complicated about the layout of this book: one of America's most influential poetry critics, Stephen Burt, presents in chronological order sixty American poems published between 1981 and 2015, alongside a short essay typically of three or four pages, providing poetic and cultural contexts and some close reading. A detailed index allows readers to pick out themes, forms, styles, and so on.

Burt chooses visiting America as an analogue for visiting its poetry: 'Contemporary American poetry is […] an image of America: it's vast, and fascinating, and sometimes baffling, because it contains so many subcultures, locales, talents, tastes, and goals.' It offers 'an enormous and varied geography, whose high points and must-sees can seem very far apart.' The book's title – as twee, out of context, as its subtitle is gratingly manual-like – is taken from the last line in the first poem, 'Paradoxes and Oxymorons' by John Ashbery, and Burt makes it giddy with positivity to encourage readers, as he puts it in the book's introduction, to 'try out, or try on, or simply encounter, the identities, the kinds of language, and the ways to see the world, that each poem opens up.' Most books on recent poetry, he argues, are 'specialized or factional', presupposing considerable prior understanding of forms and traditions, or intentionally elevating some poetries over others. The best introductions to poetry focus 'on poets such as Shakespeare and Emily Dickinson, or Sappho or Bishop or Ted Hughes or Langston Hughes of Li Po or Neruda, rather than focusing only on recent decades. That's where this book comes in.'

This is either a little disingenuous, or Burt hasn't done his homework: Ruth Padel's *52 Ways of Looking at a Poem* and *The*

Poem and the Journey: 60 Poems for the Journey of Life immediately come to mind as counterparts in the genre. But those are British books with a British focus, and there is in fact little overlap in poets between Burt's book and either of Padel's. And certainly Burt's approach is egalitarian: the only uniting principle here is that the poems are American and recent, and that the editor thinks they matter, usually in social terms as well as by dint of inherent poetic skill. They range in length from Robert Grenier's one-line (plus title) 'SHOE FROM THE WAVES' ('oh he got a shoe from the waves') to the 144 lines of 'Self-Portrait in Tyvek™ Windbreaker' by James Merrill, and a simple list of the first four poets indicates the diversity of styles in which Burt wants us to find fascination: after Ashbery, we find Tato Laviera, Richard Wilbur and Lucille Clifton. Most of the authors are well-known in contemporary American poetry, but many will be new to most British readers. The choice of poems, on the other hand, is rarely predictable, though a few of Burt's more obvious inclusions, such as Yusef Komunyakaa's Vietnam War poem 'Facing It', are simply too significant to be excluded. It is refreshing to find a book that gives equal weight and relish to avant-garde minimalism, New Formalism, and so many of the stations between.

With its chronological ordering and (somewhat coincidental but unignorable) focus on more influential figures, this book succeeds adequately as a tour both through the recent history of American poetry and aspects of history as portrayed by it, from Vietnam to the massacre of native Americans (Carter Revard's 'A Song That we Still Sing'), to that most American of constants: consumerism and its corollaries. Racial politics is one of many leitmotifs, and Burt is discreetly on point in his contextualising comments on poems such as the stylistically simple, emotionally complex 'Race' by Elizabeth Alexander. There are also poems, of course, that embody America's great multifariousness, an essence undiluted as yet by political developments slightly too recent for the volume to explore. Agha Shahid Ali's 'Tonight' is an obvious choice for inclusion – almost an 'instant classic', as Burt calls it, 'an exemplary ghazal meant to show Americans how and why we should think about the form':

> The hunt is over, and I hear the Call to Prayer
> Fade into that of the wounded gazelle tonight.
>
> My rivals for your love – you've invited them all?
> This is mere insult, this is no farewell tonight.
>
> And I, Shahid, only am escaped to tell thee –
> God sobs in my arms. Call me Ishmael tonight.

Burt's unpacking of this – the near-pun on 'gazelle', the last sentence recasting the first words of a great American novel as a vulnerable plea, the faith inherent in the ghazal form and how it is tested, and so on – is impressively light and readable. Burt is a good teacher.

From one essay to the next to the next, he is keen – occasionally too keen – to bring us back to an understanding of that most fashionable thing: how poetry might be of use, might help us better to enjoy or better to endure our lives. The analysis of Adrienne Rich's 'An Atlas of the Difficult World XIII (Dedications)' is a case in point, moving swiftly and economically through an overview of Rich's significance to American poetry, her identity as a lesbian and feminist poet, and a lively discussion of how the poem 'connects relatively fortunate, though hurried or stressed-out or lonely, readers to people in acute distress', including some pertinent observations about Rich's versification, before boiling the discussion down to a universalised take-home message: 'Poetry speaks to us differently depending on what we need, on where we began, on how we are affected by headline news', Burt writes; 'Yet it remains, as Jahan Ramazani has written, a kind of language in "vexed dialogue with the news"'. But this as false as it is true, as is the statement Burt goes on to make later in the same paragraph, that 'Poetry brings us together'. I, for one, do most of my reading alone.

Burt's habit of stretching for interpretations has its charms, and offers the encouragement some will need to read ambitiously, but inevitably it leads to some mis-focused analysis. For example, Wilbur's 'The Ride' certainly has allegories and analogues, but I remain unconvinced that the lack of a decent US welfare state is one of them – as does Burt, who describes that as a perspective 'too far' before embracing it anyway. There are other problems. Exegesis can too readily transform into a detailed explanation of the obvious, as when a discussion of Laura Kasischke's 'Miss Weariness' sidesteps into a discussion of overwork and the pressures faced by women with children. These are legitimate issues, obviously, but this still feels like a not particularly edifying foray into virtue signalling. There are also moments of awkward biographical criticism, which perversely encourage us to trust the teller and not the tale: 'Dennis has said that these characters are wholly fictional; we cannot know how [the character in the poem] got sick', he says of Carl Dennis's 'More Music', encouraging the kind of limited reading the book is elsewhere so concerned with guarding against. The blasé assertion that rhyming couplets are 'dated' is also pointedly at odds with Burt's impressively broad celebration of disparate poetries. And sometimes he is just plain wrong: there is no 'full rhyme' at the end of 'Emptiness' by Kay Ryan, and Rita Dove was not 'the first black woman to win the Pulitzer Prize' – that was Gwendoline Brooks.

The Poem is You is a big book, and gripes are almost inevitable. The poems Burt selects would alone comprise a valuable anthology of the American poetry of their times, and he is an entertaining, thought-provoking and eager guide to them, keen to ask and investigate all questions that occur in his reading, and to engage with the chicanery of thought it engenders. Each essay is obviously a product of enjoyment, and encourages us to treat poems with the same enthusiasm – to embrace difficulty and difference in exchange for the articulate and involved pleasure that perhaps poetry, of all the arts, can best provide.

Times Literary Supplement, 2016

N.B. The author of The Poem is You *is now called Stephanie Burt. This review, and of course the book, both precede that development.*

ROMANTIC, NOT QUIXOTIC

Anthony Caleshu, *The Victor Poems* (Shearsman, 2015)

Anthony Caleshu is drawn to wild tales of isolation. His previous collection, *Of Whales*, was obsessed with nineteenth-century whaling and *Moby Dick*. It is a little harder to put a finger on the identity of the eponymous Victor, who in this book-length poem comes to us only through the reported sentiments of apparent friends. We know the following: several people are on a quest, pushing through ice and wind, cold and nothingness, remembering society, sex, normality, and, above all, the wisdom of the elusive Victor, which keeps them going, but whose presence-absence poses as many questions as it answers.

The book's epigraph, from Emerson's essay 'Friendship' (1841), puts all in context: 'We walk alone in the world. Friends such as we desire are dreams and fables. But a sublime hope cheers ever the faithful heart…'. Indeed, Caleshu's poem benefits from being read alongside Emerson's essay, which includes passages such as: 'The essence of friendship is entireness, a total magnanimity and trust. It must not surmise or provide for infirmity. It treats its object as a god, that it may deify both.' This is suitably romantic (but not quixotic) poetry, desperate but never despondent: 'Who are we to be telling tales of *you*?', the speaker asks at one point, before imploring Victor to 'Come to us this winter, like spring.' Throughout the poem, society is yearned for and chided, solitude is yearned for and chided, and all are disciples of Victor, a sort of quotidian *deus absconditus*, the dream and fable who is no less real for that, who provides but is never seen:

> Even *in absentia*, you put the credit card   down.
> It's all paid for, the bartender said: round
>   after round

after round

There is too much of this poem. Moreover, the fact that, stylistically and formally, each section is about a page and a half from roughly the same template, of apparently disjointed thoughts interwoven with images of dislocating travel, will hardly appeal to everyone. All the same, this is triumphant work. Through crystalline images and lines whose apothegmatic weight is often buoyed by dry wit, Caleshu holds up a magnifying mirror before us. It is formally sprightly too, without ostentation. For example, most sections occupy a double-page spread, and about half end with the apparent closure of a drawn-out rhyming couplet (often with foot-dragging feminine rhymes such as 'equatorial' / 'boreal'), before pushing on again into ice and inquisition when we turn the page: 'For so long we've lived our life like ice, constantly melting. / How do we stop the melting? / put the ice on ice, you said one day.' This is a poem about what it is to be human, 'walking from nowhere to no-one' with a whistle and a song, 'studying hard the cracks in the clouds, neglecting the cracks in the ice', and never quite knowing whether we are doing the right thing.

Times Literary Supplement, 2016

VOICE OF SENSE ON EARTH

Peter Porter, *Chorale at the Crossing* (Picador, 2016)

Chorale at the Crossing brings together poems written between the Australian-born Peter Porter's last collection, *Better than God*, published in 2009, and his death in 2010 at the age of 81. This amounts to fifty-three pages of new work, and as such has the appearance of a final full collection, though it is unclear whether all of the poems would've made it into Porter's final cut. Moreover, though Sean O'Brien's introduction is warm and rewarding, it sheds no light on whether Porter is responsible for the ordering of the contents, nor on who served as editor, nor on why the book took five further years to appear. In any case, though it is inevitably uneven, this volume sparkles frequently with Porter's highly readable wit and wisdom, and contains some outstanding poems made all the more poignant by the fact that, for much of the time during which they were written, Porter knew he was dying.

In the opener, 'First Poem of the Last Book', the poet challenges himself to be true and forthright and to keep a steady nerve: 'no reaching for Last Things, / Not Nature's, god's, or history's armature, / Just kitchen, garden, bedroom splinterings!' The second – though, O'Brien tells us, the last of these poems Porter completed – seems to speak to us as an extended epitaph on himself:

> The sound of speech, the voice of sense on earth,
> In this adjunct seems carpentered of years.
> My richness now is nothing but a dearth
> Of tricks for the wiping-away of tears.

Death was always one of Porter's recurring subjects, though here it is all the more central not only because of its imminence, but also because of, as O'Brien puts it, the 'inevitable shrinking of horizons' illness brings. (Porter's native Australia, for example, is almost absent from these poems.) Another leitmotif is a self-questioning *ars poetica*, and the two aren't necessarily kept apart. 'A Perfect Suicide' ('I bungled my own death'), begins:

> And here I will sacrifice all rhyme,
> that is, I will avoid any of the beautiful
> consequences which may intrude on patterns
> infinitely more inter-calculable […]

Porter's poetry is in fact often both formal and metrical, and no less lithe for that. 'Lines for an English Heine', for example, uses the constraint of tetrameters with interlocking rhymes to create a reflexively emotional, emotive prism:

> Our monosyllables are fraught
> With all the things we cannot say,
> And feeling now is drawn to thought
> While thought is threadbare with delay.

This also shows something of Porter's rare skill at using abstractions in the service of verse that has real apothegmatic weight. An equal number of the poems, however, are riddled with odd syntactical inversions, wrenched metres, and trite rhymes in the service of keeping the formalist boat on course. This, from the same poem, surely asks us to forgive too much, and makes us work too hard for what it offers in return:

> Germanic hopes by tongue-tied lake
> In simple language trail the heart,
> But English words cannot awake
> From secrecy a speaking art.

The ambitious 'A Toccatina of Galuppi's', a deferential nod to 'A Toccatta of Galuppi's' by Robert Browning in Browning's rhymed tercets, also echoes its predecessor by imagining layers of time in that most precarious of cities, Venice, and ends with Browning in the place of his death:

> What hangs in minor keys and major lingers in the mind like lead.
> "Those suspensions, those solutions – must we die?" and then we're dead.
> In the Ca' Rezzonico, one Robert Browning climbs to bed.

The metre is seductively jaunty, and on the whole this is a superbly rich poem – but though it is clear what the first line wants to mean, the image is lazily illogical.

The collection ends on another high point, though. 'Hermit Crab' was written just six weeks before the poet died – and was dictated, as were all of his poems in his final illness, to his wife Christine, who typed it up:

> I have no new shell to retreat to
> Having scanned the beach (it has never
> Seemed so wide and such a tympanum
> For the thundering ocean) […]

It is a decidedly odd, clear-eyed, moving and memorable poem, full of thought's chicanery, and complemented here by an afterword from Christine Porter, in which she calls it 'a powerful hymn to death and the letting go of life'. That could serve as an epigraph for this humane, mordant and often consoling last book.

Times Literary Supplement, 2017

A SERIES OF FITS

Basil Bunting, *The Poems of Basil Bunting*, ed. Don Share (Faber, 2016)

For much of his often extraordinary life, which included spells as a prisoner and a spy, Basil Bunting was a neglected poet. His first publication, the pamphlet *Redimiculum Matellarum* (1930), meaning 'a necklace of chamber pots', was privately printed, and received one review – from his poet friend Louis Zukofsky. The same year, he had bigger success when his long poem 'Villon' appeared in *Poetry*, but it wasn't until 1950 that a full-length collection, more pragmatically titled *Poems: 1950*, was printed in an edition of 1000 copies. All the same, as Don Share has it in his introduction, 'Bunting laboured in obscurity'. The beginning of the end of this was when *Poetry* (today edited by Share) published 'The Spoils' in 1964, and, the same year, the young Newcastle poet Tom Pickard, who ran the influential Morden Tower Bookroom, invited Bunting's participation and printed an edition of the same poem. In 1965, Fulcrum Press published Bunting's *First Book of Odes,* then *Loquitur*, essentially an updated and better edited version of *Poems: 1950*; and that same year he composed 'Briggflatts', quickly regarded as his *chef d'oeuvre*. In 1966, it appeared in *Poetry*, then in book form – first in an edition of 350 copies, then quickly in a second of 3,000. That is a lot for a poetry book.

For most of the rest of his life, Bunting wrote short lyrics, and infrequently. His output had never been prolific, and success did not change that. But since the 1970s, several attempts have been made to amass Bunting's oeuvre, so that sizeable new volumes have appeared with some regularity. A *Collected Poems* was published in 1968, another in 1978, and another in 1985, the year of Bunting's death. That book's contents, together with the extant poems he had rejected, were then gathered by Richard Caddel into *Complete Poems* (2000), supplemented by a short introduction and no notes beyond those Bunting had previously provided. Since then, there have been no major discoveries of unpublished work: no caches behind cabinets, or folders hiding in the deepest dark of a university archive.

One might initially be excused, then, for wondering what the present volume can offer. In his 'Note on the Edition', Share is keen to disabuse us: a new edition is necessary 'to examine and rectify [printing errors], and to annotate his complex, allusive verse'. This latter function might well please readers, but would not have pleased the poet, who was routinely dismissive of notes to poems. In the introduction, and apparently pre-empting any criticism of the extensive scholarly apparatus this variorum edition provides, Share quotes Bunting in a letter of 1951: 'I do not see why people should want to "understand" everything in a poem', before countering that 'It is impossible to understand everything in a poem, but it is also impossible for a reader not to want to know things about a poem'. In fact, the annotations take up about 300 pages – more than the poems – the goal being to indicate analogues and sources, and 'demonstrate the textual and textural complexity of the poems in such a way as to enhance their appreciation'. In addition to providing fastidious commentaries on textual variants, Share contextualises Bunting's often abstruse or otherwise challenging poetry with background information, excerpts from correspondence, transcriptions of comments Bunting seems happy to have made at readings, and so on – nothing like which has previously been attempted. There are a few jarring moments, such as when he describes the Scots Burns and Scott as 'Northern literature' alongside Bede and others, as set against the South represented by Spenser, Milton, Dryden and Tennyson, who wasn't really a southerner. Or in the notes on 'Villon', where Share provides only the mythological gloss for 'Erebus', while context implies the geographical one, to the Antarctic volcano, would be apt: 'they have melted the snows from Erebus'. But such slips and omissions are minimal: Share is a conscientious, erudite and meticulous editor, and the end result is a considerable work of scholarship. And of course it seems fitting that the current editor of *Poetry*, which did so much for Bunting, should now be his editor.

For *Poems: 1950*, Bunting arranged everything into three categories: Sonatas (longer, multi-part poems), Odes (all short) and Overdrafts (translations and poems after others' poems). Caddel stuck to this, then added sections for 'Uncollected Odes' and 'Uncollected Overdrafts'. Share organises the poems as Caddel had done, so that again we are guided through them in an order close to what would have been Bunting's Bunting, and the contents pages of the two posthumous volumes are similar. The newly available material, if one takes that to mean poems included here but not also in Caddel's *Complete Poems*, amounts to seventeen pieces. First, there is a second version of a bitter poem of contemporary reference called 'They Say Etna', and two extra 'Uncollected Overdrafts', which squeeze in among Caddel's list of contents. Then come a handful of pieces at the end, split between the new categories of 'School Poems' and 'Limericks' (both of which had been used by Caddel for his two appendices, which include four of the five poems thus designated in the present collection), then the longer 'Fragments and False Starts', and 'Anomalies' – which is actually one 'Anomaly': another version of 'They Say Etna', differing only slightly from the other two. Together, this 'new' work comprises under a sixth of the 260 pages of poetry. In addition, some of the other poems (or unfinished fragments) are in versions apparently closer to Bunting's intentions, and there are some extensions, most notably Bunting's aborted attempt at translating Ferdowsī's 'Faridun's Sons', seventy-four lines of which made it into Caddel's book, compared to 319 here.

Bunting's gradual development is traceable in these chronologically-arranged sections. First, he is too indebted to Pound but evidently striving to find his own ways. Then, in his forties and fifties, his range expands into various languages and cultures, and his experimentation with sound is more fully realised. This is followed by the later period beginning with 'Briggflatts' and other smaller poems, often closely linked to the north-east, to which Bunting had conclusively returned. He wrote 'sonatas', 'odes' and 'overdrafts' in all of these periods. The longest are the six sonatas, Bunting's appropriation of the term emphasising sonic properties and his belief that 'poetry, like music, is to be heard'. The earliest, 'Villon', completed in 1925, is vivid and visceral:

> In the dark in fetters
> on bended elbows I supported my weak back
> hulloing to muffled walls blank again
> unresonant.

We mustn't cheapen Bunting's poetry by overstating biographical allegory. But in 1918 he was imprisoned for conscientious objection. He spent time in a military hospital with a septic ulcer, was given hard labour in Winchester prison, and eventually absconded while on sick leave after a hunger strike. He probably knew what he was writing about.

Bunting had met Pound in 1923, while living in Paris and digging roads for poor pay. He then followed Pound to Rapallo, becoming, in the words of Yeats, one of his 'more savage disciples'. Pound apparently performed a service for the young Bunting not unlike the one he had performed for Eliot, 'scratch[ing] out about half the poem', according to Bunting; the end result is the tightest and shortest sonata. Here we find early signs of Bunting's economy with language, his contemptuous humanitarianism, and his ability to play a rollicking rhythm or register against a poem's semantics:

> Remember, imbeciles and wits,
> sots and ascetics, fair and foul,
> young girls with tender little tits,
> that DEATH is written over all.

Bunting is of course best known for the last and longest sonata, his non-linear poetic autobiography 'Briggflatts' – a poem so influential that Donald Davie's contrarian study, *Under Briggflatts*, was relatively non-contrarian in its title: it is for many *the* long English late modernist poem. Bunting also saw it as his magnum opus, and in 'A Note on Briggflatts' he refers to it as 'a poem that reflects, fragmentarily, my whole mind'. 'Briggflatts' is named for the Quaker meeting house Bunting knew from his youth, though the use of two *g*s rather than one is a reversion to an older variant spelling. The poem is intertextual and allusive, drawing on Persian and Anglo-Saxon prosody, Northumbrian history and lore from Eric Bloodaxe to the Border Reivers, and much else. But though we can be grateful for Share's glosses, which point us to such instances and send us down various other rabbit holes, Bunting was ultimately right: this often sheerly moving meditation on transience, beauty, unfulfilment, 'needs no explanation':

> amputated years ache after
> the bull is beef, love a convenience.
> It is easier to die than to remember.
> Name and date
> split in soft slate
> a few months obliterate.

'Follow the clue patiently and you will understand nothing', we are told elsewhere in the poem. From its opening portrayals of first love to its tidy coda, 'Briggflatts' is a less effusive and apparently more felt counterpart to those universals explored so bluntly in 'Villon', and is perhaps the definitive poetic statement on looking, following the clues patiently because we are human, reliving our accreting losses.

The short 'odes' are divided into a longer 'First Book' of thirty-seven, and a 'Second Book' of twelve. The first includes poems up to 1949, and the second picks up in 1964; for most of the 1950s and early 1960s, Bunting effectively went on hiatus. As with the sonatas, Bunting's chosen term of categorisation is only loosely based on a usual definition: one would be hard pushed to identify in these pieces the strophe, antistrophe or epode of a classical ode, though Bunting did tell an interviewer that 'the odes are called odes because Horace called his odes.' He went on: 'An ode is essentially a sonnet to be sung, not all of mine are meant to be sung; most of them are'. We have to guess which ones; and almost none could conceivably be called sonnets – beyond the original meaning of that word (*sonnetto*, 'little song'). Most are not given a title, though all Bunting chose to publish are numbered. The first – a fragment Bunting preserved in 1924 from a longer poem – is a sort of anti-*reverdie*-cum-meditation on human proclivities, owing too much to the beginning of Eliot's *The Waste Land*, published two years beforehand, but with its own sprightly economy:

> Weeping oaks grieve, chestnuts raise
> mournful candles. Sad is spring
> to perpetuate, sad to trace
> immortalities never changing.

Bunting had written plenty of poems before this, but destroyed them. It is perhaps surprising this survived the cull: it is a youngster's poem, its epiphanies too cheap. The trouble with several of the earlier odes is that they rely on the meaningful observation of the obvious, and, in the worst of them, brevity does not preclude prolixity. Number 4, from 1926 and originally called 'Aubade', seeks to subvert received wisdoms about dawn. Of this, Bunting asked Pound: 'Have I found my voice? Everybody says it is exceedingly disagreeable of me to be unpleasant about sunrise and the loud chorus of complaints encourages me to think that I must have done something of my own at last'. He hadn't:

> In repose majestic
> vile wakening, cowering under its tyrant
> eager in stratagems to circumvent the harsh
> performer of unveilings […].

Within a few years, though, we see his desire to say something translate into him saying something, albeit at once too plainly and abstrusely: 'never a spark of sedition / among the uneducated workingmen', ends a fourteen-line poem from 1928, after taking us from the inexpensive repast of 'pigeon for dinner' to a bus ride through London. By 1930, in 'Gin the Goodwife Stint' (which translates roughly as 'If the good wife is abstemious'), Bunting is bringing much of this together successfully – and more in the vein of a Northumbrian Wordsworth than an obvious disciple of Pound. In twelve vernacular lines, he lets a circumstance speak for itself, any outrage existing behind the statements:

> The Duke can get his rent
> and we can get our ticket
> twa pund emigrant
> on a C.P.R. packet.

It is simple but moving, and in that sense has something in common with the final poem in 'The First Book of Odes', 'On the Fly-Leaf of Pound's Cantos' – a poem of high praise indeed, equating the Pisan Cantos with the Alps:

> There they are, you will have to go a long way round
> if you want to avoid them.
> It takes some getting used to. There are the Alps,
> fools! Sit down and wait for them to crumble!

Larkin liked this enough to include it in his *Oxford Book of Twentieth-Century English Verse* (1972), characteristically opting for one of the less interesting but more graspable poems by a modernist. Pound, then incarcerated at St Elizabeths psychiatric hospital in Washington, DC, liked it too, of course: a note tells us he broke down upon reading it. But like many of the poems in this 'First Book of Odes', it offers little beyond its most obvious point.

The later odes are, on the whole, wryer, more controlled, and more frequently in dramatic mini-monologue, which suited Bunting's wit and wisdom well. In the first, framed by two lines from a human narrator, a thrush's song is articulated as 'familiar things, / fear, hunger, lust'. 'O gay thrush!', translates the apparently unlistening, romantic human. It is a slight but memorable beginning to this bizarrely varied and rewarding dozen, which also includes a quasi-Georgian presentation of the River Cocquet in Northumberland, in which the water becomes a teasing nymph who 'dares me chase', in lines both limpid and clichéd. Among the others is a grim evocation of Persia, where Bunting served during the war – a counterpart to comparable evocations in the penultimate sonata, 'The Spoils': 'Canvas udders sag, drip, / Swell without splash the mirage / Between islands'.

Bunting claimed his 'Overdrafts' were written 'for the purpose of studying something', and with the help of Share's notes, we get a strong sense of this translator's struggles. In the twenty pages of overdrafts Bunting thought worth saving, there is a translation into Latin (which Bunting did not know) of a tribute to Pound by Zukofsky, versions of Horace, and Catullus's longest poem, Catullus LXIV, broken off at line 20 with the exclamation '–and why Catullus bothered to write pages and pages of this drivel mystifies me'. Especially rewarding, considering the relative paucity of such translations into English, are Bunting's attempts at works by classical Persian poets. In addition to the extended version of Ferdowsī's 'Faridun's Sons', these include an excerpt of Ferdowsī's epic *ShŌh-nŌmeh* (Bunting had tried to translate the whole poem but, characteristically, thought his effort 'no good').

Then, a mere 150 pages in, we go beyond poems Bunting sought to keep in print. The overwhelming feeling while reading the 'Uncollected Poems' – both those previously preserved by Caddel and those new to the present collection – is that Bunting often judged himself wisely, though there are few outright failures. Never close to being the one kind of modernist readers only familiar with 'Briggflatts' might imagine, Bunting in fact tried out myriad styles as well as subjects. 'The Pious Cat', for example, is a fable for children, translated from the fourteenth-century Persian of Ubayd-i Zakani. With its jaunty rhymes, rhymed tetrameters, and flirtations with gruesomeness, though, it might come across to modern readers as a better-mannered counterpart to Roald Dahl's *Revolting Rhymes*, as much as the political allegory originally intended:

> But while the high tribunal tried him
> the cat was gnawing the thongs that tied him
> till with a resolute wrench he bust his
> bonds and swallowed the Lord Chief Justice.

There are many more 'overdrafts', from classical Western and Persian poets especially, and some very English-seeming curiosities, such as 'Keep Truth', an ornate piece of juvenilia from 1916. Share reads this as 'patriotic', following Caddel who included it in an appendix with a note expressing that 'its orthodoxy is surprising'. But for all its obvious triteness, the poem strikes me as subversively ironic, guardedly turning the rhetoric of Henry Newbolt, filtered through the likes of Jessie Pope, back on them:

> Play up, and play the game.
>   What do you do for England,
>   Who does so much for you?
>   Keep troth, speak true, for England,
>   Be straight, keep troth, speak true.

What does it mean to 'speak true'? It is surely possible to read this as a riposte to jingoism from an adolescent who would soon be a victimised conchy.

Caddel also included two of Bunting's limericks in an appendix, with a note that they are the only two which can with certainty be attributed to the poet. Share adds a third, from a letter dated 1984, about a greedy guest of the Ritz: 'It did no good. He died / Of a series of fits of the squits', it ends, with that sudden halt in the penultimate line, followed by the repeated 'of' and double-stepping internal rhyme, comprising joyous fancy footwork. And the twelve poems under 'Fragments and False Starts' include more doggerel, such as the cheerily ribald 'Grandma's Complaint', apparently written to amuse Pound: 'I wish to the lord that the bloody old crock / Would leave off his trousers and get a stiff cock'. More intriguingly, it also includes flabbier versions of two of Bunting's better-known poems, 'The Well of Lycopolis', and 'On the Fly-Leaf of Pound's Cantos', where the following five explanatory lines go in the middle of the four quoted earlier:

> Ethical or aesthetic exaltations
> Are out of scale. Ridiculous
> To praise a peak, take exception to a rift.
> Sun on high snow snatches the heart, awe
> The only appropriate emotion.

A reader might initially wonder why this has been included: other poems' drafts aren't shown. But a note reveals that this was sent to Pound 1951, two years *after* he'd written the better-known counterpart. When we consider how these poems might speak to Pound, and how their relationship had become more complicated as a result of Pound's fascism, we might read between these lines.

Bunting's strict editing of his oeuvre is obviously at odds with any attempt to expand that oeuvre, and this book marks its apotheosis. But there really is no greater justification than our curiosity; and moreover, as far as is sensible, Share sees it as his duty to respect Bunting's wishes. For example, for the 1978 *Collected Poems*, the only such volume he lived to see into print, Bunting made numerous revisions to earlier haphazard punctuation. Caddel silently made further alterations, apparently for house style, but Share reverts to the 1978 versions. Where Bunting's wishes for his work are unknown, and Share has been forced into an executive decision, he has left a paper trail so we can make up our own minds. The end result is a book that remains at once deferential to its subject and to the needs and wishes of its audience. And with its additions and glosses, this volume easily supersedes its precursor. The appendices add valuable odds and ends to the poetry and notes, including a facsimile of drafts of 'The Spoils', tables of contents for previous books of Bunting's poems, Bunting's notes to poems and editions of his work, and his prefaces and forewords. There is also a fine, if concise, bibliography; only an index and a simple list of the poems in order of completion would have been sensible and helpful additions. With the exception of the magnificent *Basil Bunting's Briggflatts* (Bloodaxe, 2009), which includes essays and contextualising material alongside that poem, this is now surely the only book of Bunting's poetry any reader needs.

Essays in Criticism, 2017

OF DEATH AND CONSOLATION

Bernard O'Donoghue, *The Seasons of Cullen Church*
(Faber, 2016)

'So wistful', the first poem in Bernard O'Donoghue's sixth book of poems begins. It is a fitting opening for what is arguably the poet's most elegiac collection to date, the title poem of which refers to the church in the County Cork village where he was born seven decades ago, with its angels 'on permanent watch' and its 'rich smell of death and consolation'. As we can expect from O'Donoghue, the many short lyrics in this book tend to be finely tuned and are often unfashionably personal, with his customarily languorous, exploratory imagery: 'the sun feeling for cloud-gaps to direct / its beams on the small lakes inland which look / like inky scraps of crêpe', for example, or 'occasions unrecallable, / like a green caravan in a field corner'. O'Donoghue's world seems thronged with symbols, from 'the shearwaters who were all around us / one mystic Skellig midnight, souls returned / from their other, closed life deep out at sea', to 'the dog who, unaccountably, / stopped in the road looking uncertain'. The poems are all perfectly easy to understand, on the surface, but the imagery and unshowy mysticism of the best of them are rich and resonant enough for us to feel that we might never have reached all the way inside.

A common theme is that universal of youth and age. 'Robbing the Orchard' recalls returning to an old school, now just 'a single wall / marked by ivy', and the nearby orchard, to find all unkempt: 'no bough with strength enough to bear / even a crab apple, fighting a lost cause / amid the bitter green and bullying elders'. It is solemn without being maudlin, which isn't quite enough to save it from cliché, but the book does contain more startling and original poems about what the Welsh call *hiraeth*, and the inability to go back. The title of 'You Know the Way' is at first colloquial – 'You know the way how', the poem starts – but by the end it homes in on its subject: once, there were myriad routes through a park, a county, a town, and of course a life; now, 'at this stage of things', there is 'no right or wrong way, not much turning / on which you choose'. Surely he doesn't quite mean it, because surely it isn't quite true, but that doesn't mean it isn't honest.

As with O'Donoghue's other recent collections, this book contains some sprightly contemporary takes on classical and medieval poems. One particularly disquieting example is a sumptuously calm version of Riddle 2 from the Exeter Book, one of the 'storm riddles' – here titled 'Tsunami', giving an answer with a contemporary-seeming relevance in light of the several cataclysmic natural disasters of the past dozen years:

> You are a wise man:
> say who draws me from the depth of the ocean
> when the tide grows calmer again
> and the waves turn to melody, so deafening before.

Less successful, because it does relatively little to challenge us, is 'Riddle', which meshes the broadly Anglo-Saxon form with the contemporary in a more ostensibly political manner: 'I share my name with the unproductive bees / who do all the work. I travel in the night', it begins. Does he mean drones? Surely. But drone bees exist to breed, and are otherwise functionless. A more affecting meditation on tragedy is 'migration', an unobtrusively allusive piece about the conflicted Irish nationalist poet Francis Ledwidge, killed on the Western Front:

> Our complement of native blackbirds
> are reinforced in winter by battalions
> that fly down the North Sea and Baltic
> to escape the cold and then join up
> with the first February chorus of the spring.

It is striking how many of these poems – such as 'The Will', about inheritance and emigration from Ireland many decades ago – are powerful as anecdotes, but do not benefit from having been cut every few words into lines of tensionless verse. And considering how pellucid and economical the best pieces are, it is surprising that a fair number are neither. A poem of stargazing, for example, named 'Enif' for the star at the nose of Pegasus, seems fully aware of the overfamiliar baggage its subject carries, making a clever allusion to Donne's 'busy old fool', but ultimately just points out that the star is hot yet distant and marginal, and how this can stand as a metaphor for 'desperation and obsession'. And the carelessness of some of the phrasing, such as 'he lay on his back, supine', is confusingly at odds with this poet's manifest gift, which at other points in this book is on typically rewarding display.

Times Literary Supplement, 2017

TIPPOO CHARGING TENNYSON

Daljit Nagra, *British Museum* (Faber and Faber, 2017)

The title of Daljit Nagra's third collection (or fourth, if you count his *Ramayana: A Retelling,* 2013) indicates a departure from the exuberance of its loud, exclamation mark-bejewelled predecessors – the most recent being *Tippoo Sultan's Incredible White-Man-Eating Tiger-Toy Machine!!!,* 2011. The book opens with what at first seems just one of those many self-congratulatory poems of parental wonderment (and how frequently do such poets seem to prefer their children asleep?): 'I've simply flown upstairs / to watch you upside down again'. But the poem is rather more complex than that, for this is part of a hard-won freedom:

> In my past, I was treated
> as a child when I was a man
> and forced to remain in wedlock
> to uphold the family name.
>
> Look at me flying upstairs
> on the wings of my shame
> for my second-chance life.

Where Nagra has previously favoured sometimes cartoonish levels of declarativeness and exclamation, here he shows a predilection for questions, many of them to do with how British institutions and cultural history are shaped to represent us, and the effects they have. Unfortunately, he also favours the kinds of enjambment that as often as not seem arbitrary and lacklustre. In 'Broadcasting House', in which the BBC's headquarters is relentlessly referred to as a 'ship' in an extended metaphor that has difficulty keeping afloat, he asks, among myriad other things, 'When the flag at the Palace weeps, / say, for the death of a Saudi king, / must our vessel, as dictated by the Houses / of Parliament, echo a voice of grief?'. In 'Hadrian's Wall', which reads like a Facebook *cri de coeur*, we have:

> Where will our walls finally end? In
> the gigabytes of our biometric online
> lives, in our passports? To keep us
> from trespass, will our walls be raised
> watchful as the Great Firewall of China?

And in 'Meditations on the British Museum', a poem as long and obvious as it is politically astute and knowledgeable, he wonders: 'Is each dancing massacre, each perverse beauty, on a plate / or vase, the work of Love designed to leave us mollified?'.

A Londoner, Nagra is often also a poet of the British immigrant experience, with an unblinking seriousness of purpose (if not always of tone). In 'The Vishnu of Wolverhampton', a first-generation immigrant and widower prays that on his last day 'my peoples / will light my sandalwood pyre' and that the wife to whom his marriage was arranged 'and I will come together. / One double-big / chumchum pink / chuckling cloud'. 'The Look of Love' presents the paradox of being considered, and (partly as a result) feeling, English/not-English: 'I must not measure myself / by the wealth of your heritage / which will never be imagined as mine'. He remains a highly allusive poet at times, keen to turn that heritage to his own purposes. His most celebrated poem, 'Look We Have Coming to Dover!', drew equally on Matthew Arnold, W. H. Auden and D. H. Lawrence for its title, and 'The Look of Love' carries an epigraph from Thomas Campion ('Fairnesse seene in th'outward shape / Is but th'inward beauties Ape', that first word heavily loaded in this context). 'The Dream of Mr Bulram's English' recalls school-teaching, the poet's erstwhile day job, to 'shades-of-the-globe teenagers': 'I pray they'll honour this tongue William dared / never to conquer', and 'I hope to spin their minds / timeless with Chaucer, Donne, Keats and Byron, / with Tennyson and Browning'. The poem following it lets rip: 'if they like me they think I'm exotic / if they think I'm too English I'm a mimic [...] I'd corner you all in a corner of Adlestrop / then call for support but there'll never be enough of us [...] I'd rather be Tippoo light-charging Tennyson'. *British Museum* has its shortcomings, then, but for all that it is a book of guts, heart and fallible tensions, an honest and often polemical collection that posits on-the-sleeve, personal and public questions without implying simple answers.

Times Literary Supplement, 2017

CANS AND DESERT THISTLES

Terence Tiller, *The Collected Poems* (Eyewear, 2016)

Terence Tiller (1916–87) was once a poet of some repute, largely as a result of his poems from Egypt during the Second World War; he has since fallen into obscurity – rarely anthologised, and routinely ignored in discussions of war poetry. He published six collections: three between 1941 and 1947, while he worked as a lecturer in Cairo, and the others back in his native England, where he worked for the BBC. The stated aim of this handsome book is to bring back into print, in his centenary year, the complete body of work of what the book's (and press's) editor, Todd Swift, proclaims to be 'a rediscovered lyric-modernist genius'.

Swift's introduction is informative about the first three books, but doesn't extend to a discussion of the others – or, to put it another way, to the last three decades of the four represented in the volume. The result is that the introduction feels half-done, for all that it is long and laudatory, variously marking Tiller out as a 'quintessential poet of the Forties style' (with some justification), the originator of the Movement style long before 'its ostensible origins in 1950s Britain', and a modernist too modern to be appreciated by his contemporaries (both with considerably less justification). His response to the sometimes lukewarm reception Tiller received in the 1940s is to 'wonder if what we have here is a failure of criticism itself at the period – a moment [A. T.] Tolley, [Alan] Ross and others could not conceive of a different style, another modern way'. Tiller, Swift argues, was simply too brilliantly original to be understood properly at the time – as J. C. Squire with Eliot's *The Waste Land*, so Tolley and Ross with Tiller, whose work 'simply blows all critical fuses'. It is a shame Swift can't celebrate Tiller for the significant but wholeheartedly minor poet he was. His comments hardly prepare us for 'For Doreen', the opener to *Poems* (1941):

> *Time is the medium, not the kind,*
> *of dreaming in the actual tense;*
> *under the dreams you will not find*
> *their being, but their imminence.*

Such formal decorousness, and conventional sentiment, are not at odds with many other poems here, despite the lonely, Eliotian *flâneurie* and abrupt shifts in tone that also typify this and other of Tiller's collections. The earliest work is frequently undermined by wailing, epiphanic romanticism and over-poeticised youthful angst of a fairly silly kind – 'look down stars, you illimitable and glorious wakers, / on her delight that wakes from silks', or 'Now as I lie, owls in the dark gardens / – swift for destroying, sudden circlers – wail / for no grief; tress have their windy burdens'; and on it goes. Occasionally, this contemplative spirit is turned with grim determination to overbearing worldly concerns, though often vaguely or abstractly:

> The world is weary of harness now,
> the open, the tumultuous:
> shutter the window, let the bough
> be plucked that blossoms God knows how.
> The smell of death is over us.

A more intriguing early poem is the over-long 'Egypt 1940', with its cleverly altering refrains – 'The night finds us the body betrays us / and love devours us and time passes', then 'The body betrays us and love devours us / and time passes and none saves us', and so on – and its sense of being at a unique remove from 'the sharp / and screaming rack of Europe'.

Prefacing *The Inward Animal* (1943), Tiller wrote that the War's 'impact and the impact of strangeness must have shaken, and destroyed, many a customary self'. The collection has a tripartite structure at once obvious and sui generis: 'distress; rebellion against place and circumstance; slow mutual absorption ending in the birth of something at once myself and a new self and Egypt'. Tiller is a war poet writing from a position unlike most others – involved and yet not, and on a particular margin. Many of the poems in this second collection are linked to specific North African locations, such as 'Coptic Church' (set in 'Musturrud'), which evokes the 'memory of magnificence' that 'reared up this primitive pretence'. The collection is more formally adventurous than his first, but drops regularly into the same pitfalls of prolixity and abstraction, as in the title poem:

> The primitive revolt
> against a mind or will,
> the blood of Abel spilt
> in cups already full.
> Being and feeling and thought
> are but a naked man
> who fights what he is not,
> the animal within.

Simultaneously, the younger Tiller is prone to philosophising maxims, often boldly wearing the urgent influence of MacSpaunday: Tiller's 'World was not built for dreams' recalls MacNeice's 'Snow' ('World is suddener than we fancy it'); elsewhere, Tiller warns 'Never believe us, poets tell you lies'. He certainly takes on the big questions and has something to say about them, but it doesn't always sound like him speaking.

In these first two books, most poems are numbered; for *Unarm, Eros* (1947), Tiller abandons numbering, so each poem seems more a discrete entity, and adopts a more quizzical tone and often a narrower focus – on faces, hands, etc. 'Face' begins:

> Her soft lines over subtleties of bone
> read like a script meaning itself alone;
> we can add nothing but our own unrest.

Many of the poems are still fuelled by the least answerable questions and attendant simmering anxieties. 'Big City' is set in Cairo, but, as is typical of Tiller, it evokes its environment only insofar as the atmosphere impinges on the speaker's consciousness:

> Homeless the rolling blood that cries
> of love and Love in hidden ways
> where kisses like a bird fly back
> and bring no bounty to their Ark,
> since all about the city stands
> night […].

Elsewhere, attention is given to unease at the poet's relationship to the War in comparison to that of most other temporary British expatriates in North Africa. In the acutely observed and moving 'Lecturing to Troops', 'strange violent men' whom the speaker has come to address 'sit like shrubs among the cans and desert thistles', with 'dirty unfamiliar muscles', 'wanting girls and beer'. Before them, he is 'shy' and guilt-ridden: 'They have walked horror's coast', while 'I come taut and scatheless with a virgin air'. The sweeping generalisations about these men reveal his own vulnerability and alienation. Other moments of observation are less successful, such as the obvious irony in 'Beggar' of a hand held 'out like an offering'; but this collection marks the high point of Tiller's poetry: he has plenty to say, and has by this point developed a talent for understated formal control that usually keeps his probing meditations in check.

A decade passed before *Reading a Medal, and Other Poems* (1957), by which time Tiller had long since returned home. The poems are again often inquisitively anxious to see the details of things, and to posit ecumenical questions – as in 'Tropical Aquarium', which begins with 'the absurd / flexes of small and coloured flesh' and ends 'Must I be glad, having seen them lose the wings / that swam with rainbows, rainbows floating: them?'

To Tiller, such questions are also questions of faith, as explored in poems such as 'Three Christmas Trees', which moves from the candle-lit 'tree of night' to a sleeping son: 'There is no age in sleep; the boy is one / with infant and with patriarch'. The poem then imagines the child 'companion to that other boy / whose parents' dreams lay round him as he slept', before pleading 'do not wake too early'. It is as beautiful as it is conventional.

Of course, this collection lacks the Egyptian wartime contexts that render some of the earlier poems more than the sum of their parts, but it is otherwise another high point, when Tiller was most completely in control of form and subject. At times it owes an obvious debt to Philip Larkin and the typically understated Movement aesthetic – the debt is not the other way round – and there is even a controlled, moving poem about Victorian street performers that, like Larkin's 'Deceptions', published two years earlier, grows from a passage in Henry Mayhew's *London Labour and the London Poor* (1851).

How often do older poets appear to run out of things to say, or new ways to say things, their later work seeming suddenly slipshod? Tiller is not among the countless exceptions, and his final two collections, *Notes for a Myth* (1968) and *That Singing Mesh* (1979), are on the whole weaker and less interesting. In the former, Tiller is again at his best when moving from a focus on minutiae to the existential questions served up by his intense and religious mindset, as in 'Keepsakes', in which the 'golden locket-glass' of amber, with its 'fossil grief', becomes a counterpart to our transience. In a foreword, Tiller explains that *That Singing Mesh* is to be his final volume, and makes 'an earnest plea to friends who may possess poems of mine […] other than these printed here: destroy them'. (None appear in the *Collected*.) It abounds with sonnets and with villanelles – one of Tiller's favoured forms – and, unusually, notes to poems, though not always the most helpful sort: 'In these villanelles it will be found that each repetition of the refrains has a slightly different meaning', one begins, as though this is unusual for villanelles with any merit, the repetends acting as hinges rather than largely redundant placeholders. Unfortunately, Tiller's often fall short of his wish for them;

> The most of pain is greater than its need;
> but who shall draw the colours from the glass
> until the firing becomes death indeed?
>
> To snatch reluctant wings is baby greed
> (lust is foundry that unfuses brass):
> the most of pain is greater than its need.

It is odd for a poet to know he is writing the last poems he'll preserve, but, for all its obliquity, the closing title poem offers little doubt about his intentions: 'the last music in the sky shall be / a breaking string; and then the axes' fall'. Yes: multiple axes. And with that, Tiller ended an intriguing if deeply flawed body of work, amounting to about 270 pages.

These are not the final poems in the book, however, which closes with appendices containing poems by the poet's daughter Sarah Tiller and his grandson Matthew, in addition to seventeen monochrome photographs of the poet, taken at various points in his life, including one of him in old age smiling beside a child who might be Matthew (though the caption doesn't tell us, and is apparently misdated '1954'). Matthew Tiller's prefatory note stresses that the extra poems are included 'at Todd [Swift]'s suggestion', and that he hopes the book will be judged solely by his grandfather's work. They are nice enough and well meant; but so do I.

It is far-fetched to pretend Terence Tiller is a major poet, or even an especially good one. For all that, he is intriguing, primarily because of the time and place of his early adulthood and the sensibility he brought to bear on it in his poems. He deserves to be read and studied in that context.

Poetry Review, 2017

FULL OF SOUL

Jacqueline Saphra, *All My Mad Mothers* (Nine Arches, 2017); Roddy Lumsden, *So Glad I'm Me* (Bloodaxe, 2017)

The first two sections of Jacqueline Saphra's second full-length collection, respectively focused on young childhood and adolescence, constitute a sort of fractured coming of age narrative in the past tense. The poems are by turns sentimental and hardened about what seems at once a dysfunctional and loving upbringing for its narrator. In the prose poem 'Getting into Trouble', for example,

> My boyfriend, who was stupid but useful, told all his friends I was a virgin and forced me to see *Close Encounters of the Third Kind* three times and listen to nothing but Genesis, which I preferred to The Sex Pistols, because I never believed there was No Future, not when my mother was, at least for now, empty-wombed and full of soul, as she stirred a pot of her famous lentil soup, not yet tied by blood to the man she loved.

The poems' narratives are sometimes unreliable enough for us to have to do some work to see where the values lie. The title poem presents one woman in multiple guises, some apparently more literal than others, none allowing us to see her whole:

My mother barely spoke between her bruises:
her low-cut gown was tea-stained silk, and from behind
her Guccis or Versaces, she would serve us salty dinners,
stroke a passing cheek, or lay her head on any waiting shoulder.

[…]

My mother was so hard to grasp: once we found her
in a bath of extra virgin olive oil, her skin well slicked.

> She'd stocked the fridge with lard and suet, butter – salted
> and unsalted – to ease her way into this world. Or out of it.

The book's breathless opening poem has given this some context. It presents a mother (there is nothing in the poems to suggest it isn't the same woman, though also no indication of how much or what is true) gathering her baby into a car bought by the child's father, and ending up on the roundabout at Hyde Park Corner, 'not sure how to execute the move outwards'. It would be a superb metaphor for escape succumbing to psychological entrapment if Saphra didn't then explain it away by telling us she had never been 'properly taught how to make an exit'.

Some of the poems are straightforwardly marvellous, though – such as the acutely observed, moving and witty 'Mile End', which ends, also symbolically, with 'one hand / on my cheek, one hand on my hand'; or 'Things We Can't Untie', the sort of poem destroyed by paraphrasing, which is as moving and clinical as any poem of youthful trauma I can recall. The risk of her style is that others, such as 'Volunteers, 1978', simply don't quite do enough to transcend anecdote. The speaker, it seems, was working on a kibbutz, where 'The new girls did the bloody work, / chopping the heads off but saving / the necks', and 'I went right off chicken'.

The third section generally finds the speaker (for the collection has one consistent voice) in domesticated adulthood. Occasionally, the poems cleverly pick up strands dropped earlier in the book. 'Chicken', a few pages beyond 'Volunteers, 1978', ends with a daughter's jaded, youthful belligerence: 'If you choose to eat an animal, / you must first learn to kill it, / my daughter told me / as I snipped the plastic film'. The fourth and final section then brings the book into the present tense with a disparate cluster of pieces, some meditative and others less so. 'Spunk', an ekphrastic sonnet about Jacob Epstein's *Adam* (look that up now if you don't know it), takes something of a wry and less androcentric slant on the Origin Myth:

> Drunk on lust, pumped up with blood, he stands
> broad on his plinth and howls for cunt. Who'd dare
> to leave that call unanswered? This is where
> we find the source: that first, primeval sin:
> he forced an opening, she let him in.

And towards the end, there are poems considering love in (relative) age, and simultaneously looking back and taking stock, as in the pitch-perfect 'Everlasting': 'Sometimes at night, I lie with all my dead beside me / in the absolute dark'. There is a fair amount that is of little consequence in this book, then, but its high points are variously touching, cajoling, witty and, on occasion, immaculate. Saphra is a fine poet, with plenty to say, who eschews any hint of dogmatism, and she has written a book that is apparently personal but which never gazes at its navel.

Roddy Lumsden's tenth collection is another book of four parts: 'Till it Runs Clear', 'A Soft Leviathan', 'With All of Your Might', and 'Kippers and Glitter'. In the opening poem, 'Simone's Cookie', he writes, 'I'm thinking about everything', and that would pass as a more practical, perfunctory title for the volume: few collections cover as much ground as this, or seem to reveal such a lithe and obsessive mind.

The cover displays a photograph of Sandy Denny, lead singer of Fairport Convention. If you've never heard of her, you are perhaps especially likely to struggle with the middle two sections, dominated by what are dubbed 'conflation poems' in which, as the blurb puts it, Lumsden has 'knocked the square peg of one subject through the round hole of another – often music-related'. 'Coldplay/Foreplay', like most others, brings musical allusions into an anecdote – here beginning with a woman apparently masturbating to Coldplay, as one does: 'Amber Eyes has pulled her top up to her neck / and her hands are down her barely-there shorts. / She's on the floor. She is blaring out "Clocks"'. By the end, 'I will jump ship and join her, / and you can guess where my hands will go'. Down your barely-there shorts?

'Amber Eyes' is the human subject throughout the second section, including the joyously odd 'Back-up Flats':

> Amber Eyes is trying out her stilettos,
> Criss-crossing the seagrass rug. She
> Is brushing up for Beating Retreat,
> The annual military ceremony in town.
> Music? Anything but Snow Patrol,
> I tell her and she plays a full hour
> Of Chopin. [...]

This is all very readable in its way, but the ultimate feeling is of wasting time rather than filling it. The third section of the book cuts deeper in places, but is equally allusive – and, at times, equally happy to embrace a febrile version of the male gaze. 'In Bath with Madonna' finds the speaker and Queen of Pop soaking and small-talking to post-rock chamber music: 'We are awkward and listening to Rachel's, / the *Music for Egon Schiele* album. We fit, / just about. Of course, we play with soap / and eye each other.'

Though billed on its dust jacket as Lumsden's 'most optimistic and accessible book since *The Book of Love*' (his second collection, published in 2000), it is frequently neither. Many of the poems heap impression on top of impression in a manner that is simultaneously chatty and inscrutable. 'Passing Pond Road' begins: 'The demons give us symmetry, ducks synching / on the Princess pond, couple with prammed twins, / yoghurt which pretends but is a gluey composure / of diabolic symmetry. Swing door mood.' The poem in fact reaches towards a portentous concluding epiphany about our inherent need for 'duality' and oneness: 'We climb / to each other, aching a little, then, rocked to rest, / yearning so blithely to be that impossible – one'. A part-complementary, part-contradictory sentiment is at the heart of 'Simone's Carousel': 'Then shirk the us. Us being the downtime / of the self. I need alone'. But such poems, quantum-leaping between staccato images and sentences, can be painfully difficult to unpack. Others are perhaps too straightforward, but don't get us far. 'Twenty-four Hours of People Saying Nope' is nearly fifty lines of sentences that might be moved around with no obviously deleterious effect:

> Nope declares Faycal, everyone talks
> to themselves and they are lying if they
> say they don't. Nope says Calum, quietly,
> the shop will not be open at this hour.

'I do promise / to stop this listing', he writes in 'Tending to the Reliable', and his poems are often more effective when he does. Others turn a choppy, compressed style to fine effect, though, such as 'Work Crush', which marries Lumsden's slaloming style to a scenario that feels like Arab Strap channelling David Brent: 'Deborah, her sweater blooming, bites / her bottom lip and all the hormones trip. [...] I have nothing, nothing / this evening but telly and ready meal'.

Among those 'optimistic and accessible' poems is a little masterpiece, the quiet, vivid 'The Hoopoe', set in Barcelona: 'there it is: // a hoopoe on a branch. "A hoopee?" she says. / Hoopee. I go sweet for this still on anxious days'. Then: 'one night a month on, she wakes me: // "I liked the hoopee," talking in her sleep. / Which is all the answer I will ever need'. This is vulnerable, hearty, alert to what we should most treasure. And even in its less successful moments, this is a book of considerable humanity.

Poetry Review, 2017

Cecil Day Lewis, *The Golden Bridle: Selected Prose*, ed. Albert Gelpi and Bernard O'Donoghue (OUP, 2017)

The introduction to this book begins by asserting that Cecil Day-Lewis (1904–72) was 'one of the major figures in twentieth-century English poetry by any objective measure'. This was undoubtedly true in his time: he served as Poet Laureate and Oxford Professor of Poetry, among many other things. His reputation has declined since his death, however. A once-prominent poet of what is often called 'the Auden Generation', he is now largely famous in name only, his poetry overlooked and his criticism virtually forgotten.

And he wrote a lot of criticism, steadily, over a long career in the public eye; at over 400 pages, *The Golden Bridle: Selected Prose* is not exactly a small book, but nor is it comprehensive. Albert Gelpi and Bernard O'Donoghue have cut ruthlessly, and perhaps too deeply, in the service of creating a reader-friendly volume: about half of the nineteen pieces it contains are excerpts, all bearing detailed contextualising headnotes. Several are from lectures given during Day-Lewis's various prestigious guest lecturing appointments at Cambridge, Oxford, Hull, and elsewhere. Others are introductions to poets – Wilfred Owen, George Meredith, Robert Frost. Towards the back are chapters from a memoir, and part of a previously unpublished, if hardly revolutionary, typescript on Day-Lewis's poetic methods and motivations.

Day-Lewis (he dropped the hyphen when he published: 'a piece of inverted snobbery', he said, that had 'rather mixed results') was born in Ballintubbert in County Laois, the son of a Church of Ireland rector, and educated at Sherborne and Oxford. More ardently than W. H. Auden or Stephen Spender, he was a left-wing idealist and, from 1936, the year after he left his teaching post at Cheltenham School, a card-carrying member of the Communist Party. (He never renounced communism, though later joined Labour). He was a keen activist, and proud of the reputation he gained as the 'Red' poet in the wake of his poetry collection *A Time to Dance* (1935), his Marxist morality play in verse *Noah and the Waters* (1936), and the volume of essays he edited and introduced, *The Mind in Chains: Socialism and the Cultural Revolution* (1937). He firmly believed in a poetry that engaged with these principles, and in 'Revolutionaries and Poetry', published in the *Left Review* in 1935, explained how he thought it might do so by appealing 'to the mass through the individual': 'Poetry is of its nature more personal than "straight" propaganda: the latter is the heavy artillery, the former is the hand-to-hand fighting'. However, as he had cautioned in *A Hope for Poetry* (the relevant extract is included here), 'propaganda verse is to be condemned when the didactic is achieved at the expense of the poetic'. In the same essay he bemoans those poets who are showing a 'slackening of communist enthusiasm': the 'rats' who are 'swimming back to a ship which does not seem to be sinking this time after all'.

His poetic and political convictions never left him; and his literary enthusiasms were as strong and lasting as those convictions. Introducing the poems of Wilfred Owen in 1963, Day-Lewis brings his own poetic motivations to bear on the thwarted future he imagines for one of his heroes: 'Would the vein of savage indignation prove exhausted, or might Owen have found it renewed in the struggle against social injustice which animates some of his poetic successors?' He is good at putting across his points in succinct, memorable and occasionally simplistically fervent phrases, some of which come to us now from the eye of a storm long since abated, as in his descriptions of several immediate literary precedents. D. H. Lawrence is 'the extreme point of individualism in this century's literature, its zenith or its nadir'; the ideas of T. E. Hulme are sometimes 'repulsive – and his manner of expressing them still more so'.

An abiding bugbear is what he saw as the elitism of literary modernism: he advocated modern poetry that was more continuously evolved from the English lyric tradition, speaking clearly and appealing to the heart, and, in *A Hope for Poetry*, described poetry becoming 'a preserve for the intellectual' as a 'thoroughly unfortunate state of affairs'. Unsurprisingly, he is also vehemently opposed to much of the criticism produced by his contemporaries, not least the 'practical criticism' of I. A. Richards, which he dismisses in *A Hope for Poetry* as 'the Cambridge laboratory school of literature': to Day-Lewis, literature should not be, cannot be, divorced from its social and personal contexts. His introduction to Robert Frost's *Selected Poems* (1972) develops from a consideration of Frost the farmer and countryman, who has 'the countryman's relish for a grim or a humorous tale about his neighbours, his ancestors, his district, combined with a subtlety of insight beyond the reach of any crudely instinctive process'. Moreover, his own responses to poets are certainly personal. The introduction (from 1940) to George Meredith's *Modern Love*, and his meticulous unpacking of its emotional intensity, replete with asides such as 'Love cannot be renewed by an act of will or an aspiration of conscience', is perhaps rendered more intriguing when we know that, as he wrote it, he was living a doomed double life between his first wife and lover.

The editors might usefully have edited their own substantial critical apparatus: by page twenty-five, we have already been told three times what we probably knew already, that it was the right-wing poet Roy Campbell who coined the derogatory compound soubriquet 'MacSpaunday' for Day-Lewis and his fellow poets of the 1930s. Moreover, there are some errors and inconsistencies attributable to poor copy-editing: in some places it is 'MacSpaunday', in others 'Macspaunday'; 'meter' is consistently spelled thus (this is not an American book); who is 'Wilfrid' Owen? But on the whole *The Golden Bridle* is sympathetically and helpfully compiled and edited, an act of love as much as of scholarship. Day-Lewis is not always the most original or adventurous thinker (or poet), but he was too important in his time to suffer his current disregard, and this is a valiant attempt to address that injustice.

Times Literary Supplement, 2017

JACKS OF ALL TRADES

Jacob Polley, *Jackself* (Picador, 2016)

Jackself, Jacob Polley's fourth collection, the surprise winner of this year's T. S. Eliot Prize, is a phantasmagorical assortment of mini-narratives which combine to tell a coming of age story, in part through various Jacks of myth, legend, and nursery tale. It is really one fragmented work, which benefits from being read patiently and in sequence. The setting is the fictional Lamanby, an isolated homestead somewhere in the Cumbrian border country – a world of farmers tending to the 'blackest sheep / the hawk-man with a rag of meat / in his leather glove', and the harsh childhood staple of school, with 'Miss Clout's chalk stick on the blackboard'. The central figures are two boys who spend much time ribbing one another: Jackself and Jeremy Wren, who suddenly hangs himself – 'thinking fuck I've left / no note until he's fucking dead' – two thirds through the book, and yet continues to be present to Jackself in death. Everything is both normal and blatantly not. Intermittently, Wren and Jackself end up in an array of circumstances that are typically bizarre but will be familiar to almost anyone who grew up in the English countryside, as when the two are 'among the hedgerows', 'drunk on white cider and Malibu', and kicking 'the froth / of the cowparsley spunk'. And Wren intermittently interrogates his companion: 'who the fuck / has a goose shed', he says to Jackself, whom he has just found in a goose shed.

The multifarious Jacks – from the makers of the House that Jack Built to Jack-O'Lantern, Jack Sprat to Blackjack – effectively wear different clothes to present facets of the one Jackself as he struggles to make sense of a world of heady changes. We observe from all kinds of angles, then, but never quite get Jackself whole. And what we do see is often a bundle of quotidian concerns wrapped in myth or fantasy. From 'Jack Frost':

>   would it really all go to shit
> if he went home before sunrise, leaving untouched a gutter-trickle
> here or a windscreen there
>   fuck it
>   Jackself wants a hot chocolate and a digestive biscuit

It is inherent to the eeriness of *Jackself* that it so often has one foot in English tradition and the other in the wilderness. We are sure to recognise most of Polley's allusions, many of which are to children's reading, without having to undertake research. But any sense of safety they seem to provide is often dashed pretty quickly. Of course, most nursery rhymes and children's tales perturb more than comfort, and Polley is toying with our penchant for nostalgia as much as with the tales themselves. And even when the book is witty or funny, as it often is in a suitably schoolboyish way, it can also be quietly sinister. 'Every Creeping Thing' takes its title from the Genesis story of Noah, and the point at which God orders disembarkation: 'Bring out [...] every creeping thing that creepeth upon the earth; that they may breed abundantly'. Polley's counterpart offers a snapshot of where we might have come to, in what are essentially limerick stanzas:

> By the wet socket of a levered stone
> by a dog-licked ice cream cone
>   by spores, mildew
>   by the green atchoo
> by the yellow split pea and the bacon bone [...]

I have never previously known limericks to adopt an incantatory tone – which admittedly doesn't quite excuse the flailing of some rhymes and the more awkward jolts in the metre.

Jackself is Polley's most adventurous book, formally and thematically, generally breaking away from his previous disposition for uniform stanzas, and often dropping the safety rail of the left-hand margin. His poetry has always been alert to mythology and tradition, and sought to do new things with both, but here he is keener than ever to toy with the possibilities of both free and received forms. The weaving of mythologies into a coming-of-age poem set in Reiver country might ostensibly call to mind Basil Bunting's 'Briggflatts', but the structure, tone and posture owe more to Ted Hughes's *Crow*; while the frequent testing interactions between Jackself and Wren are perhaps indebted to John Berryman's *Dream Songs*, to which this book sometimes seems a younger, even more overtly playful cousin. Really, though, *Jackself* stands on its own. There is nothing quite like it, though the narrative behind it, such as it is, is itself well worn. That is quite an accomplishment. The risk, which Jacob Polley doesn't entirely overcome, is that the poetry can seem too cocksure, too aware of its cleverness, and that Jackself might just not be enough of a lived-in presence or personality for us to really care about him one way or the other. Nonetheless, *Jackself* is a haunting, witty, memorable, complex book.

Times Literary Supplement, 2017

INWARD, IS ABSORBED

> Terrance Hayes, *American Sonnets for My Past and Future Assassin* (Penguin, 2018); Terrance Hayes, *To Float in the Space Between: A Life and Work in Conversation with the Life and Work of Etheridge Knight* (Wave Books, 2018)

The prolific American poet Terrance Hayes's seventh collection presents seventy – three-score and ten – unrhymed and unmetered, but for the most part tightly disciplined fourteen-line poems, each named 'American Sonnet for My Past and Future Assassin'. Most explore racism and political oppression against a backdrop of Donald Trump's Republican America, 'the land of a failed landlord with a people of color / Complex', in which 'Newshounds ponder the tweets of a bullhorn', and yet, perhaps – with a pun like something from a demonstration placard – 'Love trumps power'. There are witty quips here, some sprightly and often ridiculing passages of verbal gymnastics ('The umpteenth thump on the rump of a badunkadunk / Stumps us'), some moments of calculated introspection, and many fistfuls of tempered anger.

It is fashionable at present, not least in American poetry, to make a sudden leap from one sentence-length statement about something to another about something else, and so on, and Hayes is prone to this. When it gels, the parts create tacit meanings and extensions of meanings between one another, through economical contraction, elision, the subtle and not-so-subtle creation of subtexts. At others, it can be a bit of a skittish mess: 'I love poems more than money & pussy. / From now on I will eat brunch alone. I believe / Eurydice is actually the poet, not Orpheus.' But Hayes is a strikingly clever poet, both accessible and fruitfully allusive. While distinctly American, this sonnet sequence, with its page after page of ragged-edged rectangles of text, visually resembles its Renaissance counterparts, which typically interrogate the agonies of unrequited love, corseted in monuments to a moment or a thought. Hayes pins himself to this tradition in poems that question where tradition has led us and what has been learnt and forgotten.

The parallels are often blatant. As he writes at the end of one poem early in the sequence, 'I will make you a box of darkness with a bird in its heart. / Voltas of acoustics, instinct & metaphor. It is not enough / To love you. It is not enough to want you destroyed.' These poems don't express much hope. 'Even the most kindhearted white woman', one opens, 'may begin, almost / Carelessly, to breathe *n*-words' to herself when stuck in traffic. 'What is inward, is absorbed', it ends, with perhaps over-conclusive certainty, though one can see Hayes's point and how certain it must at times feel.

This year has also seen the publication of *To Float in the Space Between: A Life and Work in Conversation with the Life and Work of Etheridge Knight*, which evolved from a series of lectures given across America. Knight (1931–91) was an elusive, sometimes mercurial poet of the Black Arts Movement: a veteran of the Korean War whose treatment for wounds left him an opiate addict, a hustler par excellence who was nonetheless a man of deep principle, and a former convict, imprisoned for armed robbery in 1960. During his imprisonment, his attention turned to poetry; his first collection was *Poems from Prison* (1968), and he went on to win the American Book Award in 1987 for *The Essential Etheridge Knight*, before dying from cancer at only fifty-nine years of age.

Behind this stark outline was a life perhaps as full and rich as any could be. This poet Hayes never met and who he has in some ways never replicated – 'My coming-of-age story is about a road I did not take', as he puts it in one of myriad instantly quotable passages – has been an obsession for him throughout his own writing life. *To Float in the Space Between* is an unconventional, consistently fascinating *bricolage* of short and often personal articles, line drawings, and poems by both Knight and Hayes himself – including the superb and unextractable 'Portrait of Etheridge Knight in the Style of a Crime Report' – and as much a book about Hayes and his own *sui generis* poetics as it is about Knight, though it succeeds on that count as well, keeping him in middle distance while also offering the kinds of insight so unlikely in a more conventional biography. 'This is not a biography', writes Hayes in the Foreword; it is in fact as much fractured autobiography as it is biography, because a poet, as opposed to a scholar, 'looks upon the work of another poet not only through a window but also through a mirror'. 'Consider this a collection of essays as speculative, motley and adrift as Knight himself', he adds. That is quite a claim, but one this unusual, candid book ultimately justifies.

Times Literary Supplement, 2018

WENDY COPE, *ANECDOTAL EVIDENCE* (FABER AND FABER, 2018)

Wendy Cope is often regarded as a gentle wit, a parodist, with a nice line in teasing and sometimes acid mockery of a man's world. However, the poems in which those talents are evident have been fewer and farther between for over two decades. Most of her earlier critics ignored the less funny poems she also wrote; now those are her mainstay, and have matured with her.

The opening poem of this, her fifth collection, serves as introduction: poetry is 'anecdotal evidence / About the human heart', and indeed, this book is full of hearty anecdotes. Many elucidate memories, solitude in the company of ghosts. In 'The Damage to the Piano', 'I am cast adrift / with all this furniture / and no-one to tell me off.' And at the end of 'Baggage', a sonnet about finding her father's battered suitcase, 'The child of his old age, I close my eyes / And join him under sunny foreign skies.' The poem's formal elements are initially quite loose: it comes 'right', softly and triumphantly, at the moment of heartbreakingly elusive connection.

Cope is famous for her incisive digs at other (usually male) poets, though here only Shakespeare and Herbert are taken on, in conversations, not parodies or ripostes. Another poem about transience and permanence, 'My Father's Shakespeare', is one of several sonnets concerning the Bard. When passing the book down, her father 'wrote, "To Wendy Mary Cope. With love." / Love on a page, surviving death and time. / He didn't even have to make it rhyme.' Her freer poems are more hit and miss, though. Some read like the brief prose memoirs collected in Cope's *Life, Love and The Archers* (2014), and are sometimes light-footed and witty, but no less so if you pretend they don't have line-breaks.

This is a contented book, despite its many intimations of mortality. In 'To My Husband', which fittingly opens and closes with tight rhymed couplets, Cope writes that 'If we were never going to die, I might / Not hug you quite as often or as tight.' Her love poems ooze with such sentiments. Most are sonnets, almost forming a short unnumbered sequence at the book's heart. Unfortunately, they tend to say the same things in different words. The few more ostensibly humorous pieces come mainly towards the end, including a dig at men telling 'anecdotes and jokes' – not as evidence of their feelings, but probably to hide from them – and 'At 70', in ludicrous couplets: 'I do a crossword every day. I play with forms poetical / with one as tough as this I sometimes get a bit frenetical.' If someone other than Wendy Cope had written those lines, she could have pinched them for the book's epigraph.

Times Literary Supplement, 2018

ANNE HAVERTY, *A BREAK IN THE JOURNEY* (NEW ISLAND, 2018)

Novelists often seem to want to be poets, perhaps as a legitimising if unremunerative sideline. Anne Haverty is best known as a novelist, and certainly her greatest gift is for novelistic depictions of lives and what disturbs them. Many of the poems in her second poetry collection present multiple lives in tandem, in which everyone seems to want what has been missed or vanquished. In 'Marriage', 'She is taking off / her face // to go to bed // as away on the billows of the sea // with him'. In the opening poem, 'The Nun and the Greyhound', both 'come to the door, one / to the hall, one to the back, / lean, ardent, lonely and sad', both seeking 'the position / of household pet'. The language is always sparse and simple, the lines normally short and taut; though many of the enjambments feel arbitrary, others serve to deliver the short shock of a realigned meaning.

Unfortunately, sentiment can topple into sentimentality, anecdote into pat observation. Yes, 'Even in grief / we can love', but was it ne'er so well expressed? Yes, as 'Poemless' (ah, note the near-pun) painstakingly points out, it's hard to be a poet if one is homeless, and people walking past are likely to 'feel the shame – / though we might protest as well / that the rules of etiquette / are not clear as yet / regarding our unhoused'. I have seen poets congratulated for having a novelist's eye for detail, but this isn't an exemplar; and Haverty's occasional penchant, as here, for hitting on one-off rhymes in conversational unmetred verse strikes more of an off-note than it hints at what Rilke called the 'goddess of secret and ancient coincidences'. Her (surely) unintended puns can get in the way, too: 'Memorial' describes being taken to a 'suitably grave' memorial by hosts who are 'dead keen' that 'we / pay homage'.

There is a lot of travel in these poems, though it doesn't always alleviate the gloom. 'Beautiful Day at Birkenau' is two pages summed up by its title. 'Strange' presents Aarhus and the

Grauballe Man, famously a subject for Haverty's compatriot Seamus Heaney over four decades ago: in 'his bog-soaked skin / he rests in his long long sleep'. The several poems about Armenia, 'a new land / for my muse', are largely celebratory, wallowing in unfamiliarity: 'I step into Asia, ground / ochre and packed as in a souk / where the merchants sell enigmatic powders'. These are poems rich with human feeling and experience, then, but there often isn't enough of anything else.

Times Literary Supplement, 2018

BACK INTO SLAUGHTER

Robin Robertson, *The Long Take* (Picador, 2018)

Essentially a 200-page historical novel mainly in unrhymed, unmetred verse, *The Long Take* is quite a departure for the Scottish poet Robin Robertson, more akin to the book-length poems of his compatriot J. O. Morgan than anything he has done previously. It follows Walker, a broken Canadian veteran of the Second World War with a dark secret, through the decade after his demobbing, as he navigates the United States from New York City to Los Angeles to San Francisco and back to Los Angeles, unable to face returning to his family in the Maritimes. He eventually gets a job as a reporter for a newspaper, but never shrugs off the horror and guilt of what he has seen and done: we constantly find him searching for himself in bars and among the down-and-outs, many of them now-forgotten heroes of a forgotten war ('when we got back home, / I thought there'd be a job for me', one confides in him), in a country riddled with racism, Mob violence, proud self-interest, and McCarthyite paranoia – but also a country of rapid progress, looking forwards as he cannot.

An essential thing war gave Walker, then took away, was comradeship: 'I used to have a family of two hundred men [...]. And after that, I'm lost', he says, in a sudden outburst of feeling. Even the cities in which he finds himself keep changing in bewildering ways: as Roberton writes, with a twist on Heraclitus, 'You can never step in the same city twice', and this is doubly true in Los Angeles, the city hell-bent on paving paradise to put up a parking lot. As his one constant friend, a black former veteran called Billy Idaho puts it, the city is 'dying from the center out', increasingly 'strangled by freeways', with sudden 'empty lots, like a bomb's fallen', and hills being flattened for homes, roads and garages. Moreover, there are hideous reminders anywhere Walker goes: waves against Manhattan shingle are 'like the distant crackle and crump / of small arms or mortars'; a sunset 'bloods' the water from San Francisco 'back into slaughter, back to / bodies on the barbed wire'.

Interspersing the verse sections are many italicised prose flashbacks, some to before the war, others to the midst of it, and many apparently brought on by Walker's current experiences:

> The trees by the East River have things
> snagged in their branches: clothes,
> fish-crates, ropes and sacks, bodies sometimes,
> people say, trapped there by the tides, the ice.

*

> *It's the wire. They're caught deep in barbed wire, and can't get free. Can't get out of the water and onto the beach. They're waving their arms and screaming but the landing craft just goes over them, the propellers just cutting them apart.*

Later, he sees the next war's versions of himself returned from Korea: 'a line of kids in their twenties, slow-eyed, / passing the jug of Thunderbird'. No doubt they are also blighted by memories not unlike his, such as '*the soldier with his jaw blown half-off, trying to hold it in place*', or looking '*men you killed*' in the eye to '*see the life dimming*'. At such stark moments one might just about be reminded of Keith Douglas. Robertson carries this predilection for cold detail into his descriptions of much of what Walker sees in the city, such as when he meets a man who has had a stroke, 'his face dragged down on one side, like it had / missed a button'.

The Long Take, then, is a version of the story of an epoch. And it is immaculately researched in terms of geography, current affairs, and its constant cultural touchstones in the Hollywood films of the time, offering up their glitzy counterparts to Walker's raw experience. But the story of a broken man left to his own devices by a country for which he has suffered in war is not, sadly, one we can confine to American or British history, and it is not hard to see much of this as a narrative for our times too. Walker is a superbly rounded character, and his tale one worth telling. Unfortunately, the book is also quite repetitive, in needless as well as effective ways, and palls in places. Moreover, some of the American and Canadian slang feels a little excessive or ventriloquised, and there are a few odd and inexplicable shifts in tense. Nonetheless, it is often moving and engrossing: a ballsy move on the part of Robin Robertson that has, on the whole, paid off – not least, perhaps, in its surprise inclusion on the longlist for the Man Booker Prize.

Times Literary Supplement, 2018

PAMPHLETING

Diana Anphimiadi, trans. Jean Sprackland and Natalia Bukia-Peters, *Beginning to Speak* (PTC, 2018));
Rakhshan Rizwan, *Paisley* (Emma Press, 2017);
Charlotte Eichler, *Their Lunar Language* (Valley Press, 2018); Steve Ely, *Jubilate Messi* (Shearsman, 2018);
Carol Rumens, *Bezdelki* (Emma Press, 2017)

I love poetry pamphlets, at least in theory, which is partly why my co-editor and I recently decided to turn *New Walk* magazine into the pamphlet publisher New Walk Editions. Among myriad other things, a poetry pamphlet can give us an early glimpse at the work of a new poet who isn't yet ready for a book, can allow an established poet to gamble on a new direction or present a discrete shorter project in its own covers, or can provide an easily digestible selection from a writer new to us, but not new elsewhere in the world. I'll use this review to give space to recent examples of all these things.

The blurb to Rakhshan Rizwan's debut, *Paisley*, claims that it 'simmers with [...] anger' and 'offers critical comment on the vexed issues of class, linguistic and cultural identity – particularly for women'. Her poems are in fact far more multifaceted and skilful than those by many of her more lauded contemporaries who often seem to think a poem can more or less get by on critical comment alone. Rizwan is a Pakistani who has moved to Germany to study; for the most part this pamphlet looks back to where she is from, and at herself looking back, and does so insightfully and inquisitively. 'Buffet' is one giddy run-on sentence:

> we sit stirring the brew,
> vapours of warm melted sugar rising,
> we stir in the evening news,
> and drown ourselves

in the tiny
teacups of our
collective conscience.

'The Nawab's Daughter' is delicate portraiture, and leaves us to work things out:

We are princesses from Kabul, from Lucknow,
no man ever laid eyes on us. Unveiled,
she stirs salt into the rice and her
wounds and recites no more Ghalib, Josh or Mir.

'Noon' meditates on 'My Urdu-Persian name', in the poet's migratory context, in our febrile times:

I still get letters in the mail –
addressed to Mr Rakhshmann – a sort
of retribution – for the verbal gymnastics
I put authority figures through – Sometimes –
I do not correct them – pleased at the Germanness
of my name

Some of these poems are a little overwritten – 'wind turbines / lacerate the air / with metal blades' – but this is a young poet with plenty to say and who generally shows the kind of admirably cool restraint that encourages our attention.

Charlotte Eichler's *Their Lunar Language* is another debut with another fashionable-sounding but slightly misleading blurb, this time telling us that the poet 'explores human relationships through our ambivalent relationships with the natural world'. This implies the work of a REF-savvy academic-poet who has charged herself with the rote 'creative interrogation' of a single idea, but again the truth is thankfully more complex. Eichler's poems are tentative, probing, frequently moving, full of sentiment, rarely sentimental. Most are short and tight, and she is apparently completely in control of rhythm and image:

> We thought we knew
>
> how things like day and night
> and love would work.
>
> I held you too hard, my nails
> made chilly little moons along your arm.

The opener, 'Divination', very much sets the tone:

> Saturdays crawled with our ladybird circus –
> from the ends of our fingers, solemn as blood,
>   we sent them to find our future husbands.
> We let them trickle down
>   our wrists into the birdbath
> to see if they'd keep walking while we drowned them,
> jealous of their early flight
>
>   from one shape to the next.
> Now, like hanged men, we want to buy futures
> and there's someone doing tarot at the end of Brighton Pier.

These unsettling and precise poems – metaphorical, mythological, comprehensible for all that – long outlast the time it takes to read them.

Steve Ely is not a new name, of course, but his *Jubilate Messi* is certainly a unique project – or at least the unique product of an abandoned one. 'My original intention was to write a poetic history of football,' he writes, 'but one thing and another got in the way and the footballing Muse abandoned me after about twenty poems.' This pamphlet contains his twelve picks from those: 'a first eleven, plus a sub'. The research is extensive, the tone often tongue-only-partially-in-cheek-devotional in keeping with the title: we move from the unorganised genesis – a 'scrum and brawl / back and forth / all day' – to the desperate attempts of toffs to hold on to the organised sport in the nineteenth century, and through several occasionally *Roy of the Rovers*-meets-*Viz* snapshots of the beautiful game as it once was:

> feeding time
> and the Lions were hungry
> BUT
>   big Norman on a loose ball
>   slipped in wee Billy
>   pick that out
>   you cocky Jock cunts

Finally, on comes Messi, a savoury saviour, 'For he has the grace of Garrincha and the guts of Gascoigne; Zola's zest, the balance of Best, and Bergkamp's balmy touch: *Let Der Bomber give praise, and Henry's heart, leap like the lenten roe.*' Ely is a lively, erudite, million-miles-an-hour, total-football poet, Cruyff-turning into new narratives and even sometimes forms mid-poem, and it can be a job to keep up. The endnotes are sometimes longer than the poems to which they refer, and often both highly necessary and enjoyable in their own right – perhaps even if you're not as much of a football anorak as he is.

Carol Rumens is one of those overlooked 'famous' poets: respected, but not that widely read. In her case, I find this as incomprehensible as almost anything else in British poetry. Perhaps it is because, after sixteen collections, there is a lot of her work out there, and new readers don't know where to start. If that is you, I urge you to begin with *Bezdelki* ('small things' in Russian), a worthy surprise winner of the 2018 Michael Marks Award. This pamphlet is in elegy for Rumens's partner Yuri Drobyshev. In 'Vidua', one of the shortest of its mainly short poems, she writes:

> I wasn't a wife.
> I'm not a widow.
> I'm no-one, trying to gather
> all the 'we weres' together.

The pamphlet partially relies on Drobyshev in another way, too: 'The Admiralty' is translated from Osip Mandelstam 'with the help of Yuri Drobyshev' – and, in its present context, develops fresh connotations:

> In the Northern capital, dusty *populus*,
> Sighing, mantles the time's transparency
> And, through green dark, a frigate or an acropolis,
> Brother to water and sky, glows distantly.

Bezdelki is more than just a record of 'Your artefacts. Laced secretly all over / by the tiny snails of your dreams / and your DNA'. It is also a reckoning, a reminder to live, plain and restrained in its telling: 'I want you to come and mend the Jewish box' is hardly, objectively, one of the most moving lines of English poetry, but Rumens can subtly fill a poem with so much hard-edged meaning that it feels like the sudden bursting of a dam.

Diana Anphimiadi's *Beginning to Speak* is another restrained, miniature collection, this time effectively a short selected poems from the past decade. It constitutes the twenty-first pamphlet from the Poetry Translation Centre, which matches poets in other languages with anglophone poets and translators. Anphimiadi is prominent in her native Georgia, and for good reason. Her poems are lyrical, nuanced, often politically intriguing. The intense joy of 'Dance Lessons (3/4 Time)' is subtly undercut by its own extended metaphor:

> Rule: look straight
> into his eyes,
> even if a gorgon

is reflected there
Adjust to his steps
as if to new shoes.

Other canny and uncanny poems consider the implications of words: 'Because' asks 'What kind of word is because? [...] Both answer and question'. 'The Trajectory of the Short-Sighted' suggests that 'Happiness is the right not to see myself / too clearly in the mirror – / I like my silhouette'. The endings can be a little pat – that poem concludes 'When I go completely blind / I think it will be paradise' – but at her best Anphimiadi's work is adroitly witty and inquisitive. One of the best things a poetry pamphlet can do is show us something we haven't seen before and make us want to see more of it, and this series from the Poetry Translation Centre does that admirably. So, I would suggest, do the other pamphlets I've mentioned here.

PN Review, 2019

TRUTH AND LIES

David Cain, *Truth Street* (Smokestack Books, 2019);
David Clarke, *The Europeans* (Nine Arches Press, 2019)

David Cain's intentions are gallant. *Truth Street* was written to mark the thirtieth anniversary of the Hillsborough Disaster, in which ninety-six Liverpool supporters were crushed to death at an FA Cup semi-final in Sheffield, as a direct result of police incompetence. No event before or since has done more to alter how football stadia are constructed and configured, or how high-profile football matches are handled by the authorities. However, the attempted cover-up by the South Yorkshire Police, assisted by swathes of the media primed to defend the establishment and to attack Liverpool fans since the Heysel Disaster a few years earlier, meant that nobody was held accountable until 2017, when six people were convicted of manslaughter by gross negligence. Cain's book, subtitled *A Hillsborough Poem*, relives the day and its immediate aftermath in a series of short, versified sections, each split into single-line stanzas; a brief preface tells us that these were 'developed from evidence' given at the inquest leading up to that verdict.

This is not a book apportioning blame – though the source of blame is obvious and comes through – and we hear from fans, family members, police officers, and others who were there. The uniformity of style, and linear narrative, encourage us to view these voices as a composite, as we are hurtled into events. 'They walked through' the exit gates opened by police 'like sand into an egg timer'. The crush built and 'He was bent very far over the barrier. / He looked around and his face was very, very red. / His eyes were very wide, distress and panic on his face.' The initial police response at pitch-side was at best confused: 'I was shouting that people were dying, let people out, / they didn't respond.' And, following the disaster, the cover-up began almost immediately. One salient scandal among scandals was the attempt to pin the catastrophe on drinking. In 'Norman Bettison', named for a senior officer (knighted in 2006) who was charged in 2017 with four counts of misconduct and then acquitted, we hear testimony from someone under his command:

> It was just myself and Norman. And Norman said,
>
> 'I've been asked by my senior officers to pull together the South Yorkshire Police evidence for the inquiry
>
> and we're going to try and concoct a story that all of the Liverpool fans were drunk
>
> and that we were afraid they were going to break down the gates so we decided to open them.'

Of course, as these poems are 'developed from' testimony, it is not always apparent where the stitching begins. The book shows a few signs of sloppy preparation beyond the sort of thing we can put down to the quoting of speech from people in highly charged circumstances. The book's epigraph, for example, is the opening few lines of T. S. Eliot's '*The Wasteland*' (sic). The chief problem, though, is that *Truth Street* essentially comprises concrete testimony, entirely devoid of abstract insight, and if that is what you are after there are considerably fuller and more detailed versions of it, such as *Hillsborough Voices: The Real Story told by the People Themselves* (2016) by Kevin Sampson and *Hillsborough: The Truth* (1999) by Phil Scraton. There is something admirable about this poet trying to leave himself out of the poetry and let the words of those who lived the experience speak for themselves, but that doesn't mean it always works. The preface points us towards the Hillsborough inquests' official website, from where Cain took his excerpts of transcripts, which is a considerably more illuminating place to spend time. Nonetheless, I found *Truth Street* as riveting as an inadequate but well-intended documentary on a fascinating subject, and devastatingly sad and angering. Few books move your heart this much, but that is down to the subject and the testimonies, more than the execution. The book ends with a list of the dead and their ages; the youngest was 10 and would now be in his forties, maybe with small children of his own.

The Europeans, David Clarke's second full-length collection, is another book about power and public opinion, though it is certainly not one in which the author ostensibly keeps his perspectives out of the frame. It has the same wry, laconic voice of much of his previous work, though ratcheted up a notch. I suspect you'll be able to guess its focus from the title, and Clarke's response to our current political climate and what led us here is febrile and exasperated, and short-tempered with regard to any pack-mentality ideology. As he puts it bluntly in 'Letter in March', we are in a country in which 'every shit / defends the *culture* he does not understand'. The prose poem 'Let Me Be Very Clear' presents a collage of contradictory, usually meaningless similes used by politicians and journalists to describe Brexit:

> It's like jumping off the Titanic, or out of a burning aeroplane without a parachute, or out of one burning aeroplane and into another burning aeroplane. It's like a war, like a new kind of freedom, like a jail with the door left open.

This book is interested in the lies people tell themselves, the ways we circumnavigate thought. Many of the poems turn on a slightly surreal conceit, of the sort often favoured by poets like Simon Armitage or Paul Farley, but with a hard reproach more akin to some of the later poems of R. S. Thomas. The speaker of 'Museum of Lies' shows us around, then implores us to

> seek out that corner where your own
> untruth turns pristine on its plinth,
> its every facet catching light.

The beguiling, acutely observed opening poem, 'Invitation', is one of many pieces warning against misplaced nostalgia and the desire to reach for simple answers. The setting is the 'Hotel Europa', an apparent metaphor for a Europe borrowing time, the name returning in each stanza like an accusation:

> As soon as we arrive in the Hotel Europa
> we long to leave, to find that little place
> you once stumbled on – its courtyard walls
> rippling with fig trees, its address a fiction.
>
> And yet we cannot fault the service
> in the Hotel Europa.

England, on the other hand, is a dowdy pub in 'The Snug', in which a 'little man' – Farage, or a cut-price Farage? – leans 'against the ale-damp bars of England' to smarm up to the landlady, grope the barmaid, and coo 'words that stick in bigots' throats'. The poem is a villanelle, using its (French) form again to ram home a proper noun in apparent disapprobation – 'England' tangoing throughout the poem with our 'birthright', symbolised by the bigot. Then, in 'To a Stately Home', England is symbolised not so much by the home itself as by the 'plebeians' who 'form / disorderly queues beneath your portico' in order to 'gawp at drapes' once owned by 'tubs of lard on horse' who let the home go 'in lieu of tax, but kept a flat, of course, /a tranche of garden, a private gate'.

This is all true enough, but what are we learning? 'Letter to George Gordon Byron', the book's longest poem and one of its last, uses Byron's *Don Juan* stanzas (though often continuing the first rhyme into the final couplet, an impressive feat he normally pulls off) to address that poet about the current state of the nation. Really, though, it does little other than reiterate, without much Byronic panache: 'A puffed-up England sneers again at all / that's foreign, toffs are cheered by plebs they despise', and 'you'd weep to see' Greece 'coshed by men in suits who seem legit, / but have a banker's taste for liberty, / i.e. not much of one'.

The book's central theme occasionally drops out of view. The better poems typically occur when it does so, and the tensions are based on more than scatter-gun opprobrium. 'When my mother worked in the asylum', for example, is at once moving, witty, hard and uncanny: 'The dementia ward was a staring contest / where God always won', and 'A crocodile // of moon-faced children stumbled across / the lawn, hand in sticky hand'. In 'The Villages', church 'spires are styluses / that scratch a dirge from Heaven's / whirling acetate'. The acuteness of Clarke's observations can be very impressive; but while these poems are as sardonic as anything else here, they show us a different side to the poet, and one we cannot either simply agree with or dismiss.

Poetry Review, 2019

SICK OF SADNESS

Jericho Brown, *The Tradition* (Picador, 2019)

Jericho Brown's second collection, *The New Testament*, was published in 2014 in his native United States. A British edition arrived three years later, when some of the better-known and more politically minded black American poets – Claudia Rankine and Danez Smith, for example – had suddenly gained significant reputations this side of the Atlantic. In that book, Brown also showed himself to be a politically charged poet speaking to his contemporary moment and the forces that led to it, particularly in terms of racial, masculine and sexual identity. Variations of that sentence could be used to describe any number of poetry books published in the past few tumultuous years, but Brown's demonstrated a particularly admirable penchant for nuance, unusual among much of the more commercially successful and heavily politicised poetry of our times. In many ways, *The Tradition* is an extension of the same preoccupations, with apparently deepened intent.

A leitmotif of *The New Testament* was the subversion of biblical narrative. *The Tradition* begins in a comparable vein, with 'Ganymede', a terse and tense single block of verse (as was his mainstay in the earlier book), here reaching back to the 'tradition' of the Classics. Brown takes for preference Homer's version of events: 'A man trades his son for horses. / [...] I like / The safety of it, no one at fault, / Everyone rewarded.' Anyone who has read *The New Testament* knows Brown won't be leaving things there, though – for stories can be obfuscations of truths as much as truths themselves, and 'This way, nobody bothers saying / Rape. I mean, don't you want God / To want you?'

The Tradition is in some ways a more personal book than its predecessor: for instance, we find the speaker making love (quite a lot), or remembering a school day with microscopes, when 'we gave up / Stealing looks at one another's bodies' to see 'Our actual selves taken down to a cell / Then blown back up again'. But it is also, and often simultaneously, a book of injustices, beatings, deaths, such as that of the man who leaps 'Dirty against the whiteness / Of the sky to your escape / Through the whiteness // Of the water'. Men can rarely touch one another unless violently, or in secret (one poem, for example, recalls stabbing 'someone I secretly loved' with a pencil), and even when they can there is a looming sense of real threat. In 'Of My Fury', Brown writes, in a rare instance of more prosodic prosody:

> I love a man I know could die
> And not by way of illness
> And not by his own hand
> But because of the colour of that hand and all
> His flawless skin.

He is not afraid to implicate or chastise himself, either. Almost everything here bears a lyric I, and then near the end of the book he writes, 'I am sick of your sadness, / Jericho Brown'.

Another 'tradition' Brown toys with is that of the technical aspects of his art. Five of these poems are in a form of his own invention, the 'duplex' – effectively a loosely syllabic sonnet with elements of repetition and return borrowed from blues and the ghazal, which he uses to swing from one thought to the next:

> My last love drove a burgundy car,
> Color of a rash, a symptom of sickness.
>
> > We were the symptoms, the road our sickness:
> > None of our fights ended where they began.
>
> None of the beaten end where they begin.
> Any man in love can cause a messy corpse.

The book closes with a set of uncompromising love poems, which also draws on its earlier preoccupations. In 'Otland', for example,

> I'm sure
> Somebody died while
> We made love. Some-
> Body killed somebody
> Black. I thought then
> Of holding you
> As a political act.

Holding, of course, has a double meaning. There is a unity and maturity to this fine collection; there is also a bit too much of the same thing done in the same way, though, which was also a failing of its predecessor.

Times Literary Supplement, 2019

NO TIME FOR INNOCENCE

Beata Duncan, *Berlin Blues* (Green Bottle Press, 2018)

As her son Stephen informs us in the introduction to *Berlin Blues*, Beata Duncan (1921–2015) came from an impressive Berlin Jewish family of artists, doctors and engineers. Her childhood was overwhelmed by the time and place in which it occurred: her father, the playwright Hans Rehfisch, was openly critical of Nazism and was arrested in 1933, at which point he fled Germany, first to Vienna. Soon after, the twelve-year-old Beata and her older brother Tom were sent to England as refugees; their mother Lilli, a psychoanalyst, would be deported in 1941, and die in the Holocaust. Duncan wrote poems and fiction throughout her life, and in later years these increasingly focused on memories of early childhood; *Berlin Blues* is the product of her last decade.

Most of the poems are anecdotal and cutely conventional in style: her brother puts the pet cat in the piano, and the strings go 'mad!'; her mother plays the piano while waiting for 'another patient, unrolling / the quiet melody of Beethoven's *Für Elise*'. Knowing something of their genesis helps, then, because even the more simple or syrupy of these narratives are implicitly part of a grotesque tragedy with no time for innocence. There are moments of subtle disquiet, though, and Duncan can be witty in revealing them. 'Cheesecake with Adler', about a visit by the psychologist known for his work on the inferiority complex, is an evocative poem of childish uncertainty: 'He takes my hand in his / and we are silent. Then I giggle // as he leans forward and whispers / "I think you are a hopeless case"'. In 'Piscator Comes to Tea', Duncan's father and the German director are heard acting out scenes in the study, 'growling like bears, // a shouting dictator', before rejoining the family: 'they smiled at us with their secrets. / We looked at them both and frowned'. The final poems, detailing the period immediately before Beata's departure, are often heart-breaking. 'The Robbers' recalls hiding toys in the house 'for our return', and the 'boys and girls in scarves / and shorts, quickly marching in the street, / staring at me'. There is no doubt Beata Duncan's story matters and should be remembered, and there is plenty here to enjoy for a reader willing to consider this book as poetry-memoir, with an emphasis on the latter.

Times Literary Supplement, 2019

WINNERS, ALL

Warda Yassin, *Tea with Cardamom* (Smith Doorstop, 2019); Faith Lawrence, *Sleeping Through* (Smith Doorstop, 2019)

With the proliferation of creative writing courses and workshops, and the democratisation of publishing, has come a bloated generation of new poets – some rather good, many awful. In addition to a near-simultaneous growth in the number of magazines and other outlets in which they might publish (or 'publish'), and the recent uptick in the number of small presses (the website *Sphinx* lists nearly one hundred active British poetry pamphlet publishers) there are now also more small prizes than ever catering for their hopes and, sometimes, expectations. Opportunity isn't a *bad* thing, of course, but where is a reader to begin to make sense of it all?

He or she might gravitate towards the prize-winners. The myriad and often well-documented problems with poetry prize culture, and what it means, have increasingly been augmented in recent years by that most enterprisingly American of practices: the poetry publication prize, often targeted at the new and eager. The hopeful masses send in their Word documents, and usually also their money; those fortunate enough to be picked off rebranded slush piles can be heralded on front covers as winners. The presses certainly win, not least because demonstrating that you nurture talent appeals to the Arts Council, a major source of potential revenue. But so do the chosen poets: it looks good to be a winner, and all but the no-hopers who help to keep the boats afloat might have their turns one day, somewhere. At the pamphlet press I co-run, New Walk Editions, we haven't succumbed to this model – but we can only publish four pamphlets a year, and never have any spare money. Surely if we changed tack, we could publish more poets we believe in. But a 'small' fee can be a lot to some people, and the few aspiring poets left in garrets metaphorical and literal might be dissuaded. And, more importantly still, what about the excellent not-new poets who have been pushed aside by this ever-replenishing trend for newness? It's complicated.

Smith Doorstop – AKA, and without irony, The Poetry Business – has recently operated three competitive schemes leading to publication, on various models, including the one so charitably outlined above. The focus is largely on 'exciting new voices', to coin a phrase, and in a world of 'exciting new voices' which are often, when it comes down to it, nothing of the sort, they've done a pretty good job at hoovering up more than their fair share of genuine talent. Their fees aren't astronomical: £28 for the International Book and Pamphlet Competition is perhaps a bit much for a glorified submission fee, but the New Poets Prize costs £8; the Laureate's Choice scheme is free, but then again it isn't open for submissions, so presumably it helps if you are known by the press – which happens to run frequent one-day workshops in the north of England, where most of their poets come from, for £35–£40 a go.

Warda Yassin is one of four winners of this year's New Poets Prize: those three words take up most of the front cover of *Tea with Cardamom*, just to make sure you know. She has an almost filmic gift for presenting a version of contemporary urban Britain:

> The breeze
>
> brings the Adaan, dubstep and sirens,
> the smell of the sauna, the smoke of incense.
>
> Out front, my father breaks his fast,
> chews dates, offers a cautious smile
>
> to those with heavy eyes across the way.

Yassin is a British-born Somali, and that heritage is at the heart of many of these poems – in sights, sounds, prayer:

We stand in rows like soldiers there to learn the ways
of the second life. *You can use whatever language you like.*

Hooyo, do not bow, there is only oath and dua between you
and Allah, stay shoulder to shoulder with your sisters.

Unsurprisingly, that heritage sometimes weighs heavy, and her debut is marked by consummately nuanced, reflexive poetry. This is mature writing, at once urgent and restrained. Some of her control comes from juxtapositions, and the complexities they can tacitly belie: 'When the war began, my aunt was detained between borders / like a pattern trapped under tapestry. // I love gold eye shadow and reading books about war.' 'I want to read a novel about Somalis that isn't trauma porn', she writes at the start of 'Tales', perhaps the finest poem here. We're then given a phantasmagorical montage, real and removed:

We are not pirates, but mermaids lazing by crystalline lagoons, shiid
hoisted to the waist, buoyant youths swimming to jaamacad in
    coral crowds,
the rainforests of our sea. On the beach there is no blood, only vendors
reciting poetry, and there are no droughts on these dry pages, turn a
    leaf

and drift to the souk at dhur and see how we barter and flirt
in the baking hours [...].

For the Laureate's Choice scheme, four pamphlets a year are chosen for publication (but for some reason not introduced – perhaps she's too busy) by Carol Ann Duffy. As the new incumbent, Simon Armitage, is a local lad – Smith Doorstop is based in Sheffield – maybe we'll find out what his choices are next year. The most consistently impressive of the current crop is Faith Lawrence's debut, *Sleeping Through*, though each of the four has something to recommend it. Lawrence's are tight and precise poems – often extraordinarily so. The subject matter is largely conventional, but she writes intriguingly enough to startle. She is evidently a newish parent, and poets who are newish parents often fail to realise that what is life-altering for them isn't necessarily very interesting for anyone else; but here, the epiphanies can be as mind-shifting as they can be cutesy, and don't outstay their welcomes. This is the entirety of 'Delivery':

> Baby, you took your time;
> nothing else was in the world
> until you found that ring
> of bone, and clever as a key
> you turned, slipped right
> through and unlocked me.

In the next poem, though, there is trepidation: 'all I can promise', she writes at the end of 'Summer Born', is 'a nest shaped to both / of us, somehow.' Notice the risk of fracture in that enjambment; notice the tension between 'promise' and 'somehow'. Lawrence is always attentive to such poetic and linguistic possibilities. All of these poems are this quick on their feet.

That isn't to say every move comes off. 'Flowering', a sequence 'after eleven paintings by Sophie Breakenridge', is pithy almost to the point of insubstantiality – and some advice on how to find the paintings might have been nice. But the pamphlet really comes alive again in the final section, with its subtly clever contradictions and interrogation of a huge theme in miniature. In 'Abduction', ostensibly about Persephone being seized and taken to the underworld, 'my heart was a bee in a half-closed fist'. In 'Afterlife', on the facing page, 'Heaven' is stifling, rose-tinted merriment, encapsulated in something reminiscent of a lifestyle magazine picture from early last century:

> a lido on the coast
> where the dead are playing catch

in swimming costumes
and flowery bathing caps [...].

'Quieting' gives a rather different version of the 'end of the world': it 'will not mean / more of everything // but less'. The pamphlet then ends with its shortest non-sequence poem, the three-line 'Gift': 'The gift of winter / is to limit us'. This could almost be taken as a metaphorical manifesto for this terse, urgent little body of work – which probably shouldn't retail for almost as much as a full collection, though that is a different matter.

In a culture of poetic bombast, quieter 'new voices' such as these two are likely to be drowned out. 'Exciting' needn't mean loud, unless that's all you are personally able to hear. So, whatever one feels about the brave new world of poetry publishing, Smith Doorstop deserves a lot of respect for giving these poets a platform.

PN Review, 2019

SILENT STRENGTHENINGS

Ilya Kaminsky, *Deaf Republic* (Faber, 2019)

Deaf Republic is written for the most part in free verse (with some sections in prose), framed as a two-act play, and set in a country in which the people are resisting occupation by a brutal authoritarian regime. The country is invented and unspecified, but the location of the action (the town of Vasenka) and the dramatis personae (Alfonso and Sonya Barabinski, Petya, Momma Galya Armolinskya) are essentially Slavic, and parallels to the USSR, in which Ilya Kaminsky was born, are not exactly occulted. (There is, for example, a town of Varenka in Kaminsky's native Ukraine.) The poems are interspersed with line drawings of hands making signs: we learn in a note at the end (why not the beginning? Perhaps to keep us no more in step with the people than we are with the authorities) that 'the townspeople invented their own sign language', and this is it.

The narrative is clear, if fractured, and laced with leitmotifs and repetitions. Petya, a deaf boy, is at Sonya and Alfonso's puppet show, but 'public assemblies are officially prohibited'. When soldiers order the audience to disperse, Petya alone remains 'giggling', and is shot, and 'The sound we do not hear lifts the gulls off the water'. The people of the 'Deaf Republic' respond by rejecting sound, as an act of resistance: 'In the name of Petya, we refuse': 'At ten, Momma Galya chalks NO ONE HEARS YOU on the gates of the soldiers' barracks. / By eleven, arrests begin. / Our hearing doesn't weaken, but something silent in us strengthens.'

Sonya and Alfonso have a child, Anushka, only for Sonya to meet a fate comparable to Petya's. She is executed in 'Central Square' – a name at once generic and tellingly specific – with a sign around her neck reading 'I RESISTED ARREST'. This story is, perpetually, plot and counterplot, action and counteraction: 'Sonya looks straight ahead, to where the soldiers are lined up. Suddenly, out of this silence comes her voice, *Ready!* The soldiers raise their rifles on her command.' Again, the instant of death is 'silenced'. A regime based on barbarism often lives on borrowed time, and 'Our boys want a public killing in the sunlit piazza. / They drag a drunk soldier, around his neck a sign: / I ARRESTED THE WOMEN OF VASENKA.' He 'begs as townspeople shake their heads, and point at their ears'. His is a death we do see in full – as we later see Alfonso hanging from a rope as 'The puppet of his hand dances'.

In Act II, Momma Galya Armolinskya, who 'is having more sex than any of us', is inciting insurgency. 'Beautiful are the women of Vasenka', we learn: they lure soldiers with sex, then do away with them – beautifully. When the repercussions so familiar from Act I are swift and sweeping, some citizens are justifiably far from supportive: 'From the sidewalks, neighbors watch two women step in front of Galya. *My sister was arrested because of your revolution*, one spits in her face.' They take Anushka, and Galya 'shouts. / They point to their ears. / Gracefully, our people shut their windows.'

I won't ruin the climax of this narrative. But the book ends with a coda, 'In Time of Peace', in which this alien country is revealed as not so different from the contemporary United States (though he does not name it), where Kaminsky has spent his adulthood, and where 'I watch neighbors open // their phones to watch / a cop demanding a man's driver's license. When the man reaches for his wallet, the cop shoots. Into the car window. Shoots.' Yes, that happened, and yes, many other travesties like it have happened recently. But, for a poet who has done such a good job of exploring a subject without the contemporary poets' curse of telling us what we know and leaving almost nothing left for us to do cerebrally, it is a surprisingly reductive end: if we were reading at all carefully, we were there already. Nonetheless, Ilya Kaminsky is a real and rare talent, a writer with a distinctive linguistic skill and ideas to match it, and this is his finest work yet.

Times Literary Supplement, 2020

DR BOB PINTLE, SENIOR LECTURER IN PROFESSIONAL CREATIVITY

Life repeats – like a triolet
thinks Bob, as the alarm clock trills
and he starts composing this triolet.

This is how Bob Pintle – Lecturer in Creativity, and star of the final poem of my second collection *Sarajevo Roses* (2017) – began life, as I stumbled awake one morning and jabbed some words into the notes app on my phone while munching on my pre-work Ready-Brek. Triolets are, almost without exception, shite, written seriously these days mainly by syllable-counting New Formalists and their hapless students. I imagined an academic in mid-career, a bit too old-fashioned for the world he is saddled with, long enough in the tooth to have worked throughout all of the recent changes to the academy, and aghast at them – for all the right reasons and all the wrong ones too. I imagined him being a poet of the 'nobody loves me, it's not fair' variety, and overburdened with the need to come up with more of his product to avoid the wrath of his managers. In other words, I invented a composite of many of the people I have met or heard about, in a slightly dystopian composite of the world in which they work. I showed this near-triolet (Pintle gives up before the end) to my colleague and confidante Andrew Taylor, and he laughed and demanded more Pintle urgently. How could I resist? So, I completed a day-in-the-life sequence called 'Tuesday', adopting multiple forms, and taking us through a seminar, a staff meeting, tutorials, and the prospect of his annual review. I dedicated it to Andrew, 'who did not inspire it', and sent it to the *TLS*. They gratefully took my Pintle, so naturally I rejoiced, then wondered whether I'd be called in to have a tough conversation with the Dean.

How could I know that the same year I would meet a postgraduate student who is actually *called* Tuesday, and another called Sofi Bajor (a member of my cast is a student called Sophie

Cage)? This could have been a disaster. Both have since graduated from the MA Creative Writing that I lead, and neither reported me.

Yes, like most of the poets I know, I am an academic – and one perhaps approaching mid-career. And perhaps the Rory doth protest too much, but Pintle is not me. Well, there's a tiny bit of me in him because I'm human and full of my own failings, but he is very much his own man. He works at Peterborough University, because there is no such place, though if one is ever established it would be welcome to use my work as promotional material. Actually, a couple of years ago I learned to my horror that Peterborough does have a burgeoning university, but that is called University Centre Peterborough, so Pintle hasn't found himself needing to move on to a new institution to avoid being sued. In fact, he has somehow been promoted at PU, and his job title has changed a little to reflect the requirements of our fool's-gold-plated age: in my new collection, *Sweet Nothings*, he is a Senior Lecturer in Professional Creativity. He gets four poems this time, and I decided that he had to become angrier as he aged: he hasn't yet quite accepted his lot. If you read these poems and identify anyone in them, then yes, that is probably who they are about, because Pintle is a cut-price monster built out of real people, and most of those people are the archetypes they pretend not to be.

I imagine Bob Pintle's versified story as a sort of Rubin's vase, or rabbit-duck illusion: look at him while in one mindset, and he is a ridiculous figure who has earned his discomfort and disgruntlement: a timid Basil Fawlty, an Alan Partridge who never had anything from which to bounce back. Look at him while in another, and he is a hapless victim of the soul-destroying neoliberal academy, and of its attempts – about as honest as those of any major corporation – to gain superficial social responsibility points while trying to claw back a dwindling body of 'customers' and 'consumers' that is in some ways less robust than before. Spoiler: he doesn't cope well, and his failings don't entirely go unnoticed:

The 'Equality and Inclusion' process didn't go so well
   for Pintle, when his reading list was scanned.
They said '*The Waste Land* stinks of whitest malest privilege,
   v. is four-letter fury, and should be banned,
and *Briggflatts* is a work of heteronormativity.
   The gender balance is not what we demand –
that's also triggering. All those in favour, do jazz hands, please'.

Pintle has provided an opportunity for me to have slightly cruel fun and to make jokes, of course, but also to raise what I think are some fairly serious questions of various kinds. What follows, which was never going to make it into the book, is a conversation he (really) once had via live webchat with an essay mill representative:

Michael – Support Wizard
Hi! How may I help you today?

Bob Pintle
Hello. I work in an HE college. I'm Dr Robert Pintle.
I need a lecture on rhyme and metre and don't know how to do it.
   Lintel.
Can you help? It's nearly term – I haven't got much time.
Would you write my undergrad lecture on metre, form and rhyme?

Michael – Support Wizard
How long and what is the deadline?

Bob Pintle
It's just one lecture. Sixty mins. Four thousand words or so
On prosody, linked to employment skills, for first years. Let me know.
I just need something passable that's good enough for them –
The deadline is on Monday morning, though, at 10am.
I have a grant to utilise, so cost is not a worry.
Can you do it, please? I'm in a bind, a flap, a hurry.

Michael – Support Wizard
Place an unpaid order on the website and we'll look for an available writer before you make the payment. Just fill in the order form please, click check out on the final step, and then go back to the previous step. Then you just need to let us know the order ID number and we'll take it from there.

Bob Pintle
Okay. What's my outlay, though? I need this for my BA
Students and they're gullible and feckless, sad to say,
So I don't think it should take long if you know rhyme and metre
But sadly I'm not very good at it at all. Egg-beater.

Michael – Support Wizard
We estimate price depending on a task while looking for a writer in such cases, because it's a special paper.

Bob Pintle
Thank you, Wizard Michael. I'll submit and cross my fingers.
They're greasy, though, which makes it hard: I'm eating chicken
    Zingers –
Something I resort to when I'm in a flappy-flap.

Michael – Support Wizard
Sure, sir. Let me know when you will be finished with order so we could start looking for writer.

Bob Pintle
I'll place the order now, and then I'll go and take a nap.

Michael – Support Wizard has left the chat

Bob never fulfilled the order. He did ask me to post the conversation on Facebook, though, where the poet Kei Miller was among those who seemed to enjoy it quite a lot. Un-Pintlesque poet-academics tend to get Pintle, for some reason.

This will read like a self-preserving disclaimer, but I don't feel much of a victim myself. A lot of modern British universities seem quite psychopathic in their pursuit of what are often lowered aims, and my soul hasn't been thrown to the crusher by any of that – not quite, not yet. I'm lucky, then; Pintle isn't, and he hasn't done much to make his own luck either. He won't be for everyone, and he isn't supposed to be. In any case, I suspect he is going to die now, or at least find himself furloughed indefinitely.

Carcanet Press blog, 2020

THE SONNET

Stephen Regan, *The Sonnet* (OUP, 2019);
Mimi Khalvati, *Afterwardness* (Carcanet, 2019);
Vidyan Ravinthiran, *The Million-Petalled Flower of Being Here* (Bloodaxe, 2019)

'The aim of this book,' writes Stephen Regan in his introduction to *The Sonnet*, 'is to provide the first comprehensive study of the sonnet in English from the Renaissance to the present.' It is surprising that no such book existed already: as Regan contends, to 'trace the influence of Milton in the sonnets of Shelley and Wordsworth and Tony Harrison, or to note the ways in which Edna St. Vincent Millay and Sylvia Plath resist the sonnet strategies of their poetic predecessors, is to have a better understanding of the sonnet tradition as a whole'. He has a point, and endeavours to bear it out through carefully chosen, cross-referenced close readings. These are aided by his habit – gifted by the brevity of the form and the fact that so many sonnets are long out of copyright – of quoting poems whole, so we might more easily judge for ourselves.

Regan's six hefty chapters each comprise an introduction and a series of sections titled by name of author, from 'Sir Thomas Wyatt and Henry Howard, Early of Surrey' (the poets credited with bringing the sonnet to English) to 'Andrew Motion and Alice Oswald'. The latter pairing is indicative of Regan's tendency to stick with the mainstream near the end of the book, though the *avant garde* certainly isn't ignored. (Ted Berrigan, for example, is given two pages, though mainly to outline his subjects and unusual technique rather than to close read any of his sonnets.) Inevitably, the central focus of *The Sonnet* is overwhelmingly English, but there are also chapters dedicated to the development of the form in Ireland and America. The book's epilogue, 'The Sonnet and its Travels', which looks at sonnets in other languages and cultures, is an attempt to indicate the adaptability of the form elsewhere, in the work of Baudelaire, Roy Campbell, Derek Walcott, and others. It feels a little piecemeal, but the alternatives – either ignoring everything outside his direct remit or producing an inevitably failed attempt at a tome covering the sonnet in all cultures – are obviously less satisfactory.

Regan is perhaps especially insightful when discussing the influence of sonnets on the development of other poems, or on poets who have written sonnets then moved away from them. The page and a half dedicated to Auden's 'Musée des Beaux Arts', for example, might raise a purist's eyebrow, but Regan's observations about how and to what effect it 'extends' the sonnet form are convincing and illuminating – and, typically, formally fastidious: 'The rhyme scheme, which appears quite casual and even erratic, steadfastly refuses to follow the quatrain patterns of the Shakespearean sonnet, even though it superficially resembles them: *abcadedbfgfge hhijkkij*.' (The third 'quatrain' does, then.) Regan also offers intriguing insights into how writing sonnets has helped poets to develop, or shifted their focus. Philip Larkin published only four sonnets in the three collections for which he is remembered, but Regan makes a convincing case that it is in the thirty often Audenesque sonnets he produced in his apprentice years that he most effectively worked towards developing his mature style, perfecting his hallmark 'shifts of perspective' and facility for affecting pararhyme, taking what he had learned into later poems that typically 'demanded a more expansive, narrative method'.

This is by no means a short book, but it is certainly short for its subject and remit. Ideas take space to unpack, and Regan is the kind of purposeful critic who really comes into his own when he slows down. His ease with discussing prosodic effects allows him to make sharp points about, say, the formal properties of Elizabeth Barrett Browning's *Sonnets from the Portuguese*, often overlooked in conventional biographical readings which are 'apt to sentimentalize' them. Regan is right to note that 'intense biographical speculation' about the sequence is partly responsible for the 'relative neglect of the earlier sonnets in *Poems* (1844)', some of which are extraordinary. Unfortunately, he then proceeds to gloss over them himself. Nevertheless, this purposefully wide-ranging, limpidly written and intellectually lithe book is a significant achievement, and a useful addition to the critical canon.

It is all too easy to identify unfortunate omissions from a book like *The Sonnet*, and Regan is as representative as is sensible. He is also up to date, and his project is of course not harmed by the recent uptick in the sonnet's popularity among living poets. The most prominent example of this is surely Don Paterson's *40 Sonnets* (2015), which Regan calls, with his usual eagerness, a book of 'wondering enquiry' in which 'the flux of consciousness is matched by a bold adventurousness with form'. Mimi Khalvati's *Afterwardness*, a collection of metrically regular sonnets that all begin Shakespearean and end Petrarchan, is also a book of enquiry, and while it appeared too late to be considered by Regan, it is a little surprising she is not mentioned by him anyway, for she has always been drawn to the form. These poems do not form a sequence, but all tend to look both forwards and backwards.

Often, they feel personal: 'You're a normal child, if a bit bewildered, / struggling to push the feelings down, the questions, / the stillborn questions never to be answered, / stretching to see a sky that simply darkens'. Sometimes, as in the title poem, they do not – but the long view remains a leitmotif: 'An eleven-year-old boy from Aleppo / whose eyes hold only things no longer there / – a citadel, a moat, safe rooms of shadow, / "afterwardness" in his thousand yard stare –'. Those quotation marks don't help: if you're going to coin a neologism, see it through with conviction. However, everything always seems well made and in its place in this collection. The formality of style typically extends to the diction, always precise and concise, often reaching towards gentle or bittersweet epiphany. These poems, for all their variety of subject, tend to say what you'd most expect them to, but they do it very skilfully and can be moving.

Vidyan Ravinthiran's second collection, *The Million-petalled Flower of Being Here*, is also a book of sonnets, though in this instance they are in free verse with occasional, usually deftly-handled jolts of rhyme and metre. This book takes its title from Philip Larkin's "The Old Fools", a desperate meditation on the end of life and how it undoes that 'flower', but Ravinthiran focuses more on the 'being here'. The constant presence, or absence, in these poems is the speaker's partner: 'I had forgotten that time isn't money / and I don't need always to be on the move / within the world you've shown me how to love'. 'Within' is awkward; then again this *is* a book about being in the middle of things, often passively, as they occur.

Despite its title, though, this is a less multifaceted collection than Ravinthiran's first, *Grun-tu-molani* (2014). Many of its 100 sonnets repeat the same textures, not so much drawing energy from leitmotifs as reiterating one another, and less could have been more. But the sonnet is the right form for these candid, linked meditations that face abruptly in myriad directions: depression, Brexit, commonplace racism, what a cat might think of love, being taught the names of birds in 'grey Durham' where the poet briefly lived while writing some of these poems, violence in his ancestral Sri Lanka. Against it all, the speaker's lover is an often-absent source of hope. Ravintharan's subjects are usually contemporary or recent, but in a sense he has taken the sonnet back to its thematic origins, in a sequence of love-longing.

PN Review, 2020

A PAST TOO CLOSE

Don Paterson, *Zonal* (Faber, 2020); Medbh McGuckian, *Marine Cloud Brightening* (Gallery, 2019)

In some ways, these books are not a natural pair: Don Paterson and Medbh McGuckian tend to write from very different traditions, and have largely stuck to them throughout what are now in both cases fairly long careers. 'McGuckian is, of course, considerably more 'experimental' than Paterson, but it is Paterson who experiments more with his technique here, dramatically increasing his range - in several senses. *Zonal*, his first collection since *40 Sonnets* (2015), is a rather emphatic shift from that collection's various moments' monuments to long-lined, multi-page poems – a neat twenty of them – adopting the rhythms of expansive speech, mostly interlinked by an image or idea. It is a long monologue of monologues.

The book has a crazy conceit. As Paterson says in a prefatory note, most of the poems 'take their imaginative cue from the first season of *The Twilight Zone* (1959–1960)', but at 'various and odd angles, moves and distances' – a phrase one can imagine him lifting for his REF impact statement at St Andrews. 'They are, for the most part, experiments in science-fictional or fantastic autobiography' and 'take great liberties with […] my own life'.

If obscure sci-fi isn't your bag, then you can both join the club, and not worry: these poems do not much require their occasional intertext. And while Paterson may have adopted a new style, the old fascinations with human vulnerability remain in abundance. 'I guess I love the future. It holds such promise', says the speaker of 'The Way We Were', a sort of futuristic *Krapp's Last Tape*. In fact, the 'future' here is shown to be rife with the same often pathetic failings as our present – the fittings have changed, but not a lot else. This is as much *Black Mirror* as *The Twilight Zone*: 'Having made the error of finally agreeing to lunch with L. – what had it been, twenty-three years? – / let's say the horror was mutual. That's a lie. She was still beautiful. Her shock was ill disguised, though.' 'Thereafter I stayed home', he adds, 'on what my wife used to call "the loser's couch", the one with the built-in surround, / before she left with the dogs. I loaded up a bunch of psychogram loops, turned on the wallscreen, / and settled back'. And here he stays, reliving old memories, ending up 'in a two-second glitch-loop' with his mother's breast in his mouth. In 'The Lonely', an android-companion dictates 'the implanted memories of her terrible childhood into her own voicemail while I rub her arches'. It's all brilliantly witty and sad, crisply imagined, and philosophically and socially intriguing – an ingenious exploration of the trite piquancy of a mid-life crisis in the digital future (and present).

But there is no getting away from the fact that some of the expected snap has gone from Paterson's verse. A few of these poems read more like essays, or notes to them. The most intriguing unspool a quandary – such as 'The Deal', a sort of *Dr Faustus* parable spoken by the instigator:

> When I give someone the choice
> of five hundred years or immortality, you'll be unsurprised to hear
>   that they all choose the
> latter.
> *Might as well,* they think, and when they say *So what's the catch* and
>   I say, like I was quoting
> them for drywall,
> *in return you will give me your soul.*

Ah, the hubris: 'On average, they ask me to kill them within about two hours': 'A clock is a clock / because of the clock inside you, which you've just destroyed'. It's over-explained, but otherwise lithe and fresh. Indeed, almost every poem is littered with delightfully irreverent and apt images: a cue ball smashed 'round the rails like a light beam round a hall of mirrors', to drop 'the nine ball in the hole like a nudge into a lift shaft'; the old-before-his-time Chet Baker looking like Charles Manson. All the same, the most successfully cohesive of these poems is the shortest one, 'The Song of the Human': a self-deprecating miniature about remembering 'I am living in a glass box marked *Earth creature in his own habitat*'. The visitors have grown bored with 'the bald ape who sits all day / scratching at a piece of paper, eating sullenly from a cereal bowl, or playing his funny little twang-box', but 'I have become institutionalised and I am disinclined to wander far'. Again, this is most of us already, more or less, isn't it? And we *are* being watched...

If time permits, almost all of the finest poets stretch themselves in different directions at different times. Paterson is one of those, responsible for as many moving, memorable, sinewy poems as anyone of his generation. This long-winded collection doesn't contain many of them, and its too-cool-for-school swagger and shruggery can grate a little, but it certainly isn't the 'colossal fucking waste of time' one poem imagines a reviewer making of it.

Medbh McGuckian's fifteenth collection begins in a vein that will seem familiar to anyone acquainted with her work. A fashionable thing to say about some poetry, including McGuckian's, is that it resists interpretation – often code for a poetry of smoke and mirrors, naked emperors, and wizards ineffectually thumbing levers behind curtains. In fact, McGuckian is usually a poet worth struggling with. Her best poems – however short – are labyrinthine, multivalent structures. 'Almost Lost Poem', early in the book, has a flat, neutral tone, and begins as downtrodden *ars poetica*:

> How can we say something new
> with old words? Nothing is flatter
> than words on a piece of paper,
> gathered about one image
> designed to injure the air.

It doesn't stay there, of course, but quantum leaps across a mind to land on several of the poet's frequent preoccupations. I defy anyone to tell me what it all means, though the ineffable impression is vivid:

> A past too close, that singular,
> medieval autumn, reddening pictures
> of fire and night, the notched
> pear leaves, the botched resurrection.
>
> Bleached, arrested, almost paralysed,
> skies filled with water, the spreading darkness
> just grazing Christ and flooding
> on to His face's smooth features,
> subject only to death.

That said, this collection is often surprisingly direct in places. A number of the poems are elegies, many for dead Irish poets of McGuckian's generation. 'Elegy after Dennis O'Driscoll' is bluntly heartfelt, even if it lacks the mystique of the finest pieces here: 'Now there will be no more rave reviews / or birthday cards from 12 The Gallops', and a voice from Tipperary 'pours through my ear, saying, Dear, / forgive me for still being here'. The second of the book's four sections is in memory of Seamus Heaney who, as one piece puts it, 'churned what it is to be human'. This is more a gathering than a sequence, as multifaceted as any of McGuckian's work, and as meant and occasionally rhetorically overblown as Tennyson's *In Memoriam*:

> Now that the pageant and effort of his life
> are laid before us, as he retreats
> into the literary hinterland,
> I have the right to stay quiet in my corner.

This book's title isn't just pathetic fallacy, though the weather is certainly a leitmotif and metaphor. 'I shall have no more winter / this year, I thought it best / to omit the season', she writes, in 'The Seed Mantra: A Gift Poem':

> I went out in a fiery field
> to find a propitious name
> for a child in the four
> afterlife realms, and something
> was bestowed, a plaited blonde
> wave-shape in faded yellow.

'Marine cloud brightening' is the name for a scheme intended to reduce global warming by reflecting sunlight rather than absorbing it. 'There may be weather wars / as we weaponize the weather', here on 'earth / where all weather occurs', she warns in the title poem. This kind of ecological awareness and warning is also typical of McGuckian, an 'eco-poet' since before the badge for that was first made. So, on the whole, this collection is a continuation: the world has evidently shifted around her, but McGuckian's response to that is often as elusive, politicised, and not infrequently beguiling as ever.

Poetry Review, 2020

CANDID PAIN

Martha Sprackland, *Citadel* (Pavilion, 2020)

Many poems in *Citadel*, Martha Sprackland's full-length debut, appeared first in two pamphlets. Readers familiar with those will not be surprised to find a lot of apparently candid pain in this book, a lot of intricate, quizzical self-reckoning, akin more to Elizabeth Bishop or (dare I say it) Sylvia Plath than to anyone else writing now. 'What do I remember?' begins 'A Room in London', early in the book. The first answer is 'roommates'. Will this be pretty nostalgia? Hardly: 'I had […] an ache, a ferrous tongue, and then an orderly struggling to hold / my shoulders like the handles of a pneumatic drill / as she told me urgently what I already knew – / that *it's done*'.

Sprackland has spent a lot of time in Madrid, and Spain infuses many of her poems, most insistently through the poet's frequently surreal copresence with the sixteenth-century Queen Joanna of Castile, historically *Juana la Loca* (the Mad). In 'Juana and Martha in Therapy', the 'crackling string' of a 'makeshift telephone […] stretches five centuries' and 'They are in the bland room / above the Pret at Bishopsgate': 'The walls of the mind are deep and moated'. In 'Cocido Madrileño', 'Juana' buys modern tins of cocido and sits for stew: 'This, she believed, would sate her, save her.' Perhaps this will seem too self-absorbed for some tastes, but Sprackland is saved from naivety by her appealingly unostentatious self-awareness. Besides, she is far too interesting a poet simply to go around whacking obvious nails on the head.

There is plenty of thematic variety here, in any case. In 'Tooth', she wittily turns her gift for clarity on the all-conquering agony of toothache: 'Ed shifts and turns against me, / skin like cotton, outside the pain, / and says through sleep – / his clean sound mouth – / Honey, are you still sore? // I can't answer / round the cobblestone, / the ship, the choke, the pliers'. 'Melr' is a limpid coming of age sequence set against the backdrop of the Irish Sea:

there is an 'oil rig balanced / like a waterboatman on the meniscus' in childhood vision then, later, teenage evenings of 'hollering and bass thump // and the sound of seething water'. Everything glowed with a gleam. The lithe 'Dappled Things', about the birth of two nephews, is a note on growing beyond 'orchid skin [...] settling / as the blood learned more, as they became solid', to 'the dark / plumage – its graduation robe or city suit', and ends in unknowing aposiopesis. This is a startling debut collection: crisp and controlled, ceaselessly inquisitive, and often moving and empathetic.

Times Literary Supplement, 2020

MAKESHIFT FLAGS

Roger Robinson, *A Portable Paradise* (Peepal Tree Press, 2020)

The Trinidadian-British poet and musician Roger Robinson's third collection, the surprise winner of this year's T. S. Eliot Prize, is community-minded and contemporary, starkly plain-speaking and at times movingly surreal. In the opening poem, the first of several about the Grenfell Tower fire, 'A hundred people start floating / from the windows of a tower'; there is no ostensible outrage, just a moving, succinct vision. 'They are the city of the missing. / We, now, the city of the stayed', it ends. In the next, 'In the lights of mobile phones, / shadows wave makeshift flags, until they no longer wave them'. Then, a few pages later, in a poem about the posters of missing persons that covered nearby walls, 'as days went on, the wind blew most of them away'. The string of incessant monosyllables is geared to make it all seem so obvious, so inevitable. Robinson gives it to us straight – Grenfell is both a 'charred black tomb' and 'the charred gravestone' – but it is what he chooses not to spell out that is most affecting.

The same might be said about many pieces throughout the book, such as the three discursive poems called 'Citizen', dedicated to the black British poet 'Zena Edwards and her mother' who, like many others originally from Commonwealth territories, was recently required by British government policy to prove her right to residency: 'Warm up / them planes, boys, we are returning a cargo called / Windrush generation'. Or the prose poem 'Black Olive', a study in power play and subtext, in which the speaker finds himself talking to a 'white woman' at a literary party:

> I'm introduced to her as a writer and she is introduced to me as the director of a literary company. She picks up a black olive and says *Black olives are better than the rest aren't they. I love me some black*

olives and she pops it into her mouth and suddenly I am in her mouth bouncing off the soft trampoline of her tongue.

Is this the male gaze, or is it the white gaze? Both.

Unfortunately, the collection's many weaker poems (and there are quite a few of them) lack this complexity, this requirement for the reader to stay alert to nuance, and instead rely on listing occurrences, or telling us what we should probably know already in remarkably unadorned language. Robinson's enthusiasm for tackling almost any subject or style is laudable up to a point, but *A Portable Paradise* is as uneven as the Himalayas. The metrically wobbly 'Slavery Limerick' isn't a high point of wit, wisdom or imaginative engagement, and the poem in the voice of a perspicacious, ageing racehorse ('I'm a lowly beast without races to run, / soon to be sold as black market meat, / though racing blood still flows in my veins') reads like something done hurriedly for Creative Writing Club. There are quite a few editing mistakes, too: 'their silhouette fades', rather than 'their silhouettes fade'; 'Gluck' instead of 'Glück' in a dedication; and so on. These flimsier poems and myriad minor flaws aren't enough, luckily, to prevent some of the book from feeling about as socially necessary as contemporary poetry can feel.

Times Literary Supplement, 2020

A LIFELONG FAN

> Clive James, *Somewhere Becoming Rain: Collected Writings on Philip Larkin* (Picador, 2020)

Many readers are unshakeably devoted to Philip Larkin's poetry, and completely unswayed by modish notions that he was talentless, or that his personal proclivities should render his oeuvre unworthy of attention. The critic, poet and broadcaster Clive James, who died last November, was one of Larkin's most outspoken devotees, and it is fitting that his final book collects a lifetime's reflections on the writer he considered 'the greatest poet of his time'.

As this slim book was amassed in retrospect, we must forgive its repetitions. James's praise – and his criticism of Larkin's detractors – comes thick and fast, over and over, often repackaging the same points. Nonetheless, this volume has variety. James takes on not only Larkin's poetry, but also his fiction, jazz criticism ('Jazz is Larkin's first love and literature his first duty'), and legacy through Tom Courtenay's play *Pretending to Be Me* and the two major biographies. He also includes in facsimile three mildly diverting personal letters of admiration from Larkin, written in the slightly unbuttoned tone the older man reserved for acquaintances he liked. And he chucks in a gently parodic poem of his own, riddled with Larkinesque diction and observations: 'Ten years, was it?', 'Intangible revetments!' (He also includes a long and well-meant elegy that could happily be filed in the shredder along with most other well-meant elegies.) Mostly, though, this is a tribute to Larkin's poems. James is good at reminding us, in impassioned and empathetic ways, why and how Larkin's poetry was moving, multivalent and memorable: 'The desperation of "The Building" is like the desperation of Leopardi, disconsolate yet doomed to being beautiful. The advantage which accrues is one of purity – a hopeless affirmation is the only kind we really want to hear when we feel, as sooner or later everybody must, that life is a trap.'

'Like all good critics', James claims while discussing Larkin's reviews, 'Larkin quotes from a writer almost as creatively as the writer writes'. We might not entirely agree with this generalisation, of a kind James is wont to make, but certainly he is such a critic himself. He quotes frequently and appositely in favour of Larkin's lyrical grace, nuance, wit. The effect – and, one suspects, the aim – is to push the reader straight to Larkin. This is critical generosity. But James is also quite the wit himself: Larkin's compendium of salvaged ephemera, *Required Writing*, 'would be a treasure house even if every second page were printed upside down. Lacking the technology to accomplish this, the publishers have issued the book in paperback only, with no index.' He is also unusually observant. His parallels between Larkin and Montale are elucidating, for instance; as is his criticism of the 1988 *Collected Poems* edited by Anthony Thwaite: James carefully makes the case that Larkin's mature volumes are 'tightly integrated, making the feeling of falling apart fit together', and that in repositioning their poems in chronological order, alongside poems Larkin left out, 'that hard-fought-for poise is quite gone. Larkin now speaks a good deal less for us all, and a good deal more for himself': 'the question of how the suppressed poems should be published has now been answered: some other way than this'.

Nonetheless, James is usually a courteous critic: Thwaite is 'meticulous', and even Larkin's most recent and hagiographic biographer James Booth, though 'not very exciting', is 'an excellent guide to just why a Larkin poem can merit being called great'. James welcomes Booth's attempt at a corrective biography; it is just a shame he didn't write that book himself.

Times Literary Supplement, 2020

WE ONLY KNOW

> Raymond Antrobus, *All the Names Given*
> (Picador, 2021).

Raymond Antrobus's second collection of poems, a Poetry Book Society Recommendation, largely resembles his first. Again, we find many poems remembering the tensions of a family at once tumultuous and tender. One recalls asking his father how his parents' terminated relationship 'ever worked out': '*The sex* he smirked, *the sex / was that good*. I was twelve, and betrayed. But / I'd seen him in my mother's garden that / summer, growing sunflowers.' Another recounts how his father 'hit my pregnant mother / and my grandmother shouted *You black devil*'. There are moments of self-reproachment ('I'm one self-pitying prick of a son'), and several anecdotal poems reflecting, often tangentially and in combination, on the poet's identity: his 'Black / White' heritage, partial deafness, and Norse-origin name traced back to the village of Antrobus, Cheshire, where a farmer asks whether he is descended from 'Sir Edmund Antrobus, (3rd baronet) / slaver'; 'I shake my head'.

The book is more cohesive than Antrobus's debut: the 'caption poems' inspired by sound artist Christine Sun Kim (who, a note tells us, 'rewrites captioned text from films in order to revise the listening experience from hearing centric to Deaf centric') connect what might otherwise be the volume's sections of grouped poems. The best pieces are also more lithe and controlled than anything in his first book – 'At Every Edge', for example, which moves from past to present tense as it homes in on an encounter with a prison inmate during a writing workshop led by the speaker: 'his stubble sandpapered / my softer jaw. He tells me what he did'. But often the writing is too slack and plain, and sometimes too ostentatiously self-indulgent, to transmit much of what the poet evidently feels. 'Heartless Humour Blues' is a fine idea but strains every sinew to find its rhymes: 'My mother tried again and the next man abused her – // another man with a drink and cigarettes to drug, / laughed with my father's heartless sense of humour.' Another presumably unintentionally depicts a resurrection:

> When she died no giant
> monuments were passed
>
> our way. But she sat up
> in her hospital bed [...].

'How clearly I can hear her / and those children now', he writes at the end of the poem, but he doesn't do much to help us share the experience: we only know he had it. Antrobus has intriguing and moving stories, but these poems are regularly complacent in the telling of them.

Times Literary Supplement, 2021

BLESSED BREACH

Poetry Birmingham, issues 1–5

There's been a *Poetry London* since 1988; it took the name of the short-lived *Poetry London* of the 1940s. The title of this new quarterly, founded last year, hints at boldly comparable ambitions. The first issue of *Poetry Birmingham* includes this epigraph from Sir Philip Sidney's *The Defence of Poesy*, which might serve as an aspirational mission statement: 'Nature never set forth the earth in so rich / Tapestry as divers Poets have done'. If you think Birmingham an unlikely omphalos for a magazine with universal pretensions, the editors, Suna Afshan and Naush Sabah, probably have strong words for you: their first editorial is in part a paean to Birmingham, 'our city' of art and inspiration. But it is also a universal rallying cry, inspired by Donald Davie's 1980 consideration, published in *PN Review* in 1980, of the 'wish to *purify* poetry – to purify it of politics, of logic, of intentionality behind the poetic utterance, and consequently of any responsibility on the poet for what he utters'. 'Thus *purged*', wrote Davie, 'poetry does neither harm nor good; it can safely be ignored, compassionately tolerated, contemptuously complimented. Poetry's enemies, and poetry's false friends, ask nothing better. Poetry conceived of in this way will count for nothing in our corporate life; and it deserves to count for nothing.' 'Strains of this observation have cropped up in conversation between us for years now', write Afshan and Sabah. They hope that their magazine will serve as a corrective to a problem that, evidently, they feel either never went away, or has returned with force.

But does *Poetry Birmingham* fulfil that hope? It is beginning to. Each issue contains the work of nearly forty poets – a lot for a new little magazine. The few better-known ones in the first number, such as Alison Brackenbury and Gregory Leadbetter, are generally represented by very short poems, which suggests they might have been approached in an attempt to give the issue ballast. That sort of thing is perfectly normal for a new venture in the poetic cottage industry, and it is what a little magazine does thereafter that typically determines whether it becomes a part of the culture. Happily, Afshan and Sabah know how to take their time in a hurry, and every issue is an improvement on the last in terms of quality, and a real variety show of styles.

The fourth, for example, begins with three engrossing poems by the underrated experimentalist Khaled Hakim, including the witty and pointed 'Commoner' ('goo up to a bunch of alders & ask them *Wat ar yu doing here* – then ask them to sine a petisshon agenst th bypass & pin an Anarkhy badg on thir throte / look, dere are literaly cuples of peple dispoiling da fens th qwiksands th lickwifyd sheep & cows of commoners / they too are abzorbed in natur thir senses speking synasthezia all leeding to þe wonpoyntedness of – *How can I fit this into a funding applicashiun?*' Hakim's work is followed by a cutely observed, more traditional lyric by Imogen Forster (who is yet to publish a book), in which everything is imperfect, claustrophobic until 'in a flood of honeyed light, / a line of trees turns golden': 'We stand still, making that / rift, that blessed breach, / the day's whole reason.' Later in the issue we find strong and varied poems by Isobel Dixon, Khairani Barokka and Jessica Mookherjee, all unfashionable but substantial poets who belong to different parts of the largely unseen backbone of our poetry culture, and a host of highlights from less established poets writing in myriad traditions.

Very quickly, then, *Poetry Birmingham* has become a magazine in which a promising variety of poets evidently want to be seen. And no wonder, for Afshan and Sabah are to poetry magazines, in our times, what an opened window is to a sweaty room. Their often intellectually lithe and provocative editorials prove it, each a passionate and measured meditation on the art and its contexts: 'This is a literary culture too contingent on nebulous avowals of acclaim or censure [...]. There's a renewed need for editorial attention based on the specifics of poems,' Ashfan writes in the third issue. 'I see the melting pot that is Oxbridge', Sabah writes in the fourth: 'I am looking at publishers' lists and seeing Oxbridge colleges, Instagram/Twitter follower numbers, adopted performative identities and their branding.' This is unusually spirited in our frequently invertebrate age.

The magazine is attractively produced, and substantial, each issue containing about a hundred pages, with the last few left blank for your notes in all but the fifth and most recent issue. That's a novel idea, and probably doesn't deserve to catch on. The first four issues contain no critical prose, and while some magazines might benefit from swapping their reviews section for a few empty sheets, it is hard not to feel that presenting criticism only in editorial monologue isn't quite in keeping with this project's inherent spirit of plurality and, well, 'impurity'. But new little magazines can struggle to attract good prose. The fifth issue – slightly larger in format than the previous four – is the first to include criticism, and comes good on a promise: 'Last autumn, we expressed a sense of duty towards robust criticism', write the editors in a slightly belaboured introduction, 'and we publish, here, our first attempt at discharging that duty.' Several of the reviews engage in dialogue beyond the magazine's pages, as does Hakim's review of Rishi Dastidar, Nisha Ramayya and Bhanu Kapil: 'There are reviews of *Saffron Jack* which outline the 'plot' and themes without a word on it as 'poetry'. Is that where I got the idea of it as a mutated novel?' The prose is pleasingly eclectic: there is also a short article by Colin Bancroft on Robert Frost and astronomy that might usefully have been a little longer, and an entertaining and informative 'conversation' between the poets Roger Robinson and David Wheatley, as well as several pieces by first-time critics, most of whom have something to say and all of whom have evidently been given the freedom to say it. *Poetry Birmingham* seems to be in the process of augmenting its increasingly impressive spread of poetry with the kind of incisive and dynamic critical section that has gone missing a little in some glitzier forums in recent years.

Times Literary Supplement, 2021

ON 'LIKE FATHER'

Shortly after the Autumn 2019 *Poetry* Review appeared, the poet Katy Evans-Bush wrote on Facebook: 'Rory Waterman's poem in *Poetry Review*. Consider this a standing ovation'. This was lovely to read, but the poem makes me nervous, so it also gave me an anxious jolt. I'm fairly private, and the poem is not; what if someone asks me about it? Someone then speculated about the poem, at which point I said I'd rather offer no comment. 'No, let the poem stand', wrote Katy. Yes, and thank you. Then, a few days later, *Poetry Review* asked me for a piece on the poem, and I decided to do it – though that eventually fell through. Still, it seemed I did want to offer commentary after all, and now that poem has appeared in my new collection, *Sweet Nothings*, it seems right to resurrect that commentary. Yes, poems should stand on their own; but that doesn't mean I should hide behind one when invited not to – especially one that is so obviously autobiographical. I hope what follows doesn't sound too prim. Any lack of detail is an attempt to ensure the poem does indeed stand, without this inadvertently seeming like an attempt to provide a full and necessary counterpart.

I was born in Belfast, and my dad taught at the University of Ulster. My mum – his fourth wife – left him when I was two, moving us to her mother's house in Lincolnshire: a tiny cottage a mile from the nearest village. This was devastating for him. The comment in the poem about my grandmother's teeth refers to an incident a little later, when my father broke into that house through a window, leaving a rental car full of nappies down the lane, and was arrested. I'd seen this unfold, of course, and my earliest memory is of believing I had a 'good daddy' and a 'bad daddy', two entirely separate people; my mum convinced me I'd never have to see 'bad daddy' again, but I did, eventually. We had trees and Victorian metal fences and a mystically dark water-butt and an untidy garden full of herbs and vegetables, and not quite enough money. Nan slept on a fold-out armchair in the living room, right until her final trip to hospital. That is the kind of woman she was, but she died when I was 15 and I never did much to repay her, which has grown into one of my biggest regrets. My childhood was punctuated by custody and access hearings (about which my father kept me rather too well informed in ways that suited him, and my mother said nothing), monthly weekends with my dad in English guest houses (I'd been made a ward of court and couldn't leave England and Wales until I was 10) then also longer stays in Ireland, and simmering resentment at the adult world of those I had repeatedly been told had abducted me from my rightful Irish home. I hated (and loved) those loveable women. It was, I firmly believed, all their fault I wasn't 'normal' – a concept I had been conditioned to hold dear, not understanding it doesn't really exist. 'There's nobody nice for me here', I'd scream at my mother as a five- or six-year-old when the taxi dropped me off from another access visit. 'You're not nice and Nanny's not nice. I hate you. I want to be with Daddy in Ireland.' And then I'd burst into tears and run for a big cuddle and she'd read me Beatrix Potter.

My dad was my immaculate, otherworldly hero until, between about the ages of 10 and 13, I started to work out, and learn first-hand, that the truth was more complicated. Having my own mind did not always go down well with him, and I was an assiduous cross-examiner because the things he said rarely matched up very well with the things I was beginning to see or think for myself. We learn to improve our behaviour, in part, by recognising when and how we have messed things up and wanting to fix them, and people who never recognise their worst mistakes or tendencies for what they are lack the capacity to do better in future. The bad things simply never happened, and you are wrong. You can't just shut up, either: you must agree you are wrong. The new truth must be observed. Reality is a construct. By then, I had seen many things no child should see, one way or another, and had felt or witnessed an almost infinite array of manipulations. But I loved my dad, and I knew he loved me. We did nice things together. He taught me so much. And he was convincing, too – almost impossible not to believe. I'd also falteringly come to the realisation that we had many of the same interests. In some ways, at least, I really was a hell of a lot like him, I thought – just not as good at anything. We always had something to talk about, to laugh about.

And then, as I stumbled through two sets of A levels (flunking the first ones) and tried to be the frontman in what I thought was a punk band, I wrote several mawkish, immature poems, some of them about my complicated relationship with my father. I had feelings to explore, and not just those concerning my raging teenage hormones. Writing poems might help me to understand them. I liked the quiet and graft, the solipsism of the act, and the way things I hadn't known I'd thought would emerge, however awkwardly expressed, in the extremely private notebook in front of me. I knew the poems wouldn't be much cop, but I didn't have an audience in mind so that didn't matter.

By the time I came to write the first poems that would make it into my first collection *Tonight the Summer's Over*, a decade or so later, I was in some ways a different human, who felt more valid and stable. I'd long since moved past those early 'poems'. I could barely remember them, and certainly didn't care to. However, I did write some new ones about my upbringing, about five of which made it into the collection. Having then felt I'd moved past all of that, I didn't touch upon the subject again for a decade: my second book *Sarajevo Roses* is mute on it. At one reading for that collection, a well-meaning older woman in the audience proclaimed: 'You say you don't write poems about your childhood any more. But they're the ones I *like*'. Fair enough, I thought, but 'Woe is me' is a terrible look for a poet, and Daddy issues do not a poem make. I'm now a balding man in his late thirties! And there's nothing new I can say about it. I suggested she not bother with my second book, and I think she took the advice.

I don't want to repeat myself in collection after collection. Some poets do just that, which is why much of the modishly insular poetry of our times is bound to blow itself out on a principle of diminishing returns. But there are things I didn't say in those earlier poems, not for 'artistic reasons' but because I had a relationship to maintain with my father. That relationship finally broke down, and has since been carted off: he has developed alcoholic dementia and has been confined to a nursing home in Norwich. I visit often, we talk about airbrushed versions of my childhood and his and not at all about anything since then apart from football, and periodically he shouts impotently: *There is nothing wrong with me. You should take me home immediately you useless cunt. You are a cunt. What are we talking about? You're a good lad, son.* I have no power to remove him from the nursing home, because he has given that power to someone else who wants him to stay there – but that is a different story.

The poem slightly predates my father's 'hideous inverted childhood', my reconciliation with a man who doesn't remember there is anything to reconcile and would've pretended there wasn't if he did. About a year ago, a friend and poet I trust commented that there must be more I want to write about my childhood, and that it's a shame I haven't tried. This was a small thing to say, but it had a big impact. Perhaps the time is right, and I have another poem about this in me, I thought. On my next visit to my mother's house in Lincolnshire, I went digging in drawers, found my heartfelt teenage gibberish, cracked new joints in my toes while reading it, and decided to make a palimpsest – to have a conversation with myself then and myself now. That became 'Like Father'. I hoped it would connect with others – and had it not, it wouldn't really have been a poem at all. My formative experiences were less difficult than many people's. I'm not exceptional. But that probably has something to do with why the poem seems to work for some readers.

The Friday Poem, 2021

(GOOD) PERSON POEMS

The host lets me into the reading just in time. The little wheel spins and suddenly a huge happy face fills my laptop. 'Our first reader is the wonderful [X], who has just published a debut pamphlet, *Pieces of My Big Heart*, with Fuzzy Emotions Press. I'm *so* excited to see this.' He puts his hands together and smiles like a cartoonish primary school teacher. Simpsons hand-clap emojis fire off across the screen as it switches to the moving mugshot of a smart-shirted [X], camera slightly off-centre to reveal a Telecaster on its stand, a Velux window framing some foliage, a bit of bookshelf. The poet smiles back, thanks the host, thanks the audience, waves the new pamphlet at the screen, opens it, and settles suddenly into a meditative stare.

'My poem is for [Y]. They have recently experienced [Z].'

He then follows with some proclamation about equality, leavened with a declaration that he is working class, and another that he can't speak for communities to which he doesn't belong. It's very wholesome.

Good poems have been written about [Y] and [Z], but I quickly discover that this is not one of them, and that the introduction was a perfect précis of the poem. It keeps on coming, simply and solemnly, for the allotted seven minutes, at which point the host once again says how wonderful the poet is, before moving on to the next poet, who is equally wonderful. Messages in the chat amplify the wonder. 'Thanks', I write. One should be encouraging. It is nice to be nice. We are social animals, just as we are selfish readers.

I have altered a few details, but they are minor. You have probably experienced something like this several times during the past year and a half of Zoom obligations, and might not have listened as attentively as you pretended to have done. [X] could be any poet invited to do a reading at any point in the history of poetry readings. Hosts are not supposed to show their powers of discernment when introducing poets. Again: we are social animals. [␣Y] and [Z] are real people and circumstances that do merit attention. The attention the poet has given them is what everyone in attendance already thinks anyway, or at least knows they are supposed to think: the boundaries are often blurry.

In the example that comes most readily to mind, I certainly agreed with the poet, and on some level that has nothing whatsoever to do with poetry. I was glad the poet seemingly cared about these circumstances at least as much as I do. But the poem simply told us that the poet is a Good Person. We learned nothing else from it, and the [Y] presumably went on not knowing that they had had a poem written for them and read out in a leafy London suburb, with the poet placed front and centre as a self-proclaimed working-class ambassador with a pamphlet and Twitter profile to promote.

Good Person Poems are usually in the first person, which seemed unfashionable when I started taking a keen interest in contemporary poetry. 'Why should a reader care about the poet?', a then-modish poet told me fifteen or so years ago. Anyone familiar with my poems will be aware that I don't tend to agree with this view. In any case, the first person is back with a vengeance, emboldened by the kind of right-thinking that now dominates many corners of arty social media where what happened a couple of decades ago has been forgotten. Its lyric *I*s might be sages, inquisitors, examiners, but they are rarely flawed beings. After all, it is dangerous to reveal personal moral complexities and inconsistencies: one might be accused of some kind of impropriety. But nobody really wants to read poems that avoid moral complexity, do they? 'What oft was thought but ne'er so well expressed' does not mean 'what oft is agreed with and that is that'. And while I want to live my life to the best of my moral ability, I also don't want to avoid examining my failures in poems I write about myself.

I recently had a slightly beery conversation with a good friend who also happens to be an editor. As we talked, he mentioned several poems that had affected him particularly deeply in his youth, and we spiralled out from that point. Douglas Dunn's 'Terry Street Poems' from the collection *Terry Street* did as much as anything to make my friend fall in love with the art. That is not simply a sequence in which a working-class community is documented and adored; it is quizzical, at times self-consciously othering in its compassion. Tony Harrison's 'v.' spoke to my friend's own disenfranchisement. In part, it is a poem about meeting your alter ego and realising he is a racist thug so perhaps you might have become one too under different circumstances, about feeling as though you have let down your parents in a way that is inescapable, about moving beyond your working class community and as a result not quite having a community any more, about that community changing and those you love not being ready to accept it, about a nostalgia that implies you might not quite be ready to accept it yourself.

In the sort of quantum leap that occurs in rapid conversation, I then brought up Carrie Etter's 'Greek Salad', one of the outstanding poems from her collection *Imagined Sons*. In it, the child she gave birth to as a teen and 'gave up' for adoption comes back 'brutally transformed' as a talking olive; she silences him by swallowing it whole. Then we moved on to Togara Muzanenhamo's *Gumiguru*, and in particular the short poem 'Kubvumbi', in which the speaker sleeps 'with a layered peace' beside his newborn as farmers outside the window curse the floods that ruin their crops. R. S. Thomas's uncompromising poems after the death of his wife were mentioned next, and then Hardy's poems of 1912–13. These poems, at least in large part, are motivated by regret, and acute awareness of personal shortcomings. And Hardy led to Larkin: 'a bastard, but what a poet!', opined the friend/editor, simplifying in a way that always makes me a little uncomfortable. His evidence? 'Love Again', Larkin's last significant poem, which perhaps does as good a job as any poem can do of nailing personal flaws and demonstrating how unhappy they can leave you. Finally, we talked about Elizabeth Bishop's 'One Art', to my mind the finest poem I know about not quite facing up to assumed losses, which uses its slightly broken repetends to force home like a screw what is, to the speaker, still – at least performatively – ineffable.

A poem, even one that seemingly implicates its author, doesn't need any of these self-chastising tensions in order for us to respond to it with something more than a nod of moral approval. However, it is perhaps surprising how many have one as their engine, and how few of them would have been written if their authors had fought against the risk of appearing 'problematic'. Poets who self-consciously avoid that can never appeal to the sense of self-reproach that most of us experience frequently. They can't speak directly to our constant search for self-improvement either, which is ironic.

All of the poems I've mentioned have a huge, knotty tension at their heart, of one kind or another. By refusing the modern, statesperson-like ambition to give voice to a community or simplified grievance, they give voice to a facet of humanity. They aren't resolved, and in fact they can't be resolved. All of them make me want to cry, or laugh, or both. I carry many of them with me wherever I go, for a good short poem can be taken anywhere whole in a brain, unlike almost any other type of work of art. None can be summed up sufficiently in prose. None is concerned with making me admire the morality of its author, though they display the moral strength of honesty. If you respond to them as I do, as the editor I mention does, it will be because of what they do to you. And, when the seal-clapping has finished and the show has gone on and on, I suspect they will still be remembered.

'Happiness writes white', said Larkin (the bastard) in an interview, shortening Henry de Motherlant's aphorism '*Le bonheur écrit à l'encre blanche sur des pages blanches*' ('Happiness writes white ink on a white page'). That isn't always true, but usually – perhaps too frequently – it is. At present, sanctimonious certainty frequently writes straight into the notes feature of an iPhone or perhaps a Word doc in black 12pt and is then stapled or perfect-bound, bearing the name of one of an apparently endless conveyance of avowedly unimpeachable poets who will not be remembered in two decades' time when they have succumbed to the ageist cult of newness they seem so keen to embrace. You can apply your own list of poets to this, and I invite you to wait and see which of them will still be read twenty years from now. The best poets of any age challenge that age, but they are also not afraid to challenge themselves.

Poetry London, 2021

N.B. This piece received a lot of praise online; it then, in turn, provoked considerable condemnation on Twitter, including accusations of 'dog whistles' for various bigotries. At least one of the vicariously aggrieved threatened to try to get me fired from my job, and another accused me of taking aim at the working class, which indicates that she at least glanced at the article, but didn't actually read it. The editor who commissioned it (based on a conversation we had had), André Naffis-Sahely, had warned me this sort of thing might happen: we are in strange times. People inclined to behave in such ways rarely read books or journals, I suspect, but the article was published online as an op-ed, and was therefore shareable on social media. This experience hardened my resolve to say what I think to be true.

I WAS NOTHING BUT A HERETIC CORMORANT

Steve Ely, *The European Eel* (Longbarrow, 2021)

On the front flap of Steve Ely's *The European Eel*, Matthew Gollock (*not* Pollock) writes: 'I remember [Ely] saying how he felt European eels had "chosen" him as a subject – in part due to his name'. We call this nominative determinism, and it is indeed odd how often a person's job or pursuit corresponds with the name with which he or she has been bestowed: Arsene Wenger becoming the longest-serving manager of Arsenal FC, Bernie Madoff running the largest Ponzi scheme ever, Boris (as we are encouraged to refer to him) consistently proving himself to be a Johnson, with a Johnson that should have got him in a lot more trouble than it has, because he is as slippery as a proverbial eel.

And I have digressed already. But this is somewhat in keeping with the book in question, which weaves in and out of its ostensible subject with eel-like acuity. In three parts, it imagines an eel's birth in the Sargasso Sea and journey to the Yorkshire pool where Ely captures her for a summer, and then her route back again to the spawning ground. The poem, all fifty pages of it, is in loose blank verse: not metrical, quite, but faltering around five-stress lines. The effect is frequently frenetic:

> [...] billions more
> track east along the Channel, in the rumbling
> diesel effluent of the 'busiest sea lane in the world',
> its freight of towering container ships,
> the rise and swell of Afghan refugees.
> Onward they flow, making five or six miles daily;
> over Hurd's Deep – where the MoD
> dumped its phosgene shells and plutonium-239 –
> and the paleo-valleys and fossil meanders
> of the Weichselian Glacial Maximum.

> In the Wreckage of Dunkirk and 1588,
> they bury themselves among pieces of eight
> and the little boat bones of drunken sailors.

'I'm making it up as they go along', he writes later in the poem: 'Almost nothing demonstrated, almost / everything inferred'. Indeed, we have thus far learned little about how European eels behave in maturity in the wild – and I know this because Ely tells us in a copious section of notes at the end, which also help us to make sense of some of the poem's more esoteric references. In any case, human lives are happening around the eel and her coincidental fellow travellers without being aware they are doing so. And as the ever-dwindling shoal pushes its way up (and eventually back down) the Humber, River Don, and a series of ever-smaller tributaries, in frantic, semi-submerged counterpart to Alice Oswald's bucolic if uncompromising *Dart*, the 'survivors persist' despite significant despoliation: 'blue shit seeped from chemical toilets', 'grey froth of used condoms and sanitary towels', 'Nitram, Roundup, / Viroxide Super, Supalyx Equine Mineral Lick'. Eventually, they find cleaner water, where they wait 'buried under banks, in the clefts of rootballs, / wherever the beck finds a yard or so of depth', including the specific star of the show, who 'knots her tail / in the crevice of a rootball and pokes out / her gape in a predatory billow of breathing'.

The poem's short metapoetic middle movement is a pause for breath in prose, an account of taking custody for the purposes of what we might call 'poetic inquiry' (and what Ely's managerial apparatchiks at Huddersfield University, where he teaches Creative Writing and which he thanks for a 'small research grant', might term 'a research output'): *I tipped her in, and watched her circle in whiplash panic the walls of her glassy cage. "Just for the summer", I told her. "Just for the poem. You'll be back in your pool by autumn."* Without labouring his point, the speaker invites us to consider our unwelcome intrigues, and attempts to bring us eye to eye with a being we can never understand, whatever we might known 'I was nothing but a heretic cormorant, one that toyed and would not kill, unaccountably parallel with her living.' The third part of the poem then returns us to the form of the first, and follows the eel back out on her onward journey. The poem is again in the third person, as she shoots 'from the H&B culvert like a cork', out into the swell, and eventually back to the wide Sargasso where the life cycle begins anew with

                                        gusher
after gusher of glittering golden ova,
sparks from the cornucopian flame
of Archaea's unkillable, dark pleroma,
quickening though the mist of sperm and rising
through the photocline to join the thermonuclear
microplankton of the drifting epipelagic.

But, I imagine many of you thinking, I'm not very interested in the minutiae of an eel's existence, and certainly don't want to read an entire book about it. Poetry doesn't work quite like this, though, does it? We turn to poetry, those of us who do, in part because of the euphoric quantum leaps of semiotics a good poem might cajole our brains into making. The mind's eye can do things the body's eyes cannot. The mind's eye can be given a fleeting glimpse through another – even a very other – mind's eye. Ely's command of image is such that he can achieve this, and often does, as above.

In Ely's native Yorkshire, and in the company of the poet Matthew Welton, I recently attended the ceremony for the Laurel Prize: 'an annual award for the best collection of nature or environmental poetry to highlight the climate crisis and raise awareness', as the prize's website puts it. Simon Armitage introduced proceedings, and told us how important he thinks the award is; Seán Hewitt won with his celebrated debut collection *Tongues of Fire*, published by Cape. Ely's book was published at almost the exact cut-off point for this year's shortlist, might be eligible for the next, and would be a worthy winner. That won't happen: he is one of the country's several perennially overlooked poets who doesn't deserve to be, a true original with a voice and a mind all his own. At fifty pages, the poem in places feels too long, and yet it remains engrossing, fevered, and rich with image, allusion, truth, and imaginative fabrication. It does not need them, but is accompanied by seventeen pleasingly ethereal full-page monochrome artworks by P. R. Ruby: on one, a map of the Humber is laced with a huge eel and trees and wind turbines apparently constructed from calendars and tape measures; on another, a lattice of pale eel stencils rubs out the background murk. This is an attractive, odd, fulfilling volume.

The Friday Poem, 2021

ENDLESS PRESENT

Martyn Crucefix, *Cargo of Limbs* (Hercules Editions, 2019); Monika Cassel, *Grammar of Passage* (Flap, 2020)

In our current cultural moment, we are fervently encouraged – by corporations, much of the media, some politicians and definitely not others – to focus (often superficially) on certain kinds of inequality at home, or in America. Others are routinely ignored. So, often, are the lessons we might learn from the past. And so, increasingly, is whatever is happening anywhere else in the world, however awful it might be. (Tigray, anyone?) In this review, I want to draw attention to two pamphlets that engage perceptively and meaningfully with, respectively, fraught places and times that are not our own. We might learn from thinking about them, but these pamphlets are the work of poets, not proselytisers, and what we take from their works is up to us.

Martyn Crucefix's *Cargo of Limbs*, a long poem in sometimes disorienting short-lined quatrains, takes as inspiration Aeneas's journey into the Underworld in Book VI of the *Aenead* to depict the plights of Syrian refugees in the Mediterranean during the refugee crisis that we are now implicitly encouraged to believe has ended. The narrator is an on-scene photojournalist who, at the end of the poem, is relieved of his camera by Andras – the poem's Aeneas? – who is also a journalist:

> I raise my camera still
>
> he lifts his feeble hand
> and by what rule say
> by what moral right
> does he smash it to the ground

The narrator is a coolly objective character, eye to viewfinder, and Andras a man of empathy. The narrative is caught between two ways of witnessing and recording, as well as between recording and experiencing. It is frenetic, purposefully confused in places, a running set of fragmentations, and hard to focus on in one sitting – though it begs to be read that way, and at a speed to induce anxiety:

> she pummels her breasts
> on his cheek yellow dust
> of poison breeze running
>
> into the trunks of trees
> suddenly blind shrieking
> before the militia –
> shaken from mattress
>
> Old Age scarcely able
> forced at gunpoint
> a pink nightdress hurried
> under tarpaulins on flat-
>
> bed trucks eyes steeled

I am not convinced the poem would work very well on its own: this sort of writing, emotive though it can be and in this case often is, can all too easily seem like a banal thought exercise, untethered emotionally to the circumstances that occasioned it. However, *Cargo of Limbs* is a particularly successful multimedia collaboration, and the poem is shown to best advantage. Hercules Editions pamphlets are beautiful little square booklets, just long enough to be perfect-bound. The poems Hercules publishes are always matched with the work of visual artists – in this case, often clandestine-seeming, awkward-angled stills from the superb documentary *Purple Sea* (2019). As Amel Alzacout, who took them, says in an endnote to the volume, 'I had with me' – at the Turkish port city of Izmir and on a 'small wooden boat' intended for Lesbos – 'an action camera which I tied to my wrist and hid under my jacket sleeve. Smugglers usually confiscate mobile phones or cameras if they spot someone filming'. In apparently out-of-sequence images we see queues of would-be refugees as shadows, a tantalising view of Greece from a dusty concrete harbour wall, the boat filling with sparkling seawater. It is the perfect accompaniment, from an artist apparently poised between the perspectives of the poem's two main characters.

There are many frenetic moments too in the American poet Monika Cassel's debut pamphlet, *Grammar of Passage*. The opening poem, 'Arrival', is one long sentence of impressions and movement:

> a kiss on my grandmothers' cheek – high up and surprisingly soft in
> the face with the stern eyes, forbidding lips – white-tablecloth
> lunch of Kassler Rippchen und Sauerkraut on the balcony with a
> quick sip of mother's beer, parges puttering coal-smoke along the
> Rhine below, and a nap behind the rattling jalousies that admit
> only particles of afternoon light […]

What follows is a series of ten poems, each an atmospheric glimpse of a family caught up in Nazi Germany and its aftermath, and each dated to between 1941 and 1956, with two further poems set in the twenty-first century at the end. Several are presented as what might be directions for a screenplay:

> Cut to a boy pulling a dachshund on a leash,
> cut to soldiers
> marching ten Russian POWs down the street.
>
>   On the street, deep-gabled houses.
>
> Cut to the kids who play
> in the dirt lane by the iron fence,
> to my mother, two years old,

rubbing her eyes (she's crying),
her flowered pinafore
fastened over her sweater.

This style almost eliminates editorialising, of course, and allows Cassel to present emotive circumstances as unencumbered as possible by the contexts in which we usually put them. We are never told what to think, but are instead encouraged to understand that the quotidian aspects of life might be harder for some to navigate than almost any of the rest us can imagine. We sympathise with the family, though at the same time we can never quite be sure of the extent of their complicity. In 'Thrift, ca. 1946',

She made me a new red dress
when the schools opened again:
pulled the old flag out from a drawer,
clipped the stitches
from the circle in the center, held it up […]
A lot of girls wear red
these days.

The last two poems maroon all of this in the uncanny past. In the title poem, subtitled 'train through south Germany', we move through 'ancestral fields' and 'past a brewery, past warehouses', speeding 'towards, away, unknown – / each second we articulate, it changes':

Everything's punctuation, a *there* and *there* and *there*,
the apple trees arrayed across a hill,
the now now now of the pigeons who strut the city platform
an endless present, heads a-bobbing as they range:
They're here, they change.

It's not perfect, is it? 'That', not 'who', would be preferable grammatically – the irony! – and surely 'bobbing' would do on its own. But it is still vivid, and emotionally complex, and truthfully unresolved.

PN Review, 2021

ANDREW WATERMAN, 1940–2022

Below is the text of the eulogy delivered at my father's funeral at Colney Woods Burial Ground, Norwich, on 8 February 2022. He contributed to this magazine regularly for decades, from its inception until 2012. This was the year in which Carcanet ceased to publish his books, which he took as an affront. His final collection, By the River Wensum, *was published by Shoestring Press in 2014. He leaves behind a hurricane of difficulties that do not receive mention in the text below. Lazy comparisons between his poetry and mine often frustrate me, though I accept they are inevitable. And, much as I loved him, I hope nobody ever has cause to draw many non-poetic comparisons between us.*

*

This is the right place for my father's funeral, though sadly he has never been here before today. His best friend, at least as far as my father was concerned – who was one of the kindest men I've ever met and a true father and husband – passed away last summer, and had a very moving, well-attended funeral right here. Sadly, despite my best efforts, my father was unable to attend it, for reasons some of you know about. But that evening on the phone, as my partner and I stopped in Kings Lynn on our way back home to Nottingham, he asked me to describe the funeral to him. My father had an excellent imagination, so I'd like to think he saw it anyway, in his mind's eye.

My dad was born in London in 1940, just after the Phoney War had come to an end and just before the Blitz began. He was born to Irish parents, one of whom he later got to know and whom I called granddad. But he was adopted, and grew up mainly with his adoptive mother, my gran born in 1900, and then his younger sister – his wonderful younger sister. Until 9, he lived in Woodford, North London, with both adoptive parents, and then his mother moved with the two children to Croydon. He never saw his father again.

His favourite childhood pursuits were things like: climbing trees in Epping Forest, and later playing tennis in Ashburton Park; inventing tinpot dictatorships and then going to pretend war with his friend Chris (my dad's was Ludicrania, Chris's was Plonkvitia); running long distance races (pretty well, I gather); and, briefly, playing in a skiffle group, though he freely admitted to having no aptitude for music whatsoever, much as he liked listening to it. (When I was a child he'd give me tapes of folk music that he'd made, and later blues, both faces of each cassette bearing his characteristic almost-illegible scrawl of song titles on a thick layer of Tippex.) He was always the sort of person who'd like to have a go at things. But his childhood was complex, and so was he. At 17, and being a troubled and troublesome adolescent, he was ordered by police to leave the family home, and began several years of working at various jobs: bank clerk, bookshop worker, hotel porter. He took A Levels in his early twenties, then went to the University of Leicester to study English. He then began a DPhil on the poet Edward Thomas at Oxford, but left without finishing, because he'd secured a job as a lecturer in English at the New University of Ulster – first in Derry, and then in Coleraine. He arrived in 1968, just before the Troubles began in earnest.

In 1974, he published his first book of poems, *Living Room*, with Marvell Press. It was the first of ten books: eight collections, a *Selected Poems* and a *Collected Poems*. My dad was talented with words, the sleights they afforded, the control they gave him. Often, he rewrote truths, making them more manageable, then believing them. But he could also be poignant, moving, and funny: in one poem about gardening, he wrote: 'Concrete the bloody things over and leave yourselves free'. He might have said the same as a metaphor for the things he had done and seemed so capable of forgetting he'd done. But I think his reputation as a poet deserves to be higher than it now is.

He met my mother, his fourth wife, in 1980, when he was

exactly the age I am now. Soon she was pregnant. His friends in Ireland hoped it would settle him, but it didn't: he wasn't one for being settled. She left him in 1983, and took me, a toddler, a wee wain, with her to Lincolnshire (thankfully). I think it is this distance that helped my childhood experiences of him to be so overwhelming, and they still are in my mind.

I'll always remember with passion our short, intense access visits when I was a small child, in Lincoln and elsewhere – including often here in Norwich. Him hiding behind the statue of King George III in Lincoln Castle and pretending to answer my questions in a gruff voice. Us making paper boats, decorating them with silly pictures, and racing them between bridges of the River Witham, unless the swans got them first. Him scurrying with me through the canopies of trees in the treehouses in the grounds of Belton House near Grantham. And, though I didn't then understand the implications, us sitting a while of an afternoon in the lounge of the Wig and Mitre pub in Lincoln, a pint on his side of the sticky little table, a glass of gloopy pineapple juice and ice cubes on mine, and a bag of cheese and onion crisps, dry roasted peanuts, or whatever gaping in the middle.

And we'd go to football sometimes. He took me to my first game in 1988, at Carrow Road, with his friend Chris. Norwich lost 1–0 to Liverpool, and Chris got me Kenny Dalglish's autograph – but from that moment on, I was a Canary, and from that moment on, so was my dad. Have a little scrimmage, dad. Never mind the danger. He always wanted us to cram as much as possible into those special monthly access visits and he was, in that respect, an inspiration.

He also told me, very frequently, that Ireland was my 'real home'. He'd put green t-shirts on me, emblazoned with the word 'IRELAND', and then take them back at the end of the weekend, because he said my mother would destroy them if he didn't. He also taught me words: judge, social worker, affidavit. I was semi-fluent in legalese at a surprisingly tender age. And I remember him proudly showing me a newspaper report, after he'd had a punch up at work with the Dean of Humanities. I didn't understand it, being about five at the time, but he assured me it was hilarious. This might not sound like excellent parenting. And it wasn't. But, along with the force of his personality, it all conspired to make him my hero when I was a little boy. He belonged to another planet, and I wanted to go there, and he wanted me to go there, and wanting didn't stop us from doing. Soon enough, I'd start to see him a little more as others did. And he didn't like that.

At the age of 50, my dad was registered as a blind person, due to glaucoma. But he would downplay the blindness, telling people that – and I quote, I heard it often enough – 'in practice, I'm partially sighted.' How can anyone not admire that spirit? He didn't let partial blindness stop him doing *anything*. We'd hurtle up mountains in England and Ireland together, or navigate villages and towns and ruins and coasts in various parts of Britain and later continental Europe, his hand hooked in my arm so I might guide him. He'd take solitary holidays when I was in my twenties, and once strode purposefully off a jetty by mistake, landed up to his chest in water, clambered out, and walked back to his hotel, where he stood dripping in the lobby, proffered his hand for his key, and went back to his room. He'd fractured a bone in the process, but he thought the story at least equal parts funny and annoying, and told it to everyone for a year, punctuated by his characteristic abrupt laugh, the laugh he would use in any situation he thought warranted it, whether justified or not.

He retired in 1998, by then a senior lecturer, and moved to Norfolk – first to Cromer, where we'd spent lots of time when I was a child, and then to Norwich, essentially because his friends Chris and Joan lived here. He never returned to Ireland, and kept no friends there. Having not ever travelled abroad until the age of 42, with my mum and baby me to Austria, and rarely since, he felt he had some catching up to do, so he began going to different parts of Europe, and decided to learn Italian. He carried on writing poems. He listened to England cricket test matches whatever time of day or night, which I'll happily admit meant nothing to me, and to Norwich City games every week, after which he'd call and tell me excitedly what he knew I'd just seen or heard myself. It was a weekly ritual for decades, as the Canaries bounced around the leagues like a pinball. The last football match we went to together was about a decade ago, and he wore a radio headset tuned into Radio Norfolk, which I'd borrowed from my kind and beautiful mum. He could barely see the pitch, of course, even though we sat about three rows back so at least he'd get a shadowy glimpse whenever the ball came close. He was determined that it shouldn't matter, just as always. (And we beat Forest 2–1 that day, which both of us regarded as particularly pleasing, because I'd recently become a resident of Nottingham and had taken a slightly dimmer shining to 'the other NCFC', Notts County.)

In 2018, having made some more characteristically unwise decisions, he turned in on himself for the last time. His friends worried, as he repeatedly took to bed with bottles of wine, fell asleep at dinner tables, and at one point slipped over on the way back from Tesco, bottle in hand, and ended up in hospital. And in April 2020, early in the first lockdown, overwhelmed with disappointments, he again found himself on his own. By this time, he was clearly unwell, and almost totally isolated. Eight months later, he was taken to hospital, diagnosed with metastatic colon cancer, and given twelve weeks to live. But my father was built of tough stuff. He lived for thirteen months more, and for twelve of those at Twin Oaks Nursing Home. The staff there – Sonia, Sue, Bena, Eppie, and all the others – were superb, the sort of people who restore your faith in humanity in an instant. He wasn't in a condition to show gratitude, but I like to think an earlier version of him might have done, at least if the care had been being provided to someone other than himself. The same is true of his friend Paolo, who always tried to give my dad sage advice and sincere help, despite the odds. Thank you for being a true friend to my dad, Paolo. And the same to you, Joan. He adored you. And he was right about that.

My dad lost his final optimism in October, when he discovered he'd been blocked from any prospect of going home. Going home was all he really wanted to talk about by that point, and the dementia caused by his alcoholism made him even more assiduous on that point. He knew I tried everything I could to get him live-in care at home, despite my reservations about how safe he would then be, and I hope that offered some comfort, however cold. Nobody could get through to him by telephone in his final weeks: he'd usually just croak 'later' when the receiver was brought to him, and yelp if it wasn't taken away again. The last time I saw him, a few days before he died, a phrase from one of his favourite Philip Larkin poems came to mind: 'that whole hideous inverted childhood'. His penultimate words to me that day were 'lots of love. Best wishes.' He died alone, having spurned food for weeks. Cancer would have killed him, but hopelessness got there first. His heart broke.

I loved him passionately, though it was not always easy. His alcoholism waxed and waned, and at times he fought it gamely. At others, less so. He made a great many mistakes, enough for several lifetimes. Even so, few thought he would make the mistakes he ultimately did, which I won't name, and he deserves deep sympathy as well as other emotions: his life could have been so much more than it was. But for the moment I'd prefer us to remember him as the optimist he had often been throughout the preceding seventy-five years. In his later life, until recently when it was made impossible, we'd still talk all the time about a million things, then email one another at considerable length too. He kept up several detailed correspondences with others, as well. If he was interested in something personally, he'd talk and talk and talk. If he wasn't, he'd let you know, and tut impatiently. But *we* liked so many of the same things that we always got by, and ours was the only close family relationship of his life that endured through decades. My dad was also supportive of my own early attempts at writing, about twelve or fifteen years ago: he'd want to see my drafts, and if I let him he would make suggestions, whether I asked for them or not. Some were terrible. But all were made with pride. He'd send me his own drafts, and no doubt some of my suggestions were terrible too – he sometimes thought so. But we were two writers. He liked that. And so did I. And I admired his talent.

But, as a folk song we both loved puts it:

It's not just what you're born with, it's what you choose to bear.
And it's not how large your share is, it's how much you can share.
It's not the fights you dreamed of, it's those you really fought.
And it's not just what you're given, it's what you do with what
    you've got.

Good night, Dad.

PN Review, 2022

N.B. I did not write this with a readership in mind. Michael Schmidt, editor of PN Review *and Carcanet Press, asked to see it, then to publish it – for which reason, I added the paragraph at the top of the article.*

I SAY HEART

Naush Sabah, *Litanies* (Guillemot, 2021); Suzannah V. Evans, *Brightwork* (Guillemot, 2021); Diana Hendry, *Where I Was* (Mariscat, 2020)

I focus here on themed pamphlets. Each is very different but contains around twenty-five to thirty pages of poems: these are fairly sizeable publications, examples almost of a mid-length form between the book and what once would have been the 'standard' pamphlet, though of an increasingly common length for the medium. I do not favour absolutes, but too often, what might have been a successful themed pamphlet appears to have been bloated into a full-length collection with patently less successful poems, and increasingly I am convinced that around thirty pages is often the perfect length for such a volume. Here are three well-proportioned recent examples by way of testimony.

In 'Litany of Dissolution', on the first page of Naush Sabah's debut full-length pamphlet, we read:

> time has folded up into me
>   I've been thrown by it
> like a child down a hill
>   standing up and brushing off grass
>   to find herself a woman

The poem is a slaloming stream of consciousness, one of several here but at four pages the longest of them, and displays many of Sabah's strengths: crystalline images and muscly enjambments, enriched by a mind at once subtle and forthright. At this point, though, you might be forgiven for thinking you've read it all before in a thousand self-indulgent poems. You haven't: 'now there's day after day after day / disappearing', she continues, 'and no god in them / to hook the carcass of any hope from', and the poem doesn't compromise in its depiction of what that means.

'Fiqh makes the munafiq' (glosses inform the uninitiated that this translates as 'Islamic law makes the hypocrite'), she writes in 'On Shahada' (translation: 'testimony (of faith)'):

> I'm the hooded illusionist
>
> and you a spectator watching me
> fight against my own restraints.
> Look. by this sleight of hand
> I will make you believe I believe.

This gives a flavour of what the pamphlet puts at stake, and the certainty of its convictions. Certainty often makes poetry stale, but in this case it is the certainty of loss breeding passionately felt tensions. And passionately felt tensions can, in turn, breed self-indulgent sentimentality, but Sabah tempers them with impressive control, complexified through intertextual engagement with (or in some cases against) hadiths and Sufi songs. These poems marry their sometimes anguished conviction to an unusual panache for formal and linguistic dexterity. 'Of Monuments', a tiny poem of column-like single and double-line stanzas, comprises depictions of things presumed eternal, and ends: 'The deities have died but these columns endure.' 'Of Mercy', a two-stanza poem about an infant who might die, is one of the most affecting yet unaffected mirror poems I have read: 'if she lives / they'll praise God's mercy' and 'they'll praise God for his mercy / if she dies', each stanza either begins or ends, as 'my womb poor incubator still contracts'. The sonnet 'Of Myths and Messengers' turns every traditional element of the form – not least the expectation of unrequited love – on itself: 'The gods have needs and their messengers have pulpits: / someone must bleed, something must burn and smoke.' Who else is writing like this, now, and with at once such immediacy and breadth of reference? Sabah has a tendency sometimes to dilute by telling us what she has shown, but this is a stunning debut, that cliché for once fit for

The pamphlet is sumptuously produced, as are all things from Guillemot Press. That includes Suzannah V. Evans's *Brightwork*, which is also obsessional, this time over the items clogging a boatyard. Evans wrote these poems while writer in residence at Underfall Yard in Bristol. (I had to venture to the Guillemot Press website to learn that: despite the press's attention to production values, it doesn't print pamphlets with blurbs – or page numbers, or contents pages – which is cute but also sometimes annoying.) Often, the poems are named for what they home in on: 'The Dredger Paddle', for instance, which – surprisingly, I'm sure you'll agree – is the subject of no other poem I can think of, and which 'is gently rusting, is gently resting by the powerhouse tower.' Or 'Buoy', a concrete poem shaped like its subject but with a revivifying metaphor worth waiting for (and not spoiling) at the end. The poems are often at first apparently wide-eyed in their middle-classness: these are things other people must use for often hard work, or so it seems from the poems, which can instead meditate on the items under examination. This is from 'Slipway', one of several prose poems:

> I've seen you slide into the water, lowering yourself with an easy song, a sweet whining, a slow clanking; I've seen your wooden posts sink deeper like fins. There are other lovely things about you: your timber cradle, how you hold the hulls of boats so closely, how you keep your chocking stable, and whistle at the sight of a wooden deck. They call you a Heave-Up Slip, but the only heaving is done by the men around you, who lower poles, wind winches, puff and glance up at the sky.

'Lovely' it is, yes, but Evans often zooms out momently on the wider environment like this, so romanticisation is tempered by snatched insights into the lives of others, the lives that keep things here 'lovely' for the observer. As she writes in another poem,

> I say *elbow*, and they think of the curved piece
> of frame at the turn of the bilge, I say *heart*,
> and they picture the centre of a section of timber.

Diana Hendry's new pamphlet is also obsessed with the finer details of a setting, in this case the house in which she grew up six and seven decades ago. The opening poem, 'Before Us', speaks of 'the grief that exuded from the walls like damp / which we couldn't get rid', the 'source' of which is 'the man who'd sold us the house', father to three boys 'All killed in the war. All.' That rather gives the sense that the home is doomed from the start, and the rest of the pamphlet goes about demonstrating ways in which it was. This is an extremely moving, unsentimental pamphlet tersely unfolding its unresolvable story, in which the past also belongs to the present, but only as something relived and unalterable. 'Mother! mother! / Let's get out of here', she writes, looking back, after a vivid depiction of 'woman's work' in a stifling mid-century, upper-middle-class household where the father hides 'behind his newspaper' dreaming of the sons he hasn't had, and all is now over anyway.

Hendry does a superb job of throwing the most of us who haven't experienced it into the environment she describes. It's a bit like reading *Just William*, only with the japes and boys replaced by stoical sadness and girls, and possibility replaced by its vanquishment. In 'The Greenhouse', we learn that 'Before my father gave her away', the speaker's sister 'shut herself in there' with books and apples, as – in a perfect symbol of her predicament – 'terracotta pots of tomatoes' turned 'from green to red.' This isn't a pamphlet of lively experiments in form, but it is a meaningful tale of restriction, beautiful and pellucid in its unveiling.

PN Review, 2022

EYE OF THE STORM

The Kenyon Review 43.6 (November 2021) –
44.5 (September 2022), ed. Nicole Terez Dutton

When John Crowe Ransom founded the *Kenyon Review* in 1939, it immediately had clout, because *he* did. As a writer, editor, prominent advocate of New Criticism, and de facto figurehead of the Fugitives and the Southern Agrarians, Ransom brought with him a fierce reputation. He championed close reading, tight writing and argument; the rural American South (while largely ignoring such inconveniences as the continuation of Jim Crow laws); and 'a Southern way of life against what may be called the American or prevailing way', as the Agrarian manifesto *I'll Take My Stand* (1930) put it. Luckily, he was as interested in cultivating talent as he was in cultivating that strand of American culture: his students at Kenyon College included the likes of Randall Jarrell, E. L. Doctorow, James Wright and Robert Lowell. And from the inception of the *Kenyon Review*, he was keen to promote talent wherever he saw it, publishing the early work of a considerable number of younger writers who would become prominent.

Ransom's editorship lasted two decades; the most recent incumbent, David H. Lynn, had the post even longer. That desire to discover and foster perseveres under the journal's newest editor, Nicole Terez Dutton, appointed last year. She takes the broadly cosmopolitan approach we would now expect, and the *Kenyon Review* continues to be a literary magazine with huge significance and clout, at least in the United States. The journal is published six times a year, each issue divided almost equally between short fiction, poetry, 'nonfiction' (which in this case tends to mean personal essays) and often a fourth, themed section. This section does some of the heavy lifting when it comes to presenting new writers: in her introduction to the Young Writers' prize section in the September 2021 issue, for example, the judge, Molly

McCully Brown, dedicates several hundred words to an effusive close reading of the winning entry, Sophie Bernik's 'Come Closer', noting that 'Bernik intertwines the ordinary and the deeply consequential with remarkable restraint, conjuring the trail of disaster's continual intrusions and near misses: the way a "storm gets too strong again, // but it wears itself out ripping up trees before / it can ever get to the houses."' (How this excerpt is 'deeply consequential' she does not say.)

The November 2021 issue opens with winners of the 'Short Nonfiction Contest', judged by Roxane Gay, who was presumably too busy to provide a full introduction. The section preface notes that 'Gay describes runner-up "Blue Whale Challenge" by Christian Butterfield as "innovative, not only in form, but in function. The narrative builds slowly, inexorably, and it is beautifully rendered, haunting at times, but always remarkable."' The title of the piece alludes to an online phenomenon 'consisting of a series of tasks assigned to players over a fifty-day period, initially innocuous before introducing elements of self-harm and suicide'. Butterfield, still a teenager, is presumably in its target demographic. He writes with economy and detachment about addiction, dysmorphia, weight loss and the grim rules his narrator appears to be trying to follow in its pursuit: 'day 36: think backwards. in hindsight, the worst part about disordered eating is how easily it's labeled as accountability. day 37: learn that some paranoias are justified. your mother slips sugar cubes into your coffee, fatty deposits melting in lard-rich seas.'

Occasionally, this portion of the journal tackles a theme rather than a genre. In the July issue, 'Angry Mamas' contains poems, essays and short fiction from fifteen authors, introduced by Emily Raboteau, who explains: 'This folio takes the climate crisis as its theme, filtered through the lens of motherhood'. Agrarian, then, but also cosmopolitan. Many of the contributions are impossible to disagree with, but equally hard to feel much else about, and riddled with modish clichés, which don't exactly assuage that:

'Living like this is exhausting. Honestly I would rather not have to cultivate my anger. But we're in an existential crisis, and people fighting for their lives get tired', writes Genevieve Guenther; 'The Doomsday Clock has ticked one second closer to destruction, telling the rest of the world what mothers like Priscilla already know. The danger is everywhere', concurs Laura Picklesimer. More intriguing is Humera Afridi's resonant 'Mangroves on My Mind': 'For a while, in the diaspora, I tried to imprint on my son all that I loved when I was his age. My attempt was futile and dissonant.' Afridi ends by describing their New York City home – 'Mannahatta and her waters' – as a 'sacred topography', layering its uncolonized past back over its concreted present.

Some variability notwithstanding, readers will find in the *Kenyon Review* a compendium of substantial American writing, in a broad array of genres and styles. There is major new work by the likes of Linda Gregerson, Aimee Nezhukumatathil and Sherod Santos alongside many less familiar names. Readers won't find reviews or editorials, however. That seems a shame, considering the journal's tradition of staking claims and shaping tastes.

Times Literary Supplement, 2022

LET THE MORBID FANCY ROAM

Donald Davie, *Selected Poems*, ed. Sinéad Morrissey (Carcanet, 2022)

1922: the high-water mark of literary high modernism in English, with the publication of James Joyce's *Ulysses*, Virginia Woolf's *Jacob's Room*, T. S. Eliot's *The Waste Land*. And also the year of birth of several poets associated with that least modernist of movements, the Movement, among them Philip Larkin, Kingsley Amis, and Donald Davie. The Movement poets worth reading now rarely adhered to the formal and thematic conservatism of Movement poetics, though. Larkin and Elizabeth Jennings – admittedly an unusual pairing, which is part of my point – did, but transcended them by dint of their exceptional talents, and were thus not typical of the Movement at all, despite their constraining aesthetics. Others left the Movement behind, and largely found their enduring work elsewhere, both poetically and geographically, and later in life.

The most widely read of those poets now is surely Thom Gunn, who expanded both his world and his verse following a move to California in the 1950s. Davie is considerably less prominent a century after his birth, but he was hugely influential for much of his life: 'the definitive poet-critic of his generation'. I am quoting the poet Sinéad Morrissey, who edited this selection, and who is in turn quoting Michael Schmidt, the book's publisher, and to whom those words might also be applied. Like Gunn, though about a decade later, Davie swapped England for the US, in his case for professorships, first at Stanford, then Vanderbilt. In these august chairs, he wrote several learned, argumentative, highly engaging books on poetry – I had to replace my copy of *Under Briggflatts* when I was an undergraduate in the early 2000s because it had fallen apart from overuse – and, between 1955 and his death four decades later, twelve slim volumes of poetry, the earliest bearing most of the hallmarks of what we might regard as a Movement sensibility, and the others ranging variously beyond it.

I approach this review with an agenda: Davie, in my opinion, should not be forgotten – should, indeed, be read widely, both for his criticism and his poetry. But it feels as though he might almost have been forgotten already. And besides, where is the uninitiated reader to start? In 2002, a second and definitive *Collected Poems* appeared, edited by Neil Powell. Considering that he was an extraordinarily erudite, astute (if in my decidedly humble opinion often maddeningly incorrect) critic of other people's poetry, Davie perhaps published a little too much of his own, and that volume – much as I wouldn't want to be without it – is as uneven as it is substantial. Morrissey's introduction quotes Powell's:

> A mildly diverting, if ultimately pointless, exercise might involve winnowing it down to the equivalent of those three volumes by Larkin [*The Less Deceived*, *The Whitsun Weddings*, and *High Windows*, the very short collections on which Larkin's reputation rests]. That could, up to a point, be done; and the daunted reader would then discover a poet as approachable as Larkin.

'Pointless exercise'? One can almost see the lightbulb flickering on above Morrissey's, or Schmidt's, head, for that's essentially what this book is. Davie had in effect made his own attempt at the job in 1985, when his erstwhile most recent *Selected Poems* appeared, but he had ten years of poems left in him at that point.

In December, at the online launch of this book, Morrissey was candid about her relationship to the subject, and confessed to having barely read Davie until being approached to edit this selection. She is an inspired choice to do so: a poet with a comparably expansive unpredictability and some unusual confluences of poetic temperament, who has been able to approach Davie's oeuvre new, as will most readers of this book. She is also apparently a fine editor of her own collections, including her *Selected Poems*, published in 2020. I am comparing apples and oranges, and a concluded career with one that has not, but Davie was apparently less proficient in this regard, frequently throwing the wheat and chaff together. Morrissey seems almost apologetic that this 'is admittedly a highly personal selection', but that is its idiosyncratic triumph: this is a sampler of one of the major poets of the last generation that has been assembled by leaning into the proclivities of one of the major poets of our own.

The book presents Davie chronologically. (It is a shame there is no indication of which poems belong to which collection.) The early Davie is regularly a Movement poet par excellence – both in Morrissey's abridgement and when read more extensively: rigidly formalist, hard-edged, unsentimental, an observer and declarer, his poems often skilful thought puzzles to move the head if not generally the heart. In 'Homage to William Cowper':

> Most poets let the morbid fancy roam.
> The squalid rat broke through the finch's fence,
> Which was a cage, and still was no defence:
> For Horror starts, like Charity, at home.

That gives a flavour of Davie's preferred form at the time: tightly rhymed, tightly metrical quatrains of primly accentual-syllabic iambic pentameter, with commensurately formalised diction. 'Poem as Abstract' begins:

> A poem is less an orange than a grid;
> It hoists a charge; it does not ooze a juice.
> It has no rind, being entirely hard.

This is memorable, and encourages thought beyond reading, but ultimately it is self-advocacy masquerading as argument. 'Gardens no Emblems', on the other hand, is one of several examples here of the earlier Davie's occasionally staid formality lending his lines a vivid appositeness they could not otherwise possess:

Man with a scythe: the torrent of his swing
Finds its own level, and is not hauled back
But gathers fluently, like water rising
Behind the watergates that close a lock.

The subtle shift away from metronomic iambs in the middle lines of the stanza, then the gentle return to them, is part of the effect, experienced even if it is not noticed. You can see and feel the scene, and the closing simile, in part because of that. But this twelve-line poem transcends simple portraiture – and is, for the little this is worth, Davie at his most Larkinesque in terms of the trajectory his poem takes: 'But forms of thought move in another plane', the final quatrain begins.

Oh – to use an exclamation the early Davie loved – his poems were soon to move cautiously, determinedly away from such formalities. However, much of the restrained voice and all of the inquisitiveness would never leave him – nor would the desire to question the art he practised, a process Morrissey is evidently drawn to, as she opts to include a disproportionate number of poems doing so. One of the earliest signs of Davie's increasing breaking of the mighty line is 'The Wind at Penistone'. As Morrissey notes, 'stylistically, this is a poem of windy gaps and disjunctions, a battle between text and white space, between speech and silence.' The poem is in blank verse, 'a grid' no less, but blank verse as buffeted and cut through, yet solid, as the landscape it describes:

> The wind reserves, the hill reserves, the style
> Of building houses on the hill reserves
> A latent edge;
>   which we can do without
> In Pennine gradients and the Pennine wind,
> And never miss, or, missing it, applaud
> The absence of the aquiline;
>   which in her

> Whose style of living in the wind reserves
> An edge to meet the wind's edge, we may miss
> But without prejudice.
>   And yet in art
> Where all is patent, and a latency
> Is manifest or nothing, even I,
> Liking to think I feel these sympathies,
> Can hardly praise this clenched and muffled style.

You can sense the poem trying and failing to blow itself open.

Davie had served in the Navy during the Second World War, mainly in the Russian Arctic, though only occasionally does that become his subject – in 'Behind the North Wind', for instance, which describes 'a forgotten Front / Of 1942'. Its effects, however, are evident in several unglamorous portraits of England. In 'For an Age of Plastics', for instance:

> Chance in the bomb sight kept these streets intact
>   And razed whole districts. Nor was the lesson lost
> On the rebuilt Plymouth, how an age of chance
>   Is an age of plastics. In a style pre-cast
> Pre-fabricated, and as if its site
>   Were the Canyon's lip, it rises out of rubble
> Sketchily massive, moulded in bakelite.

There is a hint of Larkin again in 'Barnsley Cricket Club':

> 'A thing worth doing is worth doing well,'
> Says Shaw Lane Cricket Ground
> Between the showers of a July evening,
> As the catch is held and staid hand-clappings swell.

How homely this is, and every bit as vivid as Larkin's someone 'running up to bowl', but the poem hardly encourages us to go there. The apotheosis of his apparently growing distaste for

England is the opening to 'Lowlands': 'I could not live here, though I must and do / Ungratefully inhabit the Cambridgeshire fens.' 'But a beauty there is', he writes with begrudging passivity in the poem's final stanza, having undermined the opening gambit with three of the most euphorically beautiful stanzas he would ever write: 'slow light spilt and wheeling over calm / Inundations'; 'it wears like a bus-conductor / tickets of brown sails tucked into polders' hat-bands!' As so often in Davie's landscape poems, this is a depiction of a state of mind as much as of a place. If, for Hardy, 'Everything glowed with a gleam; / Yet we were looking away', for Davie things can glow with a gleam while you're looking at them, noticing them intensely, and feeling like Hardy's speaker all the while.

Frequently self-chastising, Davie is anything but a poet of simple certainties when it comes to matters of emotion or conduct. In 'July 1964', he writes:

> Love and art I practise;
> they seem to be worth no more
> and no less than they were.

Then:

> A man who ought to know me
> wrote in a review
> my emotional life was meagre.

That 'ought' is balanced, ambiguous: it might mean he should; it might mean he does. And Davie's equivalent of carpe diem is a glass half empty but held tight. 'Now is the time', he writes in 'Christmas Syllabics for a Wife',

> to measure wishes
> by what life has to

give. Not much. So be
from now on greedy.

Those are simple syllabics, but certainly he hadn't shown much interest in such principles of poetic organisation earlier in his career. What influence, specifically, did America have on Davie's poetry? In her introduction, Morrissey sees hints of Frank O'Hara in some of his later work. Poems such as 'Mornings', which she singles out, are certainly loosely conversational and frenetic, starkly at odds with the earlier 'Movement' poems in style if not underlying attitude:

> Sin, I will say, comes awake
> With all the other energies, even at last the spark
> Leaps on the sluggard battery, and one should have
> Prosopopoeia everywhere: Stout Labour
> Gets up with his pipe in his mouth or lighting
> The day's first *Gauloise-filtre*; then stout
> Caffein like a fierce masseur
> Rms him abreast of the day; stout Sin
> Is properly a-tremble.

Other of his later poems are sparse, pithy, graceful, exclamatory – often all at once, as in 'Benedictus', a single-sentence poem stretched taut over twelve short lines, and which cannot successfully be excerpted. Though raised in a Baptist home, Davie deserted Christianity for most of his adult life, before turning to Anglicanism in his sixties. This is reflected in his 1988 collection *To Scorch or Freeze*, eleven poems from which are selected by Morrissey, more than from any of his other books, and none of which were included in the earlier *Selected* because he hadn't written them yet. In 'Attar of Roses', he asks:

> do we live in a nest of boxes,
> the nubs of ourselves, so tiny, secreted in

the innermost, most reclusive, most
cramped of the boxes? If not

we have to believe in, we already believe in,
the resurrection of the body.

I for one am not wholly convinced; and, even if I were, this more didactic Davie would still leave me largely indifferent, neither scorched nor frozen – though these are not simple songs of praise. 'If I Take the Ways of the Morning' ends:

Speak if you cannot sing.
Utter with appropriate shudders
the extremities of God's arctic
where all the rivers are frozen,

and how He tempers our exile
with an undeserved planting of willows.

I find Davie most engaging when he is full of contradiction, quarrels, appears to be in dialogue – as he frequently is with other writers: Horace, Pound, Pasternak, Mandelstam, Mayakovsky (he had taught himself Russian) or, in one of his last poems, Tony Harrison, the dedicatee of 'Northern Metres', which evidently alludes to Harrison's flawed masterpiece 'v.':

Obscenities spray-painted
On parents' headstones have
Made a morass of Beeston.

Pitiful understanding
Will not disperse that stench,
Nor tidy metres quench it.

Is this nuanced admonishment? Certainly, it reads like a quarrel with Davie's younger self, and serves as a marker of how far he'd travelled.

It is a slight shame this book leaves out some of Davie's longer poems and sequences. For example, surely room might have been made for 'In the Stopping Train' ('This journey will punish the bastard'), which isn't *that* long, and is remarkable – the 1985 *Selected* included it, though perhaps that is its own argument for the poem's omission here, and the two selections are robustly different throughout. If you have the earlier book, there is therefore no reason not to read the new one, which is in any case worth the ticket price for the introduction alone; and if you have read none of Davie's poetry before, you have a small, perfectly-formed, ever-expanding universe to explore.

The Friday Poem, 2023

LOVE AND SHADOW

Peter Scupham, *Invitation to View* (Carcanet, 2022)

Peter Scupham (1933–2022) died shortly after this collection of poems was finalised and, as his last blog post for his publisher, Carcanet, makes clear, he knew he was dying. 'Time is a flip book', he writes in one of the many meditative lyrics here: 'feel the pages purr / as years fan by / in their lost variegations.' Like most of Scupham's poetry, that in *Invitation to View* is often ornately but never archly formal, and highly readable. However, here especially it often feels as if he is attempting to wrestle order from chaos, the poems providing studies in careful, quiet noticing, energised by the ultimate uncertainty:

> Her hair is shot silk;
> his jacket hangs just so,
> the bricks of their playhouse
> tingle with love and shadow,
>
> hiding the question:
> 'Where shall we go,
> when, for the last time,
> you close your eyes?'

An even stronger version of this collection would have chosen more selectively from among such pieces, which are numerous, though Scupham's panache for creating an atmosphere and settling on the right vivid image is regularly impressive. He has often felt a little like an English counterpart to Richard Wilbur, intriguing for his intricate but natural-seeming formalism and controlled juxtapositions of cool observation and emotional tumult recollected in tranquillity. One of the book's most prominently recurring images is that of impossibly distant, tantalisingly visible celestial bodies: in 'Winter Words', 'dried sap

/ knots branch to branch, / caging a star' that is 'cold to the retina / as once upon a time, / remembered pain.' The other is of a cat that, in 'The Heart of Things', 'sings to its ghost, ears cocked, / eyes bright from seeing' what we often don't.

The greatest pleasures in *Invitation to View*, though, often come from the poems that draw both on specific personal memories and on the geopolitical machinations that coincided with them. Scupham was always a poet obsessed by history's palimpsests, and that obsession is in ample evidence here. For example, 'The Cutting Edge', dated 1955, bounds along in jolly rhyming couplets and triplets of tetrameters, evoking a 'Posh tot on a chair' with 'gaiters and gloves and some buttons to spare, / I was lurking in camera, but very elsewhere, / little me.' But content then turns against form, for on the same day, 'the Lebensborn eingetragener Verein / was founded by Himmler, Reichsführer (SS), / for his black-hearted blonds in their fancy-pants dress.'

Times Literary Supplement, 2023

FIRST AS TRAGEDY, THEN AS FARCE

Karl Marx, translated and introduced by Philip Wilson, *Evening Hour* (Arc, 2022); Amanda Dalton, *Notes on Water* (Smith Doorstop, 2022); Martin Stannard, *Postcards to Ma* (Leafe Press, 2023)

Readers won't be surprised Karl Marx was an appalling poet, though they might be surprised by the kind of appalling poet he was. As Philip Wilson tells us in the helpful introduction to this dual-language selection of eleven poems from an extant haul of 120, 'The young Marx dreamed of a career as a man of letters. He wrote poetry prolifically for two years', also found time to pen a novel and a verse tragedy, and eventually came to the judicious conclusion that he 'lacked the talent'. Most of the poems in *Evening Hour* are tightly formal, wholly conventional, and inherently boring. Wilson is generous in his faint praise: 'The verse comes across as very competent pastiche: the ballads and the love lyrics ventriloquise Friedrich von Schiller and Heinrich Heine'. The following will serve as an example, and I have not cherry-picked an especially naff passage:

> Do you know the magic fulness,
> When souls flow out to meet each other,
> And pour themselves in exhalation,
> In melody and friendliness?
>
> (*Kennst Du das süsse Zauberbild,*
> *Wo Seelen ineinander fliessen,*
> *In einem Hauche sich ergiessen,*
> *Melodisch voll und Freundlich mild?*)

Souls pop up like molehills all over the neat little lawns of Marx's poems, which is perhaps surprising when one considers his maxim – more memorable than any lines of his verse – that religion is *das Opium des Volkes*. Indeed, there are few indications in this work of Marx as we know him. The closest he gets, at least in this selection, is a satirical epigram, which begins: 'In his armchair, cosy and stupid, / Sits silently our German public.' The poem never homes in as one might expect, though, but instead sails loftily, from where it can hit no marks. A short pamphlet of his poetry will be enough to sate anyone's curiosity – but isn't it intriguing to know Marx wrote like this, once? His poetry really did make nothing happen, and had he stuck to his initial ambitions, the past century of world history might have been rather different.

In (at least) one of Richmal Crompton's later William stories, written while bastardisations of Marx's non-poetic ideas were controlling the lives of half of the world's population, the dishevelled eleven-year-old hero sits scowling at his school-desk while holding a book upside down in front of him, and receives the telling off he no doubt deserves. He should've picked up Amanda Dalton's *Notes on Water*, both covers of which are front covers, and which contains two long poems bearing that title; after reading one, you turn the pamphlet upside down and start at the beginning again on the other.

One poem begins in dream or fever-dream, we don't initially know which (though that soon becomes apparent):

I'm swimming in an artificial pool
inside a broken building.
the water is deep and brown
and full of wreckage.

The poem's tight sections, separated by asterisks, then move between multivalently watery scenarios: the 'smiling boy in the car park, / little Noah, pouring rivers from a watering can', the flood 'that made the whole town one big filthy river; floating cars on Albert Street, St George's Square an artificial lake'. 'Next day the fucking sightseers block the streets. // Next day the water slings.' Stitched throughout the poem is the speaker's sister, 'kneeling in the rubble', and 'the man who will leave in winter'. The poem coheres, and is moving and evocative, but I don't want to ruin it for you. In its counterpart, a horrible, wonderful poem of memory, loss, love, pain, 'a woman waits through a long night' while a man upstairs 'lies soaked in pain / but still the doctor doesn't come'. It is all original in the telling if not in the tale, and the formatting is no gimmick: the two poems meet, joltingly, in the middle. *This* is poetry.

But then poetry is many things. Sumer is ycumen in, and Martin Stannard's *Postcards to Ma*, one 12-page stanza, is the beach read you didn't know you need. Not really – but also, why not? The poem's comically tortured, self-absorbed, Beckettian hero is on a solitary holiday (the bed is 'pleasingly firm Back / can't stand nights on anything too squishy One reason / I left wife') somewhere sun-soaked and sea-splashed, from where he sends daily postcards to Ma. The poem doesn't comprise these postcards, but is instead a frenetic, surreal, virtually unpunctuated fourteen-days-in-the-life. On day three, having arrived in 'Horse-hauled taxi cart', checked in, 'Slept like a library book nobody wants to read', sent the obligatory postcard to Ma, photographed everything and everyone in sight ('Especially receptionist in crisp / white blouse and cosmetics'), walked around town, again slept ('like a folded sheep') and 'Frolicked on sand' (another daily dalliance), he turns his attention to the local hospital and to curing 'loads of patients' of 'lupus shingles psoriasis schizophrenia (had to cure that / one twice) herpes scabies' etc, before sleeping 'like a patient etherised in a 4-star stable'.

You get the idea, but it seems apposite to go on anyway. A few days later, after an afternoon spent reading philosophers, from Socrates to Hobbes (of course) to Kierkegaard (also of course) to Superman (once more: of course – and yes, Nietzsche directly beforehand), he sleeps 'like a monk in a convent'. As the fortnight draws to a close, he finds time to acquire a BA and an MA, to learn a plethora of instruments ('piano violin cello guitar ukulele flute / piccolo trumpet bassoon oboe recorder harmonica kettle / drum triangle'), and to write a symphony, two sonatas, three violin concertos, 'some songs', two novels and a 'slim volume of award-winning poetry / *The Zenith of Our Feelings* When a man is happy / he writes damn good poetry'. He hasn't seemed especially happy most of the time; but if your brain blinks while you're reading this poem, you might miss many of its barbed little jokes. 'Could be making all this up', he later confesses. Perhaps the only thing that could make this rollicking poem any more enjoyable would be a facsimile of a postcard at the end: 'Dear Ma, Having a lovely relaxing time. Lots of love…'.

PN Review, 2023

TO HEAR THEIR VOICE BOUNCE OFF THE SHAPE OF THINGS

A. E. Stallings, *This Afterlife: Selected Poems* (Carcanet, 2022)

Many British readers of poetry will be new to A. E. Stallings – a sure sign of the transatlantic divide that still exists in modern anglophone poetry. Her reputation here is beginning to grow, though, and is likely to come of age very soon: *This Afterlife* – her first book of poems from a British, not American, press – was published late last year, and she has recently been voted the next Oxford Professor of Poetry, surprisingly beating out stiff competition from Mark Ford and Don Paterson, both of whom deserve it just as much as she does. Born and raised in Atlanta, Georgia, Stallings moved to Greece in her twenties, and quickly came to whatever prominence poets can come to in her native country following the publication of her debut collection, *Archaic Smile* (1999), half of which revivifies Greek myth. She has since published three further collections – *Hapax* (2006), *Olives* (2012) and *Like* (2018) – as well as a number of translations from ancient Greek, modern Greek, and Latin. In a time when it is extremely unfashionable to write in rhyme and strict accentual-syllabic metres, she is one of only a small handful of avowed formalists to have some kind of popular success in the past quarter century. This book, then, is overdue – and also, or so it seems in the wake of her subsequent Oxford win, prescient.

This Afterlife selects from all of her four previous volumes, and does so a little too generously, at least in the cases of the two more recent ones, which are represented almost in full. It also contains a short selection of previously uncollected and mostly underwhelming poems, and three translations from Greek of poems by Angelos Sikelianos (twice) and George Seferis. The book's title is taken from the last line of the opening poem, 'A Postcard from Greece', one of its many sonnets. The poem begins vividly, and also as conventionally as its title implies, but don't be fooled. 'Hatched from sleep', the speaker and her companion drive along a winding cliffside: 'No guardrails hemmed the road, no way to stop it, / The only warning here and there a shrine' dedicated to 'those who lost their wild race with the road':

> Our car stopped on the cliff's brow. Suddenly safe,
> We clung together, shade to pagan shade,
> Surprised by sunlight, air, this afterlife.

This gives a fairly good sense of how Stallings' poems most typically unfold. They tend to be heavily metrically and linguistically controlled, yet sprightly, and almost without exception are immediately easy to understand (you might want to look up the occasional mythological reference), their complications contained in the thoughts they prompt and appear to have been prompted by. Stallings is sometimes regarded as a New Formalist, New Formalism being a specifically American movement largely committed to the adherence to highly ordered metrical models. It has a not entirely unearned reputation for sub-Georgian levels of cosy conventionality and conservatism: most New Formalist poets (exceptions apply) look up, up, a very long way up, to Robert Frost, to Elizabeth Bishop, to Richard Wilbur, to Anthony Hecht – and so do their poems. Anyone who writes Stallings off for these failings, though, has not read her. Certainly, she has written her share of metrically conventional sonnets, triolets, villanelles and so forth, has tended until recently to favour a neat iambic pentameter, likes a well-made poem that ends with the feeling of a door clicking shut, and tends to focus on broadly conventional themes. She is also a lively if not wild experimenter within all of those parameters, which, as much as her sheer skill, sets her apart from all but the smallest handful of other (living) American formalists. Consider 'Like', the title poem of her 2018 collection, a sestina that takes the form's constraint to its singular apotheosis:

> But it's unlikely Lila does diddly. Like
> Just twiddles its unopposing thumbs-ups, like-
> Wise props up scarecrow silences. 'I'm like,
> So OVER him,' I overhear. 'But, like,
> He doesn't get it. Like, you know? He's like
> It's all OK. Like I don't even LIKE
>
> Him anymore. Whatever. I'm all like...'

(We never find out what she's 'all like', and who gives a shit?) Or 'Ajar', in both rhymed trimeter and hexameter – a metre that tends to encourage a central caesura in English anyway – which visually resembles the separation it comes to describe:

> The washing machine door broke.   We hand-washed for a week.
> Left in the tub to soak,   the angers began to reek,
> And sometimes when we spoke,   you said we shouldn't speak.

Her most off-the-shelf uses of form are often stunning, too, and subtle. The sixteen-line 'The Argument' begins with the octave of a conventional Petrarchan sonnet. Here are the opening four lines:

> After the argument, all things were strange.
> They stood divided by their eloquence
> Which had surprised them after so much silence.
> Now there were real things to rearrange.

To make a pentameter of that fourth line, by which point in the poem that metre is firmly established, it is necessary to force hard but not unnatural stresses on both the first half of 'real', slowing it into two syllables, and 'things'. Gravity. But the reader must also quicken the second 'something' in the fifth-from-last line of the poem, so no stress falls on 'would' and the line does not become hexameter. It is the quickening of an apparently irrevocable, bitter change, lives thrown off kilter, also signalled by the sudden apparent aleatory of the rhyme scheme:

> Something was beginning. Something would stem
> And branch from this one moment. Something made
> Them each look up into the other's eyes
> Because they both were suddenly afraid
> And there was no one now to comfort them.

This is remarkable poetry: organised disorganisation, complicated yet simple.

The same might be said of 'Pop Music', for one of many examples. Subtitled 'for a new parent', this poem is a laconically witty counterpart to Philip Larkin's 'Love Songs in Age', whether or not that was the intention, though that only becomes apparent towards the end. The focus, initially, is on 'The music that your son will listen to / To drive you mad', and which 'Has yet to be invented':

> As for the lyrics, or the lack thereof,
> About love or about the lack of love,
> Despite the heart's reputed amputation,
> They will be as repetitive as sex
> Without the imagination.

One of Stallings' more inconsequential poems would end there, or would at least end where a reader might well expect it to. Instead, it expands thematically, to be both abundantly mean and abundantly empathetic:

> And while you knit another ugly sweater,
> The pulsars of the brave new tunes will boom
> From the hormonal miasma of his room,
> Or maybe they'll just beam into his brain –
> Unheard melodies are better.

> Thus it has always been. Maybe that's why
> The sappy retro soundtrack of your youth
> Ambushes you sometimes in a café
> At this almost-safe distance, and you weep, or nearly weep,
> For all you knew of beauty, or of truth.

She can also be sharply witty about the roles frequently and enduringly ascribed to her sex, in a manner that is reminiscent of Wendy Cope. In 'Apollo Takes Charge of His Muses', for instance, the Muses are nine 'quiet women', recalling their introduction to the boss man: 'Of course he was very charming, and he smiled, / Introduced himself and said he'd heard good things'. 'None of us spoke or raised her hand, and questions / There were none, what has poetry to do with reason / Or the sun?' That poem is from her first collection, which most determinedly engages Greek myth, and it gives a good sense of how she does so, typically focusing on female experience and drawing the ancient into either modern life or an eternal truth.

Sometimes, though, Stallings is guilty of writing poems that really do have little consequence, such as 'Olives', which is twenty-five lines of nothing but rich celebration – though how rich that richness is:

> Sometimes a craving comes for salt, not sweet,
> For fruits that you can eat
> Only if pickled in a vat of tears –
> A rich and dark and indehiscent meat
> Clinging tightly to the pit – on spears
>
> Of toothpicks, maybe, drowned beneath a tide
> Of vodka and vermouth,
> Rocking at the bottom of a wide,
> Shallow, long-stemmed glass, and gentrified,
> Or rustic, on a plate cracked like a tooth [...]

That last line is trying too hard to find its rhyme, isn't it? But not as hard as the archaic 'I own / I've tried them both', in 'Study in White'. Nor as hard as the description of a dead garden bird in 'Cardinal Numbers': 'all that remains – a beak of red, / And, fanned across the pavement slab, / Feathers, drab.' Nor as hard as 'such a pace' and 'the insect race', describing the prey of swallows in, ahem, 'Swallows', which is a rhyme driven straight off a cliff and not worth commemoration with a shrine, at least according to this member of the mammal race. Such nosedives are conspicuous in part because of their infrequency here – they are sudden examples of wholly uncharacteristic inadequacy – and in part because the workings of Stallings' poems are so readily on display and leave nowhere to hide.

The selection has not been as selective as it might have been, then. But who could not revel in the sheer joy of her images and rhythms, even in some of the poems that don't wholly work, or don't do enough? The woman at a loom, 'The shuttle leaping in and out, / dolphins sewing the torn ocean'. Or the islands seen from a plane that are 'dribbled like pancake batter'. Or the 'expert disinterested caresses' of a hairdresser. Or the 'typing of the rain'. Or 'a lone insect's corrugated sound'. Or the bats in 'Explaining an Affinity for Bats', that 'seem like something else at first – a swallow – /And move like new tunes, difficult to follow':

> That they sing – not the way the songbird sings
> (Whose song is rote, to ornament, finesse) –
> But travel by a sort of song that rings
> True not in utterance, but harkenings,
> Who find their way by calling into darkness
> To hear their voice bounce off the shape of things.

The, well, *ringing* of those rhymes, carried along those steady pentameters, is both empathic and emphatic, perfectly so.

In the book's acknowledgments, Stallings notes that she has resisted making significant changes to any of the earlier poems, on the grounds that 'they are the work of a different, earlier me, and it is not my place to alter her work'. Undoubtedly that is both true and untrue, as it is for any poet either side of a quarter of a century, and her subjects have in some cases changed to reflect circumstance – chiefly motherhood, which has become a leitmotif. Nevertheless, the consistency of her voice – reminiscent at times of Elizabeth Bishop, Edna St. Vincent Millay, and many more besides, but always her clear and steady own too – is remarkable. She has loosened her grip on tight accentual-syllabic metres a little in recent books, and has developed a habit of varying metres within poems, but little else has changed; though one rarely thinks 'Hey, I read a poem just like this fifty or a hundred pages back'. Long may her subtle reinventions continue.

The Friday Poem, 2023

MATURE METHODS

Thomas Kinsella, *Last Poems* (Carcanet Press, 2023)

Thomas Kinsella's *Late Poems*, published in 2013, gathered his five most recent pamphlets. *Last Poems* adds to this a portfolio of thirty-two pages the poet had been assembling at the time of his death in 2021, each dated, several patently unfinished, and some accompanied by a note detailing first composition (usually 2020 or 2021, in some cases as early as the 1950s). Publishing in pamphlet form with his own Peppercanister Press had been a habit of Kinsella's since the 1970s, whereafter his work generally became more abstruse. His language is always clear, though what he is saying can be exceptionally elusive – beguilingly or bewilderingly so, depending on your proclivities.

However, there isn't as much of that mystery and mastery as one might hope for in *Last Poems*. Many affect an emotional detachment, a Kinsella speciality, but here it is frequently wedded to an evident simplicity of purpose, which can lead to some astoundingly bloodless versification. The overlong 'Retrospect', a reflection on the history of war in prim blank verse, reads like something forgotten from the seventeenth century: armies, he intones, once 'advanced in formal groups against each other / with various kinds of deadly instruments'; soon, 'With arms evolving, and mature methods, / wounds could be inflicted from a distance'; in time, 'the slaughter gained in deadliness and range'.

If there is something clever about this passivity and vagueness, Kinsella hides it well. His more customary pithiness is at times reminiscent of the later poems of R. S. Thomas, not least when he turns towards God – though, unlike Thomas, Kinsella always seems to find him: 'shining alone in the darkness / Is the one way, / The way of the timeless God / Who has pierced and entered time.' Too often, he has his arguments all settled a priori, and is happy to make do with convincing us of things we might have concluded already. One of the new final poems, 'Communism', reads in its entirety. 'An ideal system of government; / Based on goodwill, / A willingness to share. // But not practical, given / The malice and greed of the species.' This reads like the notebook-jotted epiphany of an undergraduate.

For all that, Kinsella retained the capacity to write profound little masterpieces, such as 'Summer Evening: City Centre', which begins by evoking midges in 'the last light': 'they dance among each other / to keep their places toward night and nothing.' The poem doesn't end there, and this image becomes multifaceted allegory. Thomas Kinsella is one of Ireland's most troublingly profound poets, but unfortunately his final work only rarely proves it.

Times Literary Supplement, 2023

SAINT ROBERT OF WACO

> I'm a wacko from Waco, ain't no doubt about it.
> Shot a man there in the head but can't talk much about it.
> He was trying to shoot me, but he took too long to aim.
> Anybody in my place woulda done the same.
> I don't start fights, I finish fights, that's the way I'll always be.
> I'm a wacko from Waco, you best not mess with me.

That's not me embracing a new poetic direction, nor is it about gun-hoarding and -slinging cult leader David Koresh and the Branch Davidians, names synonymous with Waco worldwide since the Waco Siege in 1993. Rather, it is the opening verse to a hypermasculine, apparently autobiographical barnstormer by the late Texan country singer Billy Joe Shaver, recalling an 'incident' in 2007, when an argument broke out in a bar after another man flirted with his wife. (Shaver, who claimed to have shot the would-be lothario 'right between the mother and the fucker' – face tattoos, perhaps – was acquitted.) In any case, in September last year I spent a couple of weeks in central Texas, with this song lodged in my head thanks to a friend who had sent it to me via WhatsApp on my first day in town.

My happy duty in Waco, before I was to have some time to myself out in the wild Texas Hill Country to the west, was to spend a few days at Baylor, the world's biggest Baptist University, to give a reading and a workshop, and attend a class for students who had been set my third collection, *Sweet Nothings*. Professor Kevin Gardner – one of those people we occasionally hear about, who buys and reads poetry but doesn't tend to write it – was my host, and a very affable and entertaining one, too. Kevin is a John Betjeman specialist, which must be a lonely pursuit in Texas. After a friendly classroom interrogation by his students, there were several hours to kill before the reading, which was to take place in the Armstrong Browning Library. We had a big Texan lunch, peered into the Baylor University bear enclosure ('My university's campus has pigeons and wagtails', I told him), and then Kevin presumably tired of my enthusiastic naivete and left me with his equally affable colleague Professor Sarah Ford at the front of the Library, so that we might look around. Okay, fine. I'd never heard of it.

Neither have many of the citizens of Waco, I suspect – perhaps even including some of the students at Baylor. They ambled along the bosky paths outside, slurping iced coffees and clutching books and gazing into phones, like extras on an excessively perfected campus-based film set. The library, pointedly in what locals think is 'Italian Renaissance-style', loomed like the all-American attempt at elsewhere that it is. It was built in the late 1940s, to house what was already at the time the world's largest collection of artefacts related to the lives and writing of Robert and Elizabeth Barrett Browning. How Dr A. J. Armstrong, then chairman of Baylor's English Department (once housed in the same building, before the expanding collection evicted it) acquired the wealth to do this remained mysterious to me throughout my visit, but in 1912, when the Brownings' son Pen died, his possessions were auctioned by Sotheby's in London, and Armstrong raised the final paddle.

We entered the sudden dim, glad to escape the sun, but were then prompted by a sprightly guide ('Hi!' – big outstretched hand – 'I'm Caleb!') to step back out and inspect the huge bronze doors through which we'd come. They are modelled on Ghiberti's famous Gates of Paradise in Florence, though here the ten panels depict scenes from Robert Browning's poems. It is a fitting introduction to what is effectively a cathedral-sized secular shrine. Back inside, we sauntered across the empty entrance hall, our footsteps rebounding from the marble floor, the marble walls, the frescoes depicting more scenes from Browning's poems, and some of this building's many heavy stained glass windows glowing with yet more scenes from Browning's poems. Most of them were obscure to me, and remained so, because Caleb didn't know what they depicted either – and I don't blame him, because they are so bountiful, and so evidently the product of a deep, narrow devotion. Across from the door, a huge painting of Robert, by Pen, stared down like a beneficent saint, over his final writing desk, placed on a dais at the back, as though it were an altar.

Next, we followed Caleb to the Foyer of Mediation, the inner sanctum. A giant chandelier hung tiny from its shallow dome, which glinted away dully in 23-carat gold leaf. An Italian garden scene with Classical adornments covered the upper walls, along with a few quotations from even more of Browning's poems, some tempting awkward comparisons:

> Man's work is to labor and leaven –
> As best he may – earth here with heaven;
> 'Tis work for work's sake that he's needing.

We were then pointed towards a little apsidal alcove at the back, the 'Cloister of Clasped Hands', presumably named thus for its alliterative properties. And there, on a little plinth, was Harriet Hosmer's famous bronze sculpture from 1853, made from a plaster cast of the couple's hands gently gripping one another, hers on his, each lopped cleanly at the wrist, homely and unheimlich. 'There are no contemporaneous portraits of the two together', said Caleb. 'This is the closest we've got'. So near and yet so far.

Walking around these grandiose rooms, it is obvious Elizabeth has lost the battle for wall space. 'So Elizabeth has the upper hand, but only literally', I quipped, feeling clever and then wondering whether this gets said at least a couple of times a day. The dynamic changed a little upstairs, in the comparatively cosy Elizabeth Barrett Browning Salon, the five stained glass windows of which depict five of her *Sonnets from the Portuguese*. Her writing chairs, tables, cabinets, were dotted around. A fat silky rope kept us at a polite distance.

'Do you have many, er, books or manuscripts?' I asked. Oh yes, and there are also very quiet reading rooms in which to consult them. The library is proud to have 25,000 visitors a year, but that's fewer than 70 a day. Electrons in an atom, not sardines in a tin. We stopped a moment at a sleepy reading room, the sort one imagines the British Library might have until one has actually been into any of its bustling counterparts, but I hadn't prepared myself for this place, wouldn't have known what to ask for nor why I wanted to see it, and besides, we were running out of time. Some manuscripts are displayed in the hall where I was to read that evening, though most of the ample cabinet space there is given over to a bricolage of first-rate curios: illustrations of the Pied Piper by the ten-year-old boy for whom Robert Browning wrote the poem; the Brownings' carriage clock with 'Bates Huddersfield' engraved on it; and what is Robert's last known bit of versification in his own hand – 'Here I'm gazing, wide awake, / Robert Browning, no mistake!' – beneath a pencil sketch, and dated 'Nov 24 '89', two and a half weeks before he died.

Of course, the Brownings had no idea their personal items and jottings would ever be on display here – nor, surely, that 'here' existed. When Robert died, Waco had only just started to outgrow its role as an outpost for cattle herders on the Chisholm Trail, the Wichita Indians having been forced out of the area a generation earlier. When Elizabeth died, it had comprised only a cluster of wooden buildings. 'Italy / Is one thing, England one', wrote Elizabeth Barrett Browning in 'Aurora Leigh', and that played in my head, but Italy and England have far more in common with one another than either does with Waco, even though the meagre Texan towns of Windsor and Milano and Clifton and Italy (and Eulogy) are each within an hour's drive.

On my final morning in Waco, a poet friend in New York sent me a message: 'Are you going to visit the Siege site before you head out of town?' I'd looked it up, of course, and had briefly considered doing so. A significant proportion of those who died during the Waco Siege had been recruited by the Branch Davidian leadership on a visit to England; several came from Nottingham, where I live; some of their relatives still reside within a mile or two of where I write this now. The victims were exactly that, whatever you make of their religious beliefs: victims, often inherently vulnerable ones, who had in most cases done nothing more malignant than seek a meaningful life, and who ended up instead dying in a manifestation of hell on earth. They deserve to be remembered, but does one ever visit such a place *only* to remember? And what could I gain from going to look at a plot of earth? In any case, I traced my way through the raggedy suburbs of Waco and down country lanes through nondescript prairie, towards where the New Mount Carmel Center complex had been until it burned down and destroyed nearly eighty people in the process, many of them children, some to the extent that their autopsy records read 'sex undetermined'. I am not a believer, but this is sacred ground.

The long driveway up to where the Center once stood is lined with sparkling granite memorials, some donated by Texan militia groups. Perhaps unfairly, I am reminded that white supremacist Timothy McVeigh murdered nearly two hundred people in Oklahoma City, two years to the day after the tragedy here, in supposed revenge at the government. What had happened to the Branch Davidians quickly became not just a rallying cry for those of all political persuasions who questioned perceived governmental overreach, it also became a white supremacist cause, though the Branch Davidians unceremoniously killed in that compound had had no such affiliations; in fact, a high proportion of them were black. A simple little clapboard chapel now stands where the building was, a 'TRUMP 2024' flag fluttering above it. Inside, Alexa Pace, the wife of the current pastor of the now greatly diminished Davidians, was very excited by my furtive entrance – I was the only visitor, after all, and she soon discovered I had 'an accent', which is all it usually takes in smalltown America. She pressed a bullet casing from the initial raid into my palm and asked me to take it home. 'Oh, my son used to dig them up all the time.' Snatches of bible prophecy, eye-watering anti-government propaganda and photographs of those who had burned to death all around us covered the walls like posters in a very odd teenager's bedroom, as David Koresh's music (he'd once dreamed of being a rock star) thumped from a speaker at the volume of shopping mall muzak. Horses cropped grass beyond the open double doors. She guided me past them, past the former swimming pool where turtles appeared and vanished in green water, across the scrubby lawn where the Center's vault had been and where several bodies had been recovered from among the cinders, and into a former storm shelter, now just a weed-strewn concrete pit with butterflies jinking in its stillness. A huge iridescent dragonfly landed on a big bloom I can't name. I opened my palm and looked at the little nub it cradled. It would have been gauche to cry. Why did I come here? Why was I glad to have done so? And more lines from 'Aurora Leigh' came to mind, more or less, although I had to wait until I was back in the car before I could look them up and remember them properly, out of context in every way and perfectly apt for all that:

> 'And see! is God not with us on the earth?
> And shall we put Him down by aught we do?
> Who says there's nothing for the poor and vile
> Save poverty and wickedness? behold!'
> And ankle-deep in English grass I leaped,
> And clapped my hands, and called all very fair.
>
> In the beginning when God called all good,
> Even then, was evil near us, it is writ.
> But we, indeed, who call things good and fair,
> The evil is upon us while we speak;
> Deliver us from evil, let us pray.

PN Review, 2023

INDEX

Ackroyd, Peter 67
Adler, Alfred 211
Ælfric 58
Afridi, Humera 276
Afshan, Suna 242–4
Agard, John 68–9
Agbabi, Patience 87–8
Aldridge, John 18, 23
Alexander, Elizabeth 143
Ali, Agha Shahid 143–4
Alzacout, Amel 259–60
Amis, Kingsley 27, 28–9, 89, 277
Amis, Martin 45–8
Anphimiadi, Diana 197, 201–2
Antrobus, Raymond 240–41
Armitage, Simon 63, 205, 215, 256
Armstrong, A. J. 302
Arnold, Matthew 167
Ashbery, John 10, 142, 143
Auden, W. H. 27, 167, 180, 226

Baker, Chet 231
Bancroft, Colin 244
Barker, George 29
Barokka, Khairani 243
Batchelor, Paul 138
Baudelaire, Charles 226
Beckett, Samuel 23, 24, 102–8, 229, 290

Beethoven, Ludwig van 211
Benn, Gottfried 114
Bergkamp, Dennis 200
Berkeley, Sara 24
Bernik, Sophie 275
Berrigan, Ted 225
Berry, Emily 4
Berry, Liz 136
Berryman, John 186
Best, George 200
Betjeman, John 27, 29–30, 49, 301
Bettison, Norman 204
Bishop, Elizabeth 10–11, 142, 234, 251–2, 293, 298
Bloodaxe, Eric 156
Blunden, Edmund 110
Boland, Eavan 20
Booth, James 45, 89–96, 99–100, 239
Bowman, Ruth 35, 37–8, 89, 91
Brackenbury, Alison 242
Bradford, Richard 89, 90
Breakenridge, Sophie 216
Brennan, Maeve 32, 43, 89
Brookes, James 136
Brooks, Gwendoline 145
Brown, Jericho 208–10
Brown, Molly McCully 274–5
Brown, Tony 70–72
Browning, Elizabeth Barrett 226–7, 301–6

Browning, Robert 150–51, 167, 301–6
Brownjohn, Alan 127
Bukia-Peters, Natalia 197, 201–2
Bunting, Basil 152–62, 186
Burnett, Archie 45, 60–63
Burns, Robert 153
Burt, Stephanie 142–6
Butterfield, Christian 275
Byron, George Gordon, Lord 8, 167, 206–7

Caddel, Richard 152–3, 154, 160, 161, 162
Cain, David 203–5
Caleshu, Anthony 147–8
Cambridge, Gerry 4
Campbell, Roy 182, 226
Campion, Thomas 167
Carey, John 79
Carson, Ciaran 19, 20, 22
Casement, Roger 18, 19
Cassel, Monika 258, 260–61
Catullus 159
Causley, Charles 51, 58
Chaucer, Geoffrey 58, 87–8, 167
Claces, Caleb 136
Clarke, Austin 18, 19
Clarke, David 203, 205–7
Clemo, Jack 139–41
Clifton, Lucille 143
Coffey, Brian 23
Collins, Billy 5, 8–9

Colum, Padraic 18
Conquest, Robert 27
Cooper, Helen 88
Cope, Wendy 4, 190–91, 296
Cotter, Patrick 136
Courtenay, Tom 238
Cowper, William 279
Crompton, Richmal 273, 289
Cronin, Anthony 24
Crucefix, Martyn 258–60
Cullup, Michael 109–11

Dahl, Roald 160
Dalton, Amanda 288, 289–90
Dante Alighieri 58, 104, 114
Dastidar, Rishi 244
Davies, W. H. 109–11
Davis, Wes 17–24
Davie, Donald 131, 156, 242, 277–85
Davitt, Michael 21–2
Day Lewis, Cecil 18, 29, 180–83,
de la Mare, Walter 110
Dennis, Carl 145
Denny, Sandy 177
Devlin, Denis 23
Dickinson, Emily 142
Disraeli, Benjamin 28
Dixon, Isobel 243
Doctorow, E. L. 274
Donne, John 165, 167
Douglas, Keith 76, 195
Dove, Rita 145
Drobyshev, Yuri 200–201

Dryden, John 66, 153
Duffy, Carol Ann 215
Duncan, Beata 211–12
Dunn, Douglas 117–18, 251
Dutton, Nicole Terez 274–6

Edwards, Zena 236
Eichler, Charlotte 197, 198–9
Einstein, Albert 115
Eldridge, Mildred E. 73
Eliot, T. S. 10, 51, 65, 66, 93, 103, 155, 157, 169, 170, 205, 277
Ely, Steve 197, 199–200, 254–7
Emerson, Ralph Waldo 147
Empson, William 95
Enright, D. J. 64
Epstein, Jacob 176
Etter, Carrie 251
Evans, Suzannah V. 270, 272–3
Evans-Bush, Katy 245

Faggen, Robert 11–13
Fallon, Peter 22, 24
Farley, Paul 205
Fenton, James 7
Ferdowsī 154, 159
Fiacc, Padraic 20
Forché, Carolyn 7
Ford, John 104
Ford, Mark 292
Ford, Sarah 302

Foreman, George 97
Forster, E. M. 64
Forster, Imogen 243
Frost, Robert 11–13, 180, 182, 244, 293
Fuller, Roy 29

Gardner, Kevin 301–2
Gascoigne, Paul 200
Gascoyne, David 29
Gay, Roxane 275
Gelpi, Albert 180–83
Gevinson, Tavi 137
Gladstone, William 28
Glück, Louise 237
Gollock, Matthew 254
Gregerson, Linda 276
Grenier, Robert 143
Grigson, Geoffrey 29
Guenther, Genevieve 276
Gunn, Thom 29, 277

Hakim, Khaled 243, 244
Hamilton, Ian 46
Hamilton, Saskia 11
Hardy, Francesca 4
Hardy, Thomas 27–8, 46, 73, 251, 282
Harrison, Tony 56, 85, 116, 128, 129, 225, 251, 284
Harsent, David 136
Hartley, L. P. 129
Hartnett, Michael 22
Haverty, Anne 192–3
Hayes, Terrance 187–9

Heaney, Seamus 5, 9, 19, 20, 58, 193, 232
Hecht, Anthony 293
Heine, Heinrich 150, 288
Hendry, Diana 270, 273
Herbert, George 10, 190
Higgins, F. R. 23
Hilbert, Ernest 56
Hill, Geoffrey 10
Himmler, Heinrich 287
Hitler, Adolf 90
Hobbes, Thomas 290
Homer 130, 208
Hood, Thomas 66
Hooper, Barbara 111
Horace 56, 157, 159, 284
Housman, A. E. 27, 46
Howard, Henry, Early of Surrey 225
Hughes, Langston 142
Hughes, Ted 71, 77, 142, 186
Hulme, T. E. 181

James, Clive 238–9
Jardine, Lisa 15
Jarrell, Randall 274
Jenkins, Alan 4
Jennings, Elizabeth 29, 277
Johnson, Boris 254
Jones, Monica 25–34, 35–44, 89
Joyce, James 18, 103, 277

Kaminsky, Ilya 218–19
Kapil, Bhanu 244

Kasischke, Laura 145
Kavanagh, Patrick 18, 19, 24, 50, 52, 71, 72
Kay, Jackie 88
Keats, John 28, 130, 167
Keyes, Sidney 92
Khalvati, Mimi 225, 227–8
Kierkegaard, Søren 290
Kim, Christine Sun 240
Kinsella, Thomas 19, 24, 299–300
Kipling, Rudyard 69
Knight, Etheridge 187, 188–9
Komunyakaa, Yusef 143
Koresh, David 301, 305–6

Laforgue, Jules 114
Larkin, Philip 2, 14–15, 25–48, 51, 60–67, 77, 79, 89–96, 98, 99–100, 130–31, 135, 158, 173, 226, 228, 238–9, 251, 252, 268, 277, 278, 280, 281, 295
Laviera, Tato 143
Lawlor, Seán 102–8
Lawrence, D. H. 27, 167, 181
Lawrence, Faith 213, 215–17
Leadbetter, Gregory 242
Leavis, F. R. 29
Ledwidge, Francis 23, 164
Leopardi, Giacomo 238
Leviston, Frances 136
Logan, William 5–16, 99

Longley, Michael 20, 21, 22
Lowell, Robert 11, 274
Lucas, John 4, 78, 98
Lumsden, Roddy 175, 177–9
Lynn, David H. 274

MacNeice, Louis 18, 21, 24, 171
Madoff, Bernie 254
Madonna 178
Mahon, Derek 19, 20, 22
Mailer, Norman 97, 100
Mandelstam, Osip 201, 284
Mansfield, Katharine 27
Manson, Charles 231
Marx, Karl 181, 288–9
Mayakovsky, Vladimir 284
Mayhew, Henry 173
McGonagall, William 68
McGuckian, Medbh 22, 229, 231–3
McVeigh, Timothy 305
Menos, Hilary 4
Meredith, George 180, 182
Merrill, James 143
Merwin, W. S. 31
Millay, Edna St Vincent 225, 298
Miller, Kei 223–4
Milton, John 28, 153, 225
Montale, Eugenio 239
Montgomery, Bruce 93
Mookherjee, Jessica 243
Moore, Marianne 14
Morgan, J. O. 194

Morrissey, Sinéad 22–3, 277–85
Morrison, Blake 133–5
Mort, Helen 122, 124, 137,
Motherlant, Henry de 252
Motion, Andrew 25, 85, 88, 89, 90, 93, 94, 133, 225
Muldoon, Paul 9, 22
Murphy, Richard 19
Murray, Les 10
Muzanenhamo, Togara 112–13, 251

Naffis-Sahely, André 4, 253
Nagra, Daljit 166–8
Nemerov, Howard 7
Neruda, Pablo 142
Newbolt, Henry 160
Nezhukumatathil, Aimee 276
Ní Chuilleanáin, Eiléan 19, 22
Ní Dhomhnaill, Nuala 22
Nietzsche, Friedrich 290
Normand, Lawrence 111
Notley, Alice 138

Ó Searcaigh, Cathal 22
O'Brien, Sean 127–32, 149–50
O'Callaghan, Conor 24
O'Donoghue, Bernard 20, 56, 57–9, 163–5
O'Driscoll, Dennis 232
O'Grady, Desmond 20
O'Hara, Frank 283

O'Loughlin, Michael 21–2
Ormsby, Frank 19
Orwell, George 69
Osborne, John 89, 94–6
Oswald, Alice 225, 255
Ovid 132
Owen, Wilfred 79, 180, 181, 182

Pace, Alexa 305–6
Padel, Ruth 142–3
Parks, Ian 116–26
Pasternak, Boris 284
Paterson, Don 227, 229–31, 292
Paulin, Tom 15, 20
Petit, Pascale 136
Picklesimer, Laura 276
Pilling, John 102–108
Piscator, Johannes 211
Plath, Sylvia 14, 225, 234
Po, Li 142
Pope, Jessie 160
Polley, Jacob 184–6
Porter, Christine 151
Porter, Peter 149–51
Pound, Ezra 65, 66, 103, 114, 154, 155, 157, 158–9, 161, 284
Powell, Neil 278
Powers, Kevin 85–6
Praed, Winthrop Mackworth 66
Prynne, J. H. 78
Pynchon, Thomas 15

Qasmiyeh, Yousif 58
Quinn, Justin 22, 24, 56–9

Raboteau, Emily 275
Rail, Evan 56
Ralphs, Camille 4
Ramayya, Nisha 244
Ramazani, Jahan 144
Rankine, Claudia 208
Ransom, John Crowe 274
Ravinthiran, Vidyan 225, 228
Reece, Spencer 137
Regan, Stephen 225–7
Rehfisch, Hans 211
Revard, Carter 143
Rich, Adrienne 144
Richards, I. A. 182
Ricks, Christopher 4
Rimbaud, Arthur 105
Riordan, Maurice 82–4, 99
Rizwan, Rakhshan 197–8
Robertson, Robin 194–6
Robinson, Roger 236–7, 244
Ross, Alan 169
Rowse, A. L. 29
Rubin, Edgar 221
Ruby, P. R. 257
Rumens, Carol 197, 200–201
Ruskin, John 114
Ryan, Kay 7, 145

Sabah, Naush 242–4, 270–72
Salkeld, Blanaid 23
Sampson, Kevin 204

Samuel, Raphael 116
San Gimignano, Folgóre da 56
Sands, Bobby 21–2
Santos, Sherod 7, 276
Saphra, Jacqueline 175–7
Sappho 142
Scannell, Vernon 75–81
Schiller, Friedrich von 288
Schmidt, Michael 4, 269, 277, 278
Scott, Walter 153
Scraton, Phil 204
Scupham, Peter 286–7
Seferis, George 292
Shakespeare, William 13, 28, 66, 68, 142, 190, 226, 227
Share, Don 136–8, 152–162
Sheers, Owen 85
Shelley, Percy Bysshe 225
Shen, Ts'en 114
Sidney, Philip 66, 242
Sikelianos, Angelos 292
Simmons, James 19
Sitar, James 13
Sitwell, Edith 29
Smith, Danez 208
Snyder, Gary 114
Socrates 290
Spender, Stephen 180
Spenser, Edmund 153
Sprackland, Jean 197
Sprackland, Martha 234–5
Squire, J. C. 169
Stallings, A. E. 292–8

Stannard, Martin 288, 290–91
Stevens, Wallace 14
Stevenson, Robert Louis 66
Sutherland–Smith, James 114–15
Sutton, Jim 37
Swift, Todd 137, 169, 174

Taylor, Andrew 220
Taylor, James Andrew 75–81
Tennyson, Alfred, Lord 153, 167, 168, 232
Thatcher, Margaret 124, 128
Thomas, Edward 56, 109, 110, 264
Thomas, R. S. 49–55, 70–74, 98, 205, 251, 299
Thompson, Luke 139–41
Thwaite, Anthony 25–34, 35, 43, 45, 46, 48, 60, 61, 94, 239
Tiller, Matthew 174
Tiller, Sarah 174
Tiller, Terence 169–74
Tolley, A. T. 46, 60, 61, 62, 94–5, 169,
Trowbridge, John Townsend 7–8, 10
Trump, Donald 187, 305
Turner, Brian 85

Vanilla Ice 115
Vendler, Helen 100
Vidal, Gore 97

Virgil 258

Walcott, Derek 226
Walford Davies, Damian 73–74
Walford Davies, Jason 70–72
Warren, Rosanna 6–7
Wain, John 29
Waterman, Andrew 263–9
Weiwei, Ai 138
Welton, Matthew 256
Wenger, Arsene 254
Wheatley, David 108, 244
Whiting, David 98
Wilbur, Richard 9–10, 143, 145, 286, 293
Williams, Hugo 136
Williams, Rowan 73, 139
Williams, William Carlos 14, 71
Wilson, Philip 288–9
Wiman, Christian 136, 138
Wootten, William 4
Wordsworth, William 158, 225
Wright, Franz 7
Wright, James 274
Wyatt, Thomas 225
Wyley, Edna 22

Yassin, Warda 213, 214–5
Yeats, W. B. 18–19, 23, 27–8, 45, 83, 89, 90, 155

Zakani, Ubayd-I 160

Zola, Gianfranco 200
Zukofsky, Louis 152, 159